Introduction to Police Work

edited by

Colin Rogers and Rhobert Lewis

WILLAN
PUBLISHING

Published by

Willan Publishing
Culmcott House
Mill Street, Uffculme
Cullompton, Devon
EX15 3AT, UK
Tel: +44(0)1884 840337
Fax: +44(0)1884 840251
e-mail: info@willanpublishing.co.uk
website: www.willanpublishing.co.uk

Published simultaneously in the USA and Canada by

Willan Publishing
c/o ISBS, 920 NE 58th Ave, Suite 300,
Portland, Oregon 97213-3786, USA
Tel: +001(0)503 287 3093
Fax: +001(0)503 280 8832
e-mail:info@isbs.com
website: www.isbs.com

First published 2007

ISBN 978-1-84392-283-4 paperback

British Library Cataloguing-in-Publication Data

A catalogue record for this book is available from the British Library

Project managed by Deer Park Productions, Tavistock, Devon
Typeset by Pantek Arts Ltd, Maidstone, Kent
Printed and bound by TJ International Ltd, Trecerus Industrial Estate, Padstow.

Contents

List of figures and tables

Figures

Tables

List of abbreviations

ACPO	The Association of Chief Police Officers
ACC	Assistant Chief Constable
APA	The Association of Police Authorities
ASBO	Anti-social Behaviour Order
ANPR	Automatic Number Plate Recognition
BAWP	British Association of Women Police
BCS	British Crime Survey
BCU	Basic Command Unit
BVPI	Best Value Performance Indicator
CADDIE	Crime and Disorder Data Information Exchange
CC	Chief Constable
CCTV	Closed Circuit Television
CDA	Crime and Disorder Act 1998
CDRP	Crime and Disorder Reduction Partnership
CHALET	Casualties, Hazards, Access, Location, Emergency services, Type
CJS	Criminal Justice System
CPS	Crown Prosecution Service
COPs	Community Oriented Policing
CPIA	Criminal Procedure and Investigation Act 1996
CPTED	Crime Prevention Through Environmental Design
CRAVED	Concealable, Removable, Available, Valuable, Enjoyable and Disposable
CRP	Crime Reduction Programme
CSP	Community Safety Partnership (CDRP equivalent in Wales)
DAT	Drug Action Team
DCC	Deputy Chief Constable
DPP	Director of Public Prosecutions
DVLA	Driver and Vehicle Licensing Agency
ECHR	European Court of Human Rights
FPN	Fixed Penalty Notice
GCHQ	Government Communication Headquarters
GPA	Gay Police Association
HMIC	Her Majesty's Inspector of Constabulary
HOLMES	Home Office Large Major Enquiry System
HVP	High Visibility Policing
IPLDP	Initial Police Learning and Development Programme
JDI	Jill Dando Institute
JTAC	Joint Terrorism Analysis Centre
LSP	Local Strategic Partnership
NAFIS	National Automated Fingerprint Identification System

NBPA	National Black Police Association
NCIS	National Crime Intelligence Service
NCPE	National Centre for Police Excellence (formerly CENTREX)
NCRS	National Crime Recording Standard
NDNAD	National DNA Database
NIM	National Intelligence Model
NOS	National Occupational Standards
NPIA	National Policing Improvement Agency
NRPP	National Reassurance Policing Programme
ODPM	Office of the Deputy Prime Minister
PAT	Problem Analysis Triangle
PACE	Police and Criminal Evidence Act 1984
PCSO	Police Community Support Officer
PITO	Police Information Technology Organisation
PNC	Police National Computer
POA	Problem Oriented Approach
POP	Problem Oriented Policing/Partnerships
PPAF	Policing Performance Assessment Framework
PSA	Public Service Agreement
RAT	Routine Activity Theory
RCT	Rational Choice Theory
RSL	Registered Social Landlord
RV	Repeat Victimisation
SARA	Scanning, Analysis, Response, Assessment
SBD	Secured By Design
SCP	Situational Crime Prevention
SFO	Serious Fraud Office
SOCA	Serious Organised Crime Agency
STAC	Spatial and Temporal Analysis of Crime
TPI	Targeted Policing Initiative
TIC	An offence 'Taken into Consideration'
TT&CG	Tactical, Tasking and Co-ordinating Group
VIPER	Video Identification Parade Electronic Recording
ViSOR	Violent and Sexual Offenders Register
VIVA	Value, Inertia, Volume and Access
YI	Youth Inclusion
YIP	Youth Inclusion Programme
YJB	Youth Justice Board
YOP	Youth Offending Panel
YOT	Youth Offending Team
ZTP	Zero Tolerance Policing

Notes on contributors

Dr Rhobert Lewis, former police officer with Thames Valley police, is currently head of department and director of the Centre for Police Sciences at the University of Glamorgan. Rhobert is the author of the following chapters: Chapter 1 'The Police Organisation', Chapter 3 'Communication', Chapter 4 'Study Skills', Chapter 9 'Forensic Support in Law Enforcement' Chapter 11 'Drug and Alcohol-related Crime' and Chapter 17 'Terrorism'.

Dr Colin Rogers, former police inspector with 30 years' service, is currently a senior lecturer in police sciences at the University of Glamorgan and author of *Crime Reduction Partnerships* published by Oxford University Press. Colin is the author of the following chapters: Chapter 8 'Crime and Disorder Reduction Partnerships', Chapter 10 'Criminal Investigations', Chapter 13, 'Operational Response' and Chapter 18 'Future Directions'.

Sarah Thomas BA MSc is currently a serving police sergeant and part-time lecturer in police sciences at the University of Glamorgan. Sarah is a former Centrex trainer and is now in charge of an area probationary training unit. She is the author of the following chapters: Chapter 2 'The Probationer Officer', Chapter 5 'Ethical Policing Values' and Chapter 6 'Race, Diversity and Equal Opportunities'.

Huw Smart is a police inspector with significant operational and training experience. He is the author of several police training books published by Blackwell's Publishers and is a part time lecturer in police sciences at the University of Glamorgan. Huw is the author of the following chapters: Chapter 14 'Arrests', Chapter 15 'The Custody Suite' and Chapter 16 'Roads Policing'.

Keith Prosser BA (Hons) is an operational chief inspector in a busy multi-culturally-diverse city. He has police training experience and is a fully qualified hostage negotiator with extensive uniform and CID experience. Keith is the author of the following chapters: Chapter 7 'The Basic Command Unit' and Chapter 12 'Anti-social Behaviour'.

Special features of the book

The book has been written from a practitioner's point of view in order to help both students and lecturer/trainers to access more easily the information contained within it. It was compiled after extensive research and consultation with serving police officers, trainers and those individuals who were recently appointed as student officers. Each chapter is laid out in broadly the same manner and contains all or some of the features discussed below.

National Occupational Standards box
At the beginning of each chapter you will find a box that contains the list of National Occupational Standards that supports the information contained in the chapter.

Chapter introduction
This highlights the main areas of the chapter and provides an indication of the scope of its content.

Exercises
A unique feature of this book is the inclusion of exercises throughout the various chapters. These exercises are linked to the information contained in the chapter and are sequenced throughout the text in a logical manner which enables you to work from a simple understanding of an idea to the more complex application of the idea in specific circumstances.

Figures
A figure or example, which includes data that supports a point made in the text, is provided in the chapter where necessary.

Tables
Tables are also included where necessary to illustrate points and to help you understand sometimes complex ideas. On occasions tables are used as part of an exercise.

Case study
Where appropriate, case studies are used to further illustrate work discussed within a chapter and to illustrate a particular point or learning experience.

Suggested further reading

At the end of each chapter you will find some books that have been identified as being useful for the student to read in support of the work contained in the chapter.

Useful websites

Also at the conclusion of most chapters there is mention of useful website(s) that are pertinent to that particular chapter. Readers are invited to explore these websites in order to reinforce the information and knowledge already covered.

Foreword

by Peter Neyroud (Chief Executive, NPIA)

Policing in the 21st Century is rapidly evolving from its 19th-century roots as the 'citizenry in uniform' into a profession with the mission to provide security to the individual, community and nation state. The impetus for the speed of this evolution is the combined pressure at individual (to reduce crime, particularly violent crime), community (to reduce anti-social behaviour) and national level (to prevent terrorism and tackle organised crime) for effective policing. Alongside health provision and education, effective policing has become a key sign to the citizen of the effectiveness of government.

The scale of these challenges mean that preparing someone for a career in policing is as important as preparing someone for a career in medicine, the law or armed forces – the more traditional professions. Increasingly policing is developing its own body of evidence-based practice in areas like neighbourhood policing, intelligence-based policing and the investigation of major crimes. There has been a very important and renewed attention to the ethics of the profession. Furthermore, 'practitioners' in policing are increasingly being required to qualify to practice, particularly where specialist practice as investigators or commanders of major operations are involved.

These changes, which are transforming policing, are well reflected in this book. There is, throughout, a strong emphasis on reflective practice, inviting the reader not just to absorb knowledge – rote learning was the dominant style in police education up until the last decade – but to think about and understand its content and rationale. The underpinning of the National Occupational Standards makes the link with the national framework that now runs from student officer training to the most senior ranks.

Written by practitioners for practitioners, this book provides a comprehensive introduction to the work of policing and will provide a useful insight for anyone, student, member of staff or citizen, seeking to understand our profession.

Peter Neyroud QPM
Chief Constable and Chief Executive,
National Policing Improvement Agency

Preface

by Dick Winterton (Chief Executive, Skills for Justice)

I am delighted to provide the preface for this excellent publication. Just a quick glance at the contents will show that it covers everything from the initial training of a probationer through to countering the modern terrorist threat. Every page is relevant, not just to those wanting to join the police service, but also to those who need to know and understand how it works, what issues it must address and what the future may hold.

Policing is high profile. If you doubt this, please find me a newspaper (on any day of the week) which hasn't got at least three news items about policing; alternatively, find me a single night when a police drama is not on the TV somewhere. But in this lies a danger! It is too easy to *think* you know what policing is all about. But is this fact? Or is this Inspector Morse's version, or Frosts'? Not good enough – it is through the expert work contained in this book that you will develop a true understanding, a scriptwriter's story.

This is an excellent book. Use it well, and use it to make <u>your</u> difference!

PART 1

THE POLICE FRAMEWORK

Chapter 1

The Police Organisation

This chapter supports the following National Occupational Standards which describe the performance and competence required of a probationer officer.

Unit No.	Unit title
1A1	Use police actions in a fair and justified way.
1A2	Communicate effectively with members of communities.
1A4	Foster people's equality, diversity and rights.
1B9	Provide initial support to individuals affected by offending or anti-social behaviour and assess their needs for further support.
2A1	Gather and submit information that has the potential to support policing objectives.
2C2	Prepare for, and participate in, planned policing operations.
2G2	Conduct investigations.
4C1	Develop your own knowledge and practice.
4G2	Ensure your own actions reduce risks to health and safety.

1.1 A brief history of the police service

The origins of the modern police service in Britain lie in the 18th century where anxieties about the capacity and ability of existing watch forces to cope with crime and disorder became widespread. First, local town watchmen were unable to deal competently with crime in increasingly densely-populated conurbations where anonymity was easily achieved. Second, large numbers of demobilised troops roamed following the end of a succession of overseas wars, causing crime waves in many towns and cities. Third, there was genuine concern at the capacity of existing authorities to control major disturbances of public order without the use of the army.

The response to these pressures and anxieties was delayed by both indecision and concerns over cost, but after many parish and private initiatives the Metropolitan Police was formed in 1829 by the then Home Secretary, Sir Robert Peel. From the beginning, the police constables were given uniforms which were obviously non-military. They wore top hats and long-tailed blue coats and they carried a wooden baton. A detective force was created within the Metropolitan force in 1842. Arguments for and against a national police force were eventually resolved and the numerous police forces that were created outside London quickly moved from Home Office to local control. The County and Borough Police Act 1856 required all English and Welsh counties to create police forces under the control of the county magistrates, and an external system of inspection was set up. A similar Act, but applying to Scotland, was passed in 1857. Initially, central government provided 25 per cent of the core costs of police forces but this contribution was later increased to 50 per cent. Most police constables were drawn from the semi-skilled or unskilled working classes, although chief constables were frequently ex-military officers. Pay was low, but it was regular work and (unusually for Victorian Britain) retired officers were eligible for a small pension.

These changes led to the current tripartite organisation of policing in the UK between the police forces, the police authorities and (in England and Wales) the Home Office. Three principles were also established, which remain important today.

The first is that since the police are paid from public funds, officers are financially independent and less likely to be corrupted. This *principle of independence* is carried over to the present, and any links between the police service and the commercial world continue to be scrutinised so that operational decisions are not compromised by such associations. Second, police officers themselves are *servants of the Crown*, meaning that they serve the law and not their employer (the Police Authority). This also means that the operational decisions of chief constables are not dictated by the Police Authority. Third, police officers have *discretion* concerning the action they take (or do not take) in response to an offence, although their actions must be fair and reasonable.

Although the justification for police forces was that they were needed to combat crime, they soon assumed responsibility for a variety of duties including missing persons and traffic. From 1890, forces were encouraged to provide mutual aid in serious and large scale disturbances in public order, a practice well honed by the time of the miners' strike in the 1980s. Nevertheless, military intervention was sometimes regarded as essential, as in the South Wales coal strike of 1910–11 when soldiers also helped with maintaining order. Irish terrorism prompted the formation of the Metropolitan Police Special Branch in 1884.

Both the First (1914–18) and Second (1939–45) World Wars greatly widened the responsibility of the police forces at a time when their resources were sorely stretched because so many officers had volunteered or been conscripted into military service. A police strike in 1918 led to an investigation headed by Lord Desborough which concluded that a national police force should be resisted, that policing was the responsibility of local authorities, and that police pay needed to be increased. Eventually, the freedom of police officers to strike was removed.

Policing after 1945 remained organised in the 'beat system', whereby officers were allocated some areas or even individual streets to patrol. In one of the biggest reforms in British policing since Peel, the 1962 Royal Commission on Policing reduced the number of police forces and introduced new technology into police work. In 1967 the Home Office encouraged 'unit beat policing' whereby officers, now armed with personal radios, were moved from foot patrols to car patrols. A series of corruption scandals, miscarriages of justice and allegations that suspect terrorists had been mistreated during interrogation proved damaging to the reputation of the police service everywhere leading to the *Police and Criminal Evidence Act (PACE) 1984*.

The way that the police service deals and consults with communities which suffer high crime was examined by Lord Scarman after the 1981 riots in several English cities. It became evident that the attitudes of many in the police service and the degree to which the police consulted and communicated with local communities (particularly minority-ethnic populations) was grossly inadequate. In 1993, the black teenager Stephen Lawrence was stabbed in London in a racist attack. The resulting Macpherson Inquiry highlighted the endemic failure of the Metropolitan Police (and by inference, all police forces) in providing a professional service to minority ethnic populations. This report was the starting-point for much of the diversity framework within which the police service works today (see Chapter 6).

1.2 The criminal justice sector and the police service

The police service in the UK is part of the criminal justice sector that includes many agencies including the *Crown Prosecution Service* (CPS), the *Serious and Organised Crime Agency* (SOCA), *HM Prison Service*, *HM Court Services*, the

Probation Service and the *Serious Fraud Office* (SFO). Crimes are dealt with at two levels, with less serious offences being tried at a Magistrates' Court and more serious or complex offences being tried at a Crown Court. The police service is the largest and most expensive part of the criminal justice sector yet the sector as a whole only runs properly if the different components work together. Co-operation between the agencies in the criminal justice sector operates at a strategic level (as when the CPS and the police service work together to reduce the time it takes for a case to reach court), and at local level (for example, when police constables work with probation officers who are monitoring sex offenders who have been released from jail). The working together of agencies was further catalysed when, in 2004, a Single Sector Skills Council and Standard Setting Body, named 'Skills for Justice', was established which applies across the whole criminal justice sector.

Police officers have very different *powers of arrest* from most other professionals involved in criminal justice (see Chapter 14), but the legal right to use physical force is constrained in exactly the same way as it is for members of the public. The use of *legal force* explains the historical origin of the term police force. The restrictions on the use of force provide an example of the kind of legislative framework under which police officers work and which the reader will encounter in later chapters. The use of such force must be:

- **Legal** (e.g. in pursuance of self-defence or in the defence of others)

- **Proportionate** to the circumstances (e.g. in the most serious cases, the use of firearms is justified)

- **Justifiable** in the sense that other alternatives (e.g. attempts at discussion) were inappropriate or inapplicable to the circumstances

- Carried out in accordance with **force policy or practice**. For example, officers should avoid striking with a baton at the head of a person.

Police officers are not the only ones working within the police service. Police community support officers (PCSOs – with lesser powers than police officers but whose powers still exceed those of ordinary citizens), traffic wardens, crime analysts, crime scene investigators and the full range of professionals required to run large organisations (including finance experts and IT managers) all work together. Special constables, who are part-time police constables (with the same powers as regular officers), form a very important part of the 'strength' of the operational police service. Overall, the percentage of 'police staff' (those who are not police officers), within the police service is increasing because many functions can often be more efficiently delivered by non-police officers. Such changes are part of the 'modernisation agenda' of central government, and included in the aim of such policies is to make the police service more expert, more professionally based and better value for money.

1.3 The organisation of police forces

Police officers have a formal rank structure similar to that of the army. The insignia of the ranks in the police service are shown in figure 1.1. The prefix 'detective' is used to denote specialist duties, but it is not a rank in itself.

In London, officers of assistant chief constable rank are known as commanders. The most senior rank in the Metropolitan and City of London Police forces is that of commissioner whereas in other forces the most senior rank is chief constable.

| Figure 1.1 | Ranks and insignia of police officers |

Copied and adapted from Met site at http://www.met.police.uk/about/ranks.htm
© Metropolitan Police Service

Figure 1.2 shows the typical organisation of a medium- to small-sized police force.

The chief constable is the most senior police officer and is ultimately responsible for the achievement of plans jointly agreed with the Police Authority.

It is the Police Authority that controls the size of the budget and is ultimately responsible for maintaining an efficient and effective police force (table 1.1). The Police Authority consists of 17 local councillors, magistrates and independent members and it is mainly through these members that the police service is accountable to the population at large.

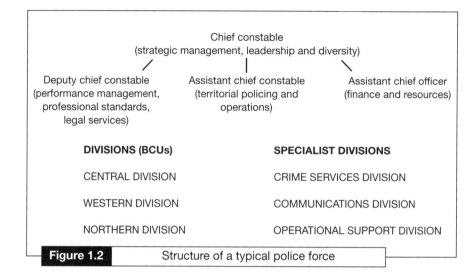

Figure 1.2 Structure of a typical police force

Chief constable	Police authority
In overall command of the force and holds ultimate responsibility for operational matters.	Holds ultimate responsibility for the efficiency and effectiveness of the force.
Drafts local plans for Basic Command Units (BCUs).	Sets overall budget and approves any additional expenditure.
Responsible for achieving local force goals.	Drafts local plans and goals for local forces. Drafts three-year force strategy in accordance with National Police Plan.
Has control of expenditure within an agreed budget.	Consults with local population.

Table 1.1 Responsibilities of the Chief Constable and Police Authority

The assistant chief officer in charge of budgeting and resources is the chief administrative officer of the force. The post-holder is not usually police officer and he or she will have responsibilities for large departments (HR, accounts, estates and finance).

Below the chief constable are the deputy and assistant chief constables. In addition to having specific responsibilities, the deputy chief constable deputises for the chief constable as required.

Below the senior management team are divisions, each headed by a police officer of the rank of chief superintendent or superintendent. The number of territorial divisions (Basic Command Units, BCUs) depends upon the size and population of the areas within the force. Each BCU may have five to ten police stations, some operating 24 hours a day. The specialist divisions have different functions. For example, the Operational Support Division includes search teams, tactical operations and firearm teams, road policing, dogs and helicopters. The Communications Division is responsible for the control rooms and call centres. Figure 1.3 shows the breakdown of a typical territorial division and of the Crime Services Division based at HQ.

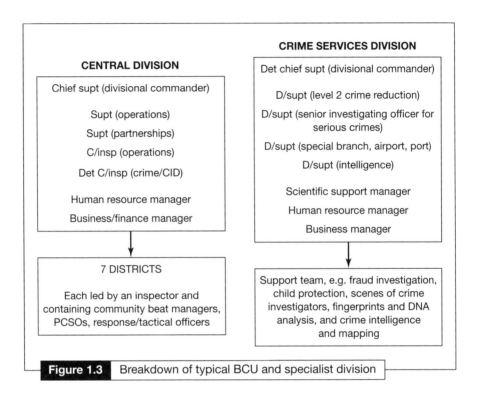

Figure 1.3 Breakdown of typical BCU and specialist division

The larger the force, the greater the number of senior officers and territorial divisions and the wider the range of specialist divisions.

The third part of the tripartite organisation of the police is the Home Office, which has become very influential in directing the work of the police service, often using specially earmarked funds to bring about improvements in crime reduction. The Home Office is a department of central government and its priorities are those of the political party in power in Westminster. Government legislation now defines the overall priorities of the police service, many of its methods of working, and even the ways in which the success of individual police forces is measured.

1.4 What is the police service for?

Exercise 1A

Take no less than five minutes over this exercise.

Suppose that you were asked to write down the main functions of the police service for a force website. What would you write? Think carefully about the wording you would use and whether or not the functions overlap.

It might surprise you to know that there is no definite answer to this exercise. There will be a variety of responses according to the standpoint and priorities of the individual, and different police forces will have slightly different priorities according to the needs of their communities.

One approach to the question 'what are the police for?' is to look at the *subjects* of police work, i.e. the 'things' that police deal with. Examples are crime, disorder, public safety (including traffic control), helping and protecting vulnerable people, terrorism and responding to major incidents and emergencies. We could then look at *what* it is that the police service does about these subjects. Taking crime as an example, the police service seeks to:

■ *reduce* the number of crimes by prevention or deterrence

■ *solve* crime by investigation

■ *reassure* the public about crime by carrying out visible patrols in cities and towns (discussed further in section 1.7).

These points are often summarised as 'reducing crime and the fear of crime'. Similar aims apply to public disorder. These examples serve to illustrate that the modern police service is not just concerned with crimes as they take place. It seeks to prevent crimes and threats to public safety from happening in the first place. It also recognises the importance of public opinion and perception – an idea that will resurface time and time again in this book. The idea that members of the public are 'consumers' of police services is relatively new, but (as in other public services) the idea helps to define the way that governments measure the success or failure of the police service. Even probationary constables in the first months of their career play a very important role in achieving success for their neighbourhood police team.

Table 1.2 shows the aims, values and policing style of Thames Valley Police, as stated on their website. This is a good indicator of the priorities of the chief officers and Police Authority of that force.

Our aim

Working with our communities to reduce crime, disorder and fear of crime.

Our values

We are people of integrity who:

■ listen and learn

■ work together and do what we say we are going to do

■ take responsibility for solving problems

■ earn trust and respect

■ are courageous, open and fair to all

■ challenge, innovate and achieve

■ hold ourselves and others accountable for performance.

Our policing style

Our policing style is working in partnership to:

■ be tough on crime and criminals

■ be accessible to people who need to call us

■ be visible to local people

■ convict and deter offenders.

| **Table 1.2** | Aims, values and policing style of Thames Valley Police |

Exercise 1B

A police constable is approached by a member of the public who asks the way to the local theatre. The constable gives the impression that she is not particularly interested in this enquiry. What might be the consequences of this 'interaction' if it were repeated on a large scale nationally?

Putting aside individual consequences for the officer (who might get an official complaint) or the member of public (who might get lost!) the real point of this question is to explore the cumulative (or *macroscopic*) consequences of many little (or *microscopic*) 'bad experiences'. Although the interaction given in the question was simply a query about direction, similar interactions occur between police personnel and members of the public hundreds of thousands of times a day. So often it is the way in which an officer deals with members of the public (whether responding to a burglary or to an enquiry about a lost wallet) that helps form public opinion and the level of support for the police in an area. In high-profile investigations, the way in which the police service deals with members of the public, including suspects and the media, is even more important.

How should police personnel deal with members of the public? As you might expect, different circumstances require different tactics. Police officers are not street entertainers. They must always exude professionalism and some authority and occasionally need to display controlled aggression. But in the overwhelming number of instances, and certainly in the example given in exercise 1B, a smile and an enthusiastic response, with eye contact and a parting 'nod', will go a long way to persuade the member of the public that 'at least some of the police are OK'. Such support, even if qualified, is always worth working for. In communities in which police–public relations are particularly tense, such support may be invaluable.

1.5 The Home Office, the National Police Plan and the performance of police forces

There is widespread agreement about the list of activities carried out by the police, but the *prioritisation* of those activities has often varied from force to force. Nevertheless, the overall priorities are now set by the government's National Police Plan, an instrument created by the Police Reform Act 2002. Individual forces must publish plans showing how they are going to achieve these priorities. Government agencies then measure the success of forces against these targets and report the results to the public.

In the 2002–8 plan, the Home Secretary defines the core role of the police as the prevention and reduction of crime and anti-social behaviour and the five key priorities are:

- Reduction of overall crime

- Provision of a citizen-focused police service

- Increase in detection rates by working with partners (especially targeting prolific and other priority offenders)

- Reduce people's concerns about crime, anti-social behaviour and disorder

- Combat serious and organised crime, within and across force boundaries.

1.6 What do the public think of the police?

There have been numerous surveys of public opinion and it has been found that the public's views of the police depend on the age and ethnicity of the respondent and upon the crime levels in the area in which the respondent lives. Here, we look at three pieces of research. All provide an interesting background to many of the modern initiatives discussed in this book. All provide 'food for thought'.

It is very important that individuals trust organisations. One interesting line of research is to study the extent to which people *trust* public services, including the police, the NHS and local councils. The study *Exploring Trust in Public Institutions* was commissioned by the Audit Commission and carried out by Mori in 2003. The Audit Commission report separated positive and negative influences upon trust and these are shown in figure 1.4. All are applicable to the police service.

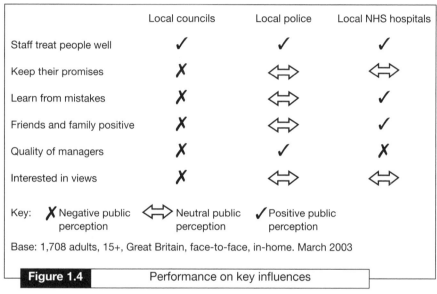

	Local councils	Local police	Local NHS hospitals
Staff treat people well	✓	✓	✓
Keep their promises	✗	⟺	⟺
Learn from mistakes	✗	⟺	✓
Friends and family positive	✗	⟺	✓
Quality of managers	✗	✓	✗
Interested in views	✗	⟺	⟺

Key: ✗ Negative public perception   ⟺ Neutral public perception   ✓ Positive public perception

Base: 1,708 adults, 15+, Great Britain, face-to-face, in-home. March 2003

Figure 1.4   Performance on key influences

Courtesy of Ipsos MORI

Exercise 1C

Can you give two reasons why NHS hospitals are rated higher for trust than the local police in figure 1.4?

There might be several explanations for this data. One is that hospitals are usually seen as 'helping organisations'. Occasionally, the police service inconveniences or upsets people (by arresting them or searching them) or by being unnecessarily aggressive in its actions. A second explanation is that patients in hospitals get more care and personal attention – not just better care – than is provided in the police service. Members of the public usually encounter the police for a matter of minutes – not hours or days. Even if the interaction is longer, the experience and the reason for such an interaction is often an unpleasant one. Unlike the health service, the police service may have to perform certain duties which make it unpopular. Nevertheless, there may be lessons to be learned and the Audit report noted that:

> '... in one sense trust is to a large extent about *satisfaction* with services and *keeping promises*. The *way in which services are delivered* is also significant; staff treating people well and equally are both important factors for all organisations.'

The second piece of research is the *Policing for London Study*, reported in 2002. Among the many conclusions were:

- Most Londoners reported that the news media, rather than their own experiences, constituted their main information about the police, especially for people over 45 years old

- Londoners have less confidence in the police than in firemen, teachers, nurses and doctors

- The proportion of people thinking that the police do a very good job continues to fall

- Young people, people in deprived areas and those of minority ethnic origin rated the police as less effective than did other members of the population

- Members of the white population sometimes viewed the police as biased towards minority ethnic groups. At the same time many minority ethnic groups continue to remain very suspicious of the police

- Londoners want policing to be more responsive to their needs, including more visible policing.

Much of the report has been used to inform improvements in the way that the Metropolitan Police Service works.

A more recent report is *Policing and the criminal justice system – public confidence and perceptions: findings from the 2004/2005 British Crime Survey*. Findings include:

- People from minority ethnic groups had more confidence than white people in the criminal justice system as a whole

- The most highly rated criminal justice agency was the police

- Of those people who had contact with the police, 82% were very or fairly satisfied with the way that the police had handled the matter

- The percentage of victims who are satisfied with the police was lower, at 58%.

1.7 Reassurance, effectiveness and efficiency

One of the duties of the police service is to reassure the public that they strongly influence and generally control the level of crime and public disorder in their communities.

Reassurance is a complex function of perception: it is how the public feel about the effectiveness of the police in achieving their goals (and, in particular, of deterring crime) that is important. Publicity, the media, individual dealings with the police service as well as speed of response to emergencies all contribute to that perception. Reassurance of the public is becoming more important as members of the public become more and more cautious about intervening in anti-social behaviour. The police are often seen as the only ones who can legitimately enforce many codes of behaviour. Yet, steps to improve reassurance are often at odds with efficiency (value for money) and effectiveness (the achievement of specific goals, such as crime reduction). This is illustrated in exercise 1D.

Exercise 1D

A police constable patrols in a car around ten streets in a town. Each street contains 200 premises. If the patrol level is doubled, so that there are two cars on constant patrol, what is likely to be the effect of the extra patrol upon the burglary detection rate?

It is entirely reasonable to suppose that (other things being equal) doubling the patrols would double the detection rate. But just what is the probability per shift that a burglar would be caught leaving premises just as a patrol car turns the corner? It is not easy to assign a probability to such an occurrence, but we know that it is tiny. Even if an extra patrol car doubles the probability of such an event, that probability is still tiny. Although there might be other benefits from two patrols (such as the availability of an extra car to attend emergency calls) the conclusion remains unaltered: two patrols are doubly expensive in terms of vehicles, fuel and officers' time and the improvement in the burglary detection rate is unnoticeable. A form of policing which is based on good intelligence rather than random patrols is more effective at reducing crime, even though it may not have the same reassuring effect in the eyes of the population.

Foot patrols are also much less effective in combating crime than in the past because of the increased mobility of the population (an offender can drive across counties in a matter of minutes or hours) and because much crime (such as identity fraud and money laundering) is now remote from our streets. 'Concealed crime' requires detailed investigation and is not appreciably deterred or detected by the presence of a police officer.

Despite these conclusions, many members of the public welcome extra foot patrols because of the reassurance factor. In this sense, effectiveness and efficiency are in conflict with reassurance, and the patrol strategy adopted (perhaps extra patrols, but only at certain times of the day) represents a compromise. Such compromises are always present in policing as in the activities of other public services. In this case, the responsibility for deciding the patrol strategy will reside at local level, perhaps with the section inspector.

Reassurance remains high on the 'wish list' of the public and so is high on the agenda of government and the police service. Reassurance is a strong theme in 'neighbourhood policing' which is being adopted by most forces over the next few years.

Exercise 1E

You are the inspector in charge of policing a small town. Suggest four sets of circumstances when you would consider providing extra (but expensive) short-term 'reassurance patrols'.

Additional reassurance patrols may be considered when:

- The community is traumatised, e.g. because a serial murderer is known to be on the loose

- Community tension is high because of a controversial arrest

- Anti-social behaviour has reached unacceptable levels and curfews need to be enforced

- A public event or bank holiday is expected to lead to disorder, e.g. drunken behaviour.

Effectiveness (the extent to which the police service carries out its functions well) and **efficiency** (whether or not the police service wastes resources) are qualities which are constantly being reviewed at force, Police Authority and governmental levels. The police service is part of the criminal justice system. In 2007, the Centre for Crime and Justice Studies at King's College, London published an independent report entitled *Ten years of criminal justice under Labour*. It concludes that the UK now spends more on criminal justice than any other state in Europe, although the effects of individual agencies (including the police) upon variations in crime figures are reported to be very hard to determine. This casts doubt about the value for money achieved by the extra expenditure.

1.8 Policing by consent

It is often said that the police service can only be effective if it has the support of the public. This is the meaning of the phrase 'policing by consent'.

Exercise 1F

Policing by consent

State three actions which members of the public could take which would support the work of the police.

Here are some of the ways in which the public could show support:

- Provide information about a crime (when, where, who …)

- Be understanding about the priorities of the police so that their expectations are realistic. (This is more subtle, and is dependent upon individual and general public opinion and upon the information and explanations that the police service provides)

- Take more responsibility for crime prevention (e.g. through the Neighbourhood Watch Scheme or by paying for security lighting on premises).

Despite the desirability of policing by consent, policing often occurs without public support. The police often have to uphold the law in difficult and unpopular circumstances and whole groups of society or districts may become overwhelmingly hostile to the police. Under these circumstances the police have no option but to police without consent, but it is the responsibility of the police service to help repair relationships with communities as quickly and as effectively as circumstances allow. Repairing such relationships is never easy and is only achieved in partnership with the communities themselves.

1.9 Themes in modern policing

We end this chapter by summarising some of the themes influencing the direction of the police service in recent years.

(a) The direction and strategy of the police service is now largely dictated by the Home Office, an influence amplified by the Police Reform Act 2002. The Home Office now contributes 51 per cent of police costs, but also controls the allocation of special funding streams, for example in January 2007 the government announced special funding for a joint initiative to provide a multi-agency approach towards anti-social behaviour in 40 so-called 'respect' areas in England.

(b) National police structures are increasing: examples are the Serious and Organised Crime Agency (SOCA) and the re-organisation of special branch under a national coordinator. The government has also suggested that the move will be towards larger and fewer police forces in the near future.

(c) The police service has adopted much of the managerial style and approach of other public and commercial concerns. 'Best value for money' initiatives (derived from the Police Act 1996) and 'performance indicators' alongside regular inspections have permeated the service. Performance is now measured and monitored at every level. While there are some concerns that such management is occasionally insensitive to public opinion (particularly since it is difficult to measure the extent to which the public feel reassured, but easier to measure, for example, a fall in the number of burglaries) the emphasis is upon management and leadership from constable to chief constable and this has had a largely positive effect in making use of scarce resources.

(d) The police service is now much more professional in the way that best practice is identified, collected and communicated to police practitioners. For example, best practice in suspect interviewing, scenes of crime management and child abuse investigation is commonly developed by inter-force groups of seconded officers working with the Home Office or the Association of Chief Police Officers (ACPO). Policing has become 'intelligence-led' and the National Intelligence Model (NIM) has introduced a uniform and organised way of gaining and using intelligence. More recently, the National Policing Improvement Agency (NPIA) has been established with responsibility for planning to meet future trends in policing, to assist forces in the implementation of national police initiatives and for improving professional practice.

(e) The greater use of PCSOs and police staff represents an acknowledgement that it is wasteful and less effective to employ police officers for many roles in the police service. PCSOs in particular provide the kind of visible reassurance that is often demanded by communities.

(f) Specialisation is increasing and even probationer police officers will specialise in one or more *career pathways* much earlier in the future.

(g) Cooperation between law enforcement agencies abroad will increase, especially in the fight against terrorism.

(h) One goal of modern police structures is to ensure that strategic and tactical plans and actions are *evidence-based*. Research is the foundation of evidence-based policing and projects and police operations are often evaluated by external agencies such as universities.

(i) Another related theme involves the use of more science and technology in crime reduction and crime detection. This is particularly important as the nature of crime changes. This is discussed further in Chapter 9.

(j) Changes in legislation have made forces adopt generic practices in sex, race and disability discrimination. The effect of the Human Rights Act 1998 has also been far reaching. In particular, any police investigation must be both justified and legal and any adverse effects upon community or an individual must be proportionate to the alleged offence.

(k) The opinions and concerns of the public are now much more important to the police than in previous decades and this is illustrated by the adoption of a form of community policing known as 'neighbourhood policing', discussed further in Chapter 8.

(l) One of the most important examples of an over-arching theme which influences the working of the police service is the way that diversity (in its broadest sense) is now seen as an integral part of the police service. This is examined further in Chapter 6.

(m) The Crime and Disorder Act 1998 recognised that the police are only one of many agencies that can influence community safety. Another type of partnership – that between the forces themselves – has also been on the increase and has often led to the next level of development: that of separate national organisations, the latest version of which is SOCA itself.

(n) Legislation has permitted police officers to use penalty notices for lower-level crime and disorder and so reduce the time that officers spend doing paperwork in the station. In 2006, over 165,000 such notices were issued. This is controversial: the use of fixed penalty tickets is sometimes felt to trivialise offences. The increasing emphasis upon 'avoiding paperwork' also needs to be examined critically. Preparing a file for court is not a bureaucratic chore; it is an essential part of the work of the police service, and one which is just as important as the arrest itself.

Suggested further reading

Rawlings, P., *Policing, A Short History* (Cullompton: Willan, 2002)

FitzGerald, M., Hough, M., Joseph, I. and Qureshi, T., *Policing for London* (Cullompton: Willan, 2002)

Wright, A., *Policing: An Introduction to Concepts and Practice* (Cullompton: Willan, 2002)

Useful websites

www.nwpolice.org/peel.html
The nine principles of Sir Robert Peel's police, all of which resonate strongly today

http://www.homeoffice.gov.uk/
The Home Office website contains a wealth of information on policing, including documents on research, policy and legislation (including the Police Reform Act 2002)

http://www.skillsforjustice.com/default.asp?PageID=1
Skills for Justice

http://www.met.police.uk/about/webinfo.htm
The Metropolitan Police Service website contains details of its structure and management and illustrates the range and complexity of functions in a very large police force

http://www.ipsos-mori.com
The official Mori poll website where many documents relating to the police and other public agencies can be found

http://www.homeoffice.gov.uk/rds/pdfs06/rdsolr0706.pdf
Policing and the criminal justice system – public confidence and perceptions: findings from the 2004/05 British Crime Survey. Home Office Report 07/06

http://www.acpo.police.uk/
The role and scope of the Association of Chief Police Officers

http://www.soca.gov.uk/
The Serious Organised Crime Agency

http://www.kcl.ac.uk/depsta/rel/ccjs/ten-years-of-labour-2007.html
The King's College Report on ten years of criminal justice under Labour

http://www.demos.co.uk/catalogue/aforceforchange/
An interesting 'think tank' report on the ways that the police service might develop

Chapter 2

The Probationer Officer

This chapter supports the following National Occupational Standards which describe the performance and competence required of a probationer officer.

Unit No.	Unit title
1A1	Use police actions in a fair and justified way.
1A2	Communicate effectively with members of communities.
1A4	Foster people's equality, diversity and rights.
2A1	Gather and submit information that has the potential to support policing objectives.
2C2	Prepare for, and participate in, planned policing operations.
2G2	Conduct investigations.
2G4	Finalise investigations.
SH1	Interview victims and witnesses.
2H2	Interview suspects.
2I1	Search individuals.
2I2	Search vehicles, premises and land.
2J1	Prepare and submit case files.
4C1	Develop your own knowledge and practice.

2.1 Introduction

It is vitally important that police training supports many of the reforms that the police service is undergoing at the present time. Further, the effectiveness of police training will influence the extent to which officers are equipped to deal with the challenges that they face. A recent advertising campaign entitled 'Police – could you?' gives a powerful insight into some of the decisions and dilemmas that challenge police officers. It is fair to say that not everyone 'could' be a police officer. The job can be very demanding and the recruitment and training process is by no means easy. The Home Office estimates that only 15 per cent of applicants each year are successful. This highlights what an achievement it is to be accepted as a police officer.

Police training in the 1980s focused on:

- Memorising lengthy pieces of legislation

- Formal examinations to test officers' knowledge

- Classroom-based training inputs at police training colleges carried out by 'instructors'

- An emphasis on discipline and obedience.

Whilst this approach may have prepared the new recruits to cope with some aspects of their work, it may not have developed the practical and interpersonal skills they needed to apply their knowledge effectively. We are currently in the middle of a period of change in police training and development. The changes implemented are designed to provide a more highly skilled service, focused on improving service to the public, with training to common national standards.

Many factors affecting society as a whole have had an impact on the police service and this is reflected in its changing approach to training. Consider the question in exercise 2A below.

Exercise 2A

Can you think of any factors affecting society that may have had an impact on police training?

You may have considered some of the factors outlined below:

- The impact of technology

- The increasing complexity of policing

- The new 'extended police family' embracing police community support officers

- The expectations society has of its police service

- Greater diversity in society.

As a result of these changes in society, police training is no longer a matter of sitting in rows of desks learning the law and legal definitions. The new 'core learning goals' provide the framework around which the new police training curriculum has been developed. These relate to:

- Understanding and engaging with the community

- Enforcing the law and following police procedures

- Responding to human and social diversity

- Positioning oneself in the role of a police officer inside the police organisation

- Professional standards and ethical conduct

- Learning to learn and creating a base for career-long learning

- Qualities of professional judgement and decision making.

2.2 Initial Police Learning and Development Programme (IPLDP)

In 2002 Her Majesty's Inspectorate of Constabulary (HMIC) carried out an inspection of the training of probationer constables. Their subsequent report entitled *Training Matters* outlined that the time was right for a fundamental review of the content and delivery of probationer training. The term 'probationer officer' is a commonly-used term to denote officers in their first two years of service; other terms used for the same officer are 'student officer' and 'recruit constables'.

2004 saw the birth of the Initial Police Learning and Development Programme (IPLDP) with the pilot adoption of the programme by five police forces. National implementation of the IPLDP followed in April 2006. The programme is overseen by the IPLDP Programme Board. Membership of this Programme Board includes representatives from the Police Federation, National Black Police Association, British Association of Women Police, Gay Police Association, the Crown Prosecution Service and the Home Office.

The primary goal of the IPLDP is to implement modernised training for student officers. The IPLDP has to be set in the wider context of police reform and modernisation and recognised for the opportunities it offers towards professionalising policing and improving performance and service-quality delivery. New recruits to the police service now carry the title of 'probationer officers'.

These probationer officers are now exposed to a more vocationally orientated programme that is made up of three interrelated elements, namely:

- Academic inputs in a classroom environment

- Achieving required national competencies

- Engagement with the community.

A key feature of the new arrangement is that forces have individual responsibility for ensuring the delivery of all stages of probationer officer training. The IPLDP curriculum is designed to allow individual forces every opportunity to tailor their programmes aligned to local needs. The training is, therefore, delivered locally. Recognising the benefits of learning alongside other groups of people from different backgrounds, some forces have adopted a procedure whereby this local police training is delivered in non-police environments, such as local colleges or universities. Additionally, wherever possible, training is non-residential to make it as family friendly and accessible as possible.

2.3 Community engagement

The IPLDP includes extensive work with local communities, with members of the public involved in all stages of the training cycle, and involves probationer officers spending extended periods of time with local community groups. Exercise 2B asks you to consider local groups within your community.

Exercise 2B

Consider which local community groups exist in your own area.

You may have identified such groups as:

- Outreach schemes

- Local authority housing

- Vulnerable groups

- Neighbourhood Watch

- Diversity groups

- Schools

- Youth associations

- Drug Action Teams

- Faith groups.

The above list is by no means exhaustive. The principle of community engagement is explicit in giving probationer officers the understanding they need of the culture, values, expectations and concerns of the people who live and work in the areas they will police. This also includes knowing and understanding the role and relationship that the police share with other members of the police family, criminal justice partners, agencies and groups.

This emphasis on community engagement is also seen as vital in terms of underpinning the new approach to 'neighbourhood policing'. We have recently seen the introduction and spread of dedicated neighbourhood policing teams, with constables increasingly working as team leaders providing the focus for approaches to achieve long term solutions to crime and disorder within local divisions working alongside community partners. Community engagement is, therefore, seen as essential to providing the responsive policing that neighbourhoods want across the country, and it is today's probationer officers who will need to learn the skills necessary to build the partnerships to achieve those goals.

2.4 Competencies and standards

The public are entitled to feel confident that police officers have the skills and abilities necessary to carry out their job competently. The probationer officers' probationary period lasts two years and in that time they will need to demonstrate their competence to become police officers. This two year period comprises a mixture of classroom-based training and practical policing. The new probationer officer is continually assessed during the whole period.

During this two year period recruits are expected to complete a portfolio of evidence, keeping accurate records of their performance on a day-to-day basis. The idea of a portfolio is that it allows probationer officers and their supervisors to see how well they are performing and to identify those areas in need of development. The document records situations that are dealt with, and includes the officer's thoughts, feelings, reactions and emotions experienced on the way to, during and after the event. Such notes assist probationer officers to reflect on events and to review their progress throughout their training. These portfolios vary from force to force, but they are all based on identified behavioural competencies.

Competencies are the lists of skills, knowledge, attitudes and behaviours that are needed in order to be an efficient police officer. The list of attitudes and behaviours that police recruits will be expected to develop is set out below.

- Resilience

- Effective communication

- Community and customer focus

- Respect for diversity

- Team working

- Personal responsibility

- Problem solving.

It is important to spend time looking at the above list and identify those areas in which you are strongest and those areas which may be in need of development. You have probably identified that you are already good at some of these things. The police recruitment process assists in identifying those individuals who can demonstrate ability in these competencies. Initial police training then aims to further develop these competencies, building on the skills and abilities that the student officer already has. Probationer officers are then expected to assess their own level of performance in these areas by receiving feedback from others and by engaging in self-reflection upon their performance.

It is important that police officers are able to demonstrate the same level of competence no matter what force they belong to. Consequently, in recent years, the police have introduced a set of National Occupational Standards (NOS) against which all officers are trained and measured. Responsibility for developing these standards was given to the Skills for Justice agency.

National Occupational Standards are a way of describing competent performance. They set out what a person needs to achieve in carrying out a particular role or job. The NOS allow a clear assessment of competence against nationally-agreed standards of performance across a range of workplace circumstances for all roles.

There are 22 NOS which describe the performance and competence required of a probationer officer. These are outlined in table 2.1 below.

2.5 Professional Development Units

The IPLDP curriculum presents forces with the opportunity to build a range of experiences from which probationer officers can draw and learn. Some will be during the classroom-based part of the programme, and others will be present during the community contact and engagement experience. A significant element will also occur during the tutor and independent workplace phases. This phase of the probationer officers' development is overseen by the Professional Development Unit (PDU) within the force.

Unit No	Unit Title
1A1	Use police actions in a fair and justified way.
1A2	Communicate effectively with members of communities.
1A4	Foster people's equality, diversity and rights.
1B9	Provide initial support to individuals affected by offending or anti-social behaviour and assess their needs for further support.
2A1	Gather and submit information that has the potential to support policing objectives.
2C1	Provide an initial police response to incidents.
2C2	Prepare for, and participate in, planned policing operations.
2C3	Arrest, detain or report individuals.
2C4	Minimise and deal with aggressive and abusive behaviour.
2G2	Conduct investigations.
2G4	Finalise investigations.
2H1	Interview victims and witnesses.
2H2	Interview suspects.
2I1	Search individuals.
2I2	Search vehicles, premises and land.
2J1	Prepare and submit case files.
2J2	Present evidence in court and at other hearings.
2K1	Escort detained persons.
2K2	Present detained persons to custody.
4C1	Develop your own knowledge and practice.
4G2	Ensure your own actions reduce risks to health and safety.
4G4	Administer first aid.

Table 2.1 The 22 National Occupational Standards

To be able to perform effectively as competent constables, probationer officers must be able to engage with real policing situations, incidents and events so they are best able to contextualise the learning. Research has highlighted that the probationer officer learns better in circumstances that provide a variety of experiences in a controlled environment. PDUs provide such a safe environment, as they provide probationer officers with the learning and development opportunities necessary for them to undertake independent patrol and become competent in the 22 National Occupational Standards.

PDUs allow probationer officers protected, reflective learning time and the opportunity to experience a range of activities and scenarios in an environment that remains operationally accountable. These PDUs carry out their role whilst mindful of the policing priorities and needs of the local community, so that officers are tasked effectively.

The probationer officers individually receive the support they need to achieve their full learning potential, and do so working with operational colleagues. PDUs are staffed by teams of qualified professionals who are dedicated to combining learning with operational experience and operational performance. Following the initial stages of their training at the training centre, the probationer officer works alongside an experienced police officer who will tutor them through real policing experiences. The role of this 'tutor constable' is to assist the probationer officer by attending real incidents and calls, allowing the new officer to take responsibility at the scene. Following this, the incident will be 'debriefed' and any developmental points discussed. The work of the tutor constable is therefore central to the training process and it is seen as crucial in ensuring that probationer officers are able to transfer their newly-acquired understanding and experience into beat work and problem solving. Once the probationer officer has demonstrated the knowledge, understanding, skills, attitudes and behaviours required to police the community effectively they are then deemed fit for 'independent patrol'.

Techniques utilised by the PDUs in police training include workplace assessment and projects. Probationer officers are required to undertake short attachments to various specialist departments within the police service in an attempt to develop their skills and learn from the expertise demonstrated by others. Probationer officers are also expected to carry out projects which encompass direct policing issues. Some will take the form of diversion or prevention of crime, and others will perhaps offer help to victims or offenders. Community regeneration and development may offer other avenues. These projects may, therefore, be completed following or during the community placements. It can be very effective, as a structured part of a probationer officer's development, to work on real issues that have a potential for a positive impact on life within the area being policed.

2.6 Approaches to adult learning

There are a number of principles of adult learning that have been applied in police training. Learning something new depends on a number of factors. Try and think about this as you complete exercise 2C below

---

Exercise 2C

Think about a recent occasion when you have tried to learn something new. Try to identify what motivated or assisted your learning.

You may have identified some of the following influences:

- You had a clear purpose for wanting to learn

- You could relate your learning to something you already knew

- You had the opportunity to use your new learning ('put it into practice')

- The effectiveness of the training given.

By the time we reach adulthood we have a wealth of knowledge and experience to draw upon. We learn by fitting new information into what we already know, and by building from simple to more complex. For example, it would be difficult to understand burglary unless you already knew about theft because theft is an integral component of the definition of burglary. By becoming involved in learning, rather than passively receiving information, adults are encouraged to incorporate new learning into their personal 'frameworks' of experience.

Throughout police training, although there are some written assessments of knowledge attained during initial training, there is an increasing emphasis on addressing attitudes and behaviour. Exercise 2D below guides you to think of attitudes and behaviour.

Exercise 2D

A probationer officer knows the law in relation to domestic violence. What other skills would they need to demonstrate before dealing with a domestic violence incident?

You may have listed such points as interpersonal skills, communication skills, the ability to show empathy, awareness of personal safety and the role of other agencies. These are skills and attitudes that could not be learnt from a book, but need practice and feedback on performance to highlight areas for development. These 'attitudes' and 'behaviours' are often addressed most effectively through group work involving role plays and discussion.

2.7 Role play

Adults need to be able to apply their new learning. This is particularly true of new skills. One of the best ways of developing new skills is through practice. Imagine trying to pass your driving test without having driven a car. In the early stages of police training it is not possible to let probationer officers practise their policing skills on the public. Instead, police training uses 'practicals' or 'role plays' to simulate police activities. During this role play the probationer officers carry out certain tasks or encounters while being observed by colleagues and trainers. The officer is then encouraged to think about how they performed. Trainers and colleagues will also identify the strengths and weaknesses demonstrated. The feedback given by the trainers and colleagues is intended to assist in improving performance, not to find fault and criticise. These role plays give the probationer the opportunity to develop their confidence and professional competence in a safe learning environment where making mistakes is without consequence.

Some forces have adopted the practice of working with members of the public, retail and security staff in commercial outlets and hotels and within other businesses to provide role players and realistic environments in which to train. There are a number of benefits to this practice. Firstly, these activities, conducted within the public gaze, allow misconceptions about police training to be addressed. Secondly, scenarios played out in retail areas or crime hotspots may even provide a preventative and reassuring presence.

2.8 Reflective practice

As mentioned earlier, pre 1980s police training saw the 'instructor' as an expert who 'lectured' learners who were assumed to know nothing. In modern police training the police trainer 'facilitates' learning with probationer officers encouraged to use their skills of questioning, observing, researching and thinking. We all have these skills, but probationer officers need to focus on them more consciously to identify their areas of weakness and develop them. You may be familiar with the idea of 'reflective practice' and 'action planning' which underpin police training. Both of these techniques relate to this principle of adult learning.

2.9 The experiential learning cycle

By the time we reach adulthood we like to see ourselves as independent-thinking individuals. We have sufficient knowledge and experience of life to form our own judgements and to act accordingly. As a result, adults learn much more effectively when they can see the relevance of what they are learning and make connections with their own experience. This is one of the reasons why police training has been designed to encourage the probationer officer to take responsibility for their own performance and identify strategies for improving it. Probationer officers are encouraged to think about what they do, hear and see, both in training and operationally. From this the officer can develop a habit of reviewing events critically, applying their own judgement and action-planning to improve their performance.

A technique that has been developed to derive grea
learning by experience is the experiential learning cyc
reflective practice cycle). It is the method on which mc
based as it provides a framework to learn from experie
action on an analysis of past events. The technique is u
class to discuss or debrief an experience, and officers are encouraged to us
their own use of the experiential learning cycle as a means of continuing their
own development. This process is known as 'reflective practice'.

Figure 2.1 below is one often used to show how the process works.

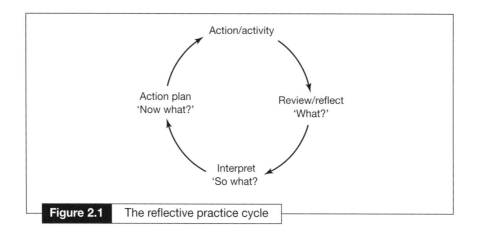

Figure 2.1   The reflective practice cycle

The first part of the process is to take part in the action or activity. During the
initial stages of training this will usually be a role play with trainers and class
colleagues. This might be a simulated, operational incident such as breath-test-
ing a motorist, issuing a fixed penalty notice or dealing with a domestic
dispute. Once the probationer officer has completed the 'experience' they will
be able to go through the remainder of the experiential learning cycle.

During the 'What?' stage the officer reflects on the event and what was
observed or felt during the experience. To assist in this process it is useful to get
the views and feelings of others involved in the scenario if appropriate.

The 'So what?' stage is about trying to make sense of what happened.
Consideration is given to how the reactions of those involved influenced the
outcome. Alternative behaviour, misunderstandings and mistakes may be
explored. Conclusions will then be drawn and theories developed as to what
might have happened if a different approach had been adopted.

The 'Now what?' stage is where a decision is made as to what to do in the
future and this approach is tried out in practice. At this stage an 'action plan'
may be developed to monitor this development.

This experiential learning cycle is presented as a continuing process. There is
no beginning or end as the learning continues with new experiences based on
that of earlier events. If this technique is adopted continuously then the
learner becomes a 'reflective practitioner'.

Another reason why the police service has taken this approach to training becomes apparent when the nature of police work is considered. Policing involves interactions with many different people, handling complex and often conflicting information and enforcing the law in widely varying, often stressful, circumstances. No two encounters will be the same and, therefore, it is impossible to train an officer to behave according to a set of rules or a formula.

2.10 Action planning

An important feature of the experiential learning cycle is 'action planning' to ensure that future performance reflects the changes that have been identified. Action planning is a critical part of a probationer officer's development, not just as part of the experiential learning cycle, but also in increasing professional competence.

The SMART action planning model is designed to help the probationer officer give structure to that process.

Specific – Be specific about what you want to improve. Examples of specific objectives might be to become competent in the completion of the right forms that must be filled in following the arrest of an individual; to become competent in the use of a piece of equipment such as a roadside breathalyser; to improve your verbal communication skills when speaking in public.

Measurable – Be sure that you can measure change when you achieve it. Measurement of your improvement may be provided by feedback from colleagues.

Achievable – Make sure your intentions are achievable. Any plan for development should be realistic in the time available using your existing knowledge and skills.

Relevant – Make sure the things you plan to do are actually achieving the things you want to achieve. It may be helpful to consider the relevant competency from the National Occupational Standards.

Timescale – You need a timescale to help focus your attention. Again, it is important to be realistic with any timescale set, as if you have not given yourself enough time then the plan may be unachievable.

2.11 Pre-reads and distance learning packages

One part of the change in the way in which training within the police service has developed is the emphasis on personal responsibility for development. This personal responsibility can be readily identified in the growing use of pre-reads and distance learning packages provided to officers during their training.

Pre-reads and distance learning packages may take the form of books, sheets or computer-based materials which are studied before the probationer attends a classroom session. Information is supplied to read and digest. This allows the probationer officer to study the subject at their own pace before attending the classroom session. This then allows the trainer to devote more classroom time to developing understanding, skills and abilities and discussing attitudes. The success of this training method depends largely on the learner taking responsibility for their own learning.

2.12 Further considerations

It is important to note that there are many other policing roles that can be done without signing up to be a sworn police constable. The training and development principles outlined above also apply to the development of special constables and police community support officers. At present, a member of police staff – for example, a police community support officer or a special constable – who wishes to become a sworn officer has no avenue available to them other than to apply in a competition which is open to the general public. While that member of police staff is likely to benefit in the tests and assessment centre from the skills and experience built up in their police service, there is no means by which they can be appointed ahead of any other suitably-qualified applicant. However, the government has recently outlined its desire to promote an easier movement from police staff or special constable to regular police officer status for those who wish to, and who can meet the national recruitment standards. It has been proposed that links should be made between the competency-based training programmes for special constables, PCSOs and other members of the policing family and the probationer package for regular officers.

The police service remains unusual, if not unique, in developing all its senior officers from those who join at the rank of constable. Some argue that this current system denies the service the opportunity to recruit those who have already progressed to a promoted position in comparable jobs – such as in the probation service, HM Customs, financial crime investigation or the armed forces. At the time of writing, the government is proposing to introduce multiple points of entry to the police service, and to remove the requirement that all police officers serve specific amounts of time at junior ranks before being promoted to more senior ranks.

At present there are several new degree courses in policing which aim to prepare individuals for police duty. These are primarily available at the universities of Glamorgan in South Wales, Central England in Birmingham and Portsmouth. Thirty-one per cent of those passing the police recruitment assessment centres in 2003–4 were graduates. The Police Reform White Paper, published in 2004 entitled *Building communities, beating crime: a better police service for the 21st century* presents the views of Ministers on the future of the police service. This report clarifies that the government intends to review whether the offer which the police service is able to make currently to graduates is sufficiently attractive. They are looking at this particularly in relation to opportunities for accelerated career development, and whether more can be done to market police careers more effectively to the graduate recruitment market.

There are already arrangements in place to identify those officers with the greatest potential through the High Potential Development Scheme. Graduates and non-graduates are entitled to apply. This is a competency-based, structured career framework which can lead to the most senior positions in the police service. It aims to turn potential into performance, whether as a highly effective middle manager in command and leadership roles, or beyond at the strategic leadership level of the police service.

Suggested further reading

Training Matters Report by Her Majesty's Inspector of Constabulary (Training) (London: HMSO, 2002)
Building communities, beating crime; a better service for the 21st century Home Office Report (2004)

Useful websites

www.policecouldyou.co.uk
The police recruitment website that contains a lot of information about being a probationer officer

Chapter 3

Communication

This chapter supports the following National Occupational Standards which describe the performance and competence required of a probationer officer.

Unit No.	Unit title
1A1	Use police actions in a fair and justified way.
1A2	Communicate effectively with members of communities.
1A4	Foster people's equality, diversity and rights.
1B9	Provide initial support to individuals affected by offending or anti-social behaviour and assess their needs for further support.
2A1	Gather and submit information that has the potential to support policing objectives.
2C2	Prepare for, and participate in, planned policing operations.
2C3	Arrest, detain or report individuals.
2C4	Minimise and deal with aggressive and abusive behaviour.
2G2	Conduct investigations.
2G4	Finalise investigations.
SH1	Interview victims and witnesses.
2H2	Interview suspects.
2I1	Search individuals.
2I2	Search vehicles, premises and land.
2J1	Prepare and submit case files.

▶

Unit No.	Unit title
2J2	Present evidence in court and at other hearings.
2K1	Escort detained persons.
2K2	Present detained persons to custody.
4C1	Develop your own knowledge and practice.
4G2	Ensure your own actions reduce risks to health and safety.

3.1 Introduction

A quick glance at a newspaper reinforces the importance of good communication at the level of the organisation: lapses in security at an airport are put down to poor communication between staff, the failure of a political party to win an election may be attributed to a failure to communicate policies to voters, and a TV advertisement may be criticised because it gives an inappropriate message about a product and so fails to increase sales. But communication at the level of 'person to person' is no less important, as illustrated by the examples in exercise 3A.

Exercise 3A

Here are some examples of communication. Complete the last columns before moving on. The first row is done for you.

Communication	Common mistakes	Possible consequences if communication is ineffective.	Possible consequences if communication is effective.
1. Officer requesting urgent assistance at scene of car accident.	Rushed message. Failing to wait for acknowledgement of receipt of the message from control.	Help is not sent to the right location.	Ambulance promptly directed to scene.
2. Elderly resident is spoken to about minor criminal damage to her property.	Officer appears uninterested *or* in a rush. High expectations of an imminent arrest are raised.	Resident is disillusioned with the police service.	

Exercise 3A continued

3. Officer is addressing two youths who have been fighting in the street.	To be too aggressive *or* too low-key, loud *or* too quiet and unimposing.	Youths resume fighting after the officer leaves and an arrest becomes necessary.	
4. Officer is asked directions to a shopping centre.	Body language and mannerism and level of voice indicate lack of interest to member of the public.	Member of public believes every member of the police service is unhelpful and lazy.	
5. Passer-by shouts abuse at a passing pedestrian belonging to an ethnic minority.	Not to firmly correct the passer-by.	The police service appears indifferent to the low-level abuse which can develop into more serious racism.	
6. Officer fails to complete a written file properly.	'Points to prove' are not clearly brought out in statements.	Prosecution may fail.	
7. Chief officer fails to communicate the strategy of a police force to her officers.	Strategy appears too abstract. There is little consultation with officers. Practitioners cannot see how they can implement the strategy in their daily work.	Police officers cannot see the value of the strategy and they see strategic aims as a 'game' to impress politicians and the media.	
8. Officer is presenting oral evidence in court.	Officer fails to study file before attending court. Officer appears nervous and does not seem to understand court procedures and the rules of evidence.	The court and public lose confidence in the officer. The prosecution case may fail because of this.	
9. Senior officer investigating a murder does not use TV and press effectively.	Too much emphasis upon details of crime and very little about the ways in which the public may be able to	provide help. Fewer members of the public feel that they are being asked for help.	

Here are some possible answers:

(2) A resident is assured and has realistic expectations of the service. She might also feel that police officers are 'human beings' too.

(3) The youths might realise that an arrest is imminent and move on peacefully.

(4) The member of public might feel 'engaged' with 'his' police service.

(5) The aggressor might now realise that there are limits to acceptable behaviour and that there are consequences of further improper actions. The passing member of the public might have more confidence in the police service.

(6) Prosecution may be successful.

(7) Police officers might change the way they work and adopt the priorities of the chief officer.

(8) Prosecution case is accepted by the court.

(9) The public is more likely to provide the 'missing piece of information' that leads to an arrest.

The circumstances surrounding the examples in exercise 3A remind us that there are several types of communication including:

- Verbal (i.e. communication by speaking)
- Mannerisms and facial expressions (communication without speaking)
- Written reports
- Web pages, posters and leaflets.

Writing reports which are concise, but also effective in that they transfer the correct information to the reader, requires practice. Success comes with determination and effort. In particular, poor punctuation and spelling give a very poor impression and may detract from what is otherwise good quality work.

3.2 Communication with the public

Communication with the public occurs at the individual level of victim, suspect and investigator and also at the organisational level through publicity (good or bad) in the media.

Every police officer has a role in maintaining and improving the standing of the police service in the eyes of the public. In Chapter 1, we noted how individual interactions with the public can influence the support that the police receive. Communication starts as soon as we arrive at the scene of an incident. How the police appear (scruffy or smart) and act (professional and fair or incompetent and biased) determines the level of trust that the public have in the police service. Above all, an understanding of the needs and predicament of the individual and a determination to 'keep their promises' avoid the negative feedback that bedevils many public organisations. The best newly-appointed officers (as well as seasoned veterans) always reflect upon how they have dealt with people on a regular basis and ask the questions: 'How did that go? If it went wrong, why did it go wrong? What will I do differently next time?' Ignore the comments of the cynical or narrow-minded: reflection is the way that we get better at our jobs. Improved ways of working not only help the police service, but also give each of us more job satisfaction because we feel we are 'doing a good job'.

Crime investigation involves many different types of communication. One particularly important example of communication is suspect interviewing, in which an officer builds up a relationship with a suspect which allows the officer to obtain the facts relevant to a case and gives the suspect an opportunity to explain his version of events.

The responsibilities of those in the rank of constable are increasing. The emphasis upon community and neighbourhood policing brings constables (as well as more senior ranks) into new roles in which they interact directly with their communities in ways such as negotiating resources, requesting information from anxious householders, placating angry residents, guiding community groups and listening to the concerned and aggrieved. These activities can only be successful if communication is effective.

A common form of communication between the police service and the public occurs through phone calls. Police forces are increasingly using call handlers to assess and grade calls according to their urgency in order to prioritise resources. An example of the classification of calls is shown in table 3.1.

Grade	Definition	Example
1	Life threatening	Multiple car crash on motorway.
2	Crime in progress	Looting is taking place in a shop at night.
3	Response required in 12 hours	Householder reports substantial criminal damage.
4	Response required in 72 hours	Advice requested regarding the secure storage of a shotgun.
5	Telephone response only required	Irate customer who has bought faulty goods is referred to her solicitor.

Table 3.1 Classification of calls from the public

Being a good verbal communicator

- An audience or individual is more likely to remember something that is important to them. Lesson: make your comments relevant to them. For example, if you wish to explain to a 12-year-old why stealing is wrong, don't speak abstractly about 'rights and wrongs'. Ask them how they would feel if their new mobile phone or iPod was stolen.

- Verbal communication must not be too lengthy. Keep comments succinct whilst not appearing abrupt. Do not get involved in side discussions and do not allow yourself to be diverted from the main message or question.

- Think of a message as being like electricity travelling down a wire: some current is wasted and never gets to the electric device. Similarly, communication is never perfectly efficient in the sense that the receiver picks up all the information, tone and urgency of the message sent by the speaker. Good verbal communication requires concentration and planning: exactly what is it that you are trying to say or trying to find out? What confirmatory questions do we need to ask in order to satisfy ourselves that the recipient has received the message?

- Body language is very important to the receiver. Try and maintain eye contact in conversations and make the intended recipient feel as if you are interested in their point of view. Above all, try and give a relaxed and confident air – without being condescending!

- Don't crowd an individual's personal space as this can heighten anxieties and appear aggressive – unless this is your intention.

- Match the communication to the audience, but never patronise people and never demean yourself by resorting to threats or swearing. 'Keeping cool' when provoked or insulted is difficult at first, but it is a very disarming tactic that you must learn.

> ### Exercise 3B
>
> Keeping police officers up-to-date about changes in the law poses logistical problems for the police service who cannot afford to take all their officers 'off the street' to be trained. For example, the Serious Crime and Disorder Act 2005 radically changed the basis on which arrests are made by police officers. Find out from police colleagues how these changes were communicated to existing officers, whether or not the communication strategy was effective and what can be done to improve such communications in the future.

3.3 Communication and the fight against crime

Whatever strategy we adopt to combat crime, it will not be effective unless the public know what part they can play in alerting the police service to crime 'hot spots' and in providing information with which to target police resources. For this reason, the government has detailed a communication strategy to help Crime and Disorder Partnerships 'spread the word'. The strategy includes:

- Using paid publicity (advertisements or posters) where appropriate
- Getting coverage from the news media and making the most of broadcast interviews
- How to avoid raising the public fear of crime
- Involving children as well as adults
- Linking with all members of the community, including those with disabilities
- Connecting with minority ethnic groups
- Involving businesses (such as local shops).

Such a communication strategy has two other functions, that of demonstrating to the public that the Crime and Disorder Partnerships exist and that the police service is serious about crime reduction. This links with the 'reassurance agenda' mentioned in Chapter 1: even if crime is reduced, the reassurance effect only comes into play if the public feel that this is the case.

Exercise 3C

'Getting the message across'

When you are next in a police station, pick out one poster on the wall, perhaps one about crime reduction. Analyse the poster. What is the purpose of the poster? Who is the intended audience? Is the message simple? Are there other ways the message could be delivered to the public? Will the poster be effective? Is the poster likely to be a waste of money?

When next there is a new initiative, such as a knife amnesty or drink-driving campaign, study how the initiative is publicised. If possible, contact the campaign co-ordinators and try and find out why they chose to publicise matters in that way. In doing so you will be preparing for the future: it is likely that you will be involved at some point in publicising police-related work in your neighbourhood and beat areas.

3.4 Communicating with the public about major incidents

Immediate communication with the public when major incidents (such as terrorist attacks) occur has two purposes: to warn the public about further danger and to stop speculation and panic. The speed at which the information can be given to the public depends critically upon the availability of up-to-date information from personnel at the scene. In the July 2005 London bombings, most of the emergency services could not communicate underground and this caused further confusion.

The police service may have to take pre-emptive action against suspected terrorists when very little concrete intelligence is available. Communication concerning anti-terrorist operations against such suspects is particularly challenging as such operations often target individuals and premises within ethnic groups. This can easily be perceived as a conspiracy against that minority and such perceptions are difficult to dispel because much of the information relating to the operation cannot be disclosed to the general public. One suggestion is to disclose the intelligence to a small number of representatives of minorities (such as the Muslim community) so that they can understand the nature of the information upon which the police aim to act and can reassure their communities that action has been taken in good faith. In this sense, the representatives are being used to communicate the acceptability (or otherwise) of police action to the wider community.

Exercise 3D

Websites

Look up four police force websites, including a major metropolitan force and a rural force. Make a list of the different ways that forces use websites (for example, to seek help from the public, to advertise success in 'crime busts', to provide information on where help can be obtained). What kind of information is displayed on the home page? Are the same kinds of documents (for example, police plans) available on each website?

3.5 Communication within the police service

Communication within a police force can be *across* the police force (e.g. from one division to another), from *top to bottom* (e.g. chief officer to constable) or from *bottom to top* (as when views about the force are obtained through staff questionnaires). Communication between police forces also occurs daily on a large scale, particularly when information is required from within another force area.

The National Intelligence Model (NIM) is partly based upon gathering, organising, disseminating (and subsequently acting upon) information that is relevant to crime. Criticisms about the implementation of NIM include the failure of officers to report information that they have obtained from patrol; without this, the crime analysts have nothing to work on and the NIM model breaks down.

3.6 Communication between the police service and other agencies

The police service is sometimes criticised for failing to collaborate properly with other agencies by sharing and receiving information.

An example of such a criticism originated in the aftermath of the tragic murders of Holly Wells and Jessica Chapman in 2002. Ian Huntley, a caretaker at Soham Village School, Cambridgeshire, was convicted of their murders. Huntley had been subjected to vetting for the post of caretaker, but no relevant information had been revealed by the checks. It later transpired that between 1995 and 1999 there had been a series of incidents involving allegations against Huntley, but this information had not been passed on to Cambridgeshire Constabulary who carried out the vetting search. This led to the Bichard Inquiry which examined the effectiveness of the relevant intelligence-based record keeping, the vetting practices in police forces since 1995 and information-sharing with other agencies. The inquiry made numerous recommendations, including the development of an improved IT infrastructure to enhance the storage and transfer of relevant information in the future.

Case study

Victoria Climbié: a case of neglect and failures in communication

Victoria Climbié was sent to the UK by her parents in Africa to escape poverty. She died aged eight after years of gross neglect and mistreatment by her aunt and her aunt's boyfriend. Victoria's case was reviewed by social workers, doctors, nurses and police officers, but no one acted to prevent her ordeal. When she died, doctors recorded 128 separate injuries on her body.

Her death was a tragic sequence of neglect and incompetence. When a consultant studied some of her cuts, she decided that they were due to a disease called scabies. The consultant later said that she assumed that someone else would investigate further. In another incident, a police officer failed to investigate the Climbié's home and a social worker neglected to read the Climbié case file properly.

The Climbié case was one in which officials from all agencies demonstrated neglect and non-compliance with existing codes of practice, but it also represented a break-down in communication between individuals and between agencies: this has been a feature of several earlier inquiries. In several cases, individuals even denied receiving information that should have 'set alarm bells ringing', and therefore indicated that Victoria Climbié was at serious risk.

Amongst the many recommendations of the Climbié Inquiry was the insistence that managers from social services and the police should be involved at the referral stage of an investigation, i.e. that senior and experienced managers should communicate and work together and not leave these matters to less senior or inexperienced staff.

The conclusions of the inquiry are of general applicability. Protecting vulnerable individuals, including children, is a multi-disciplinary task. An attitude that agencies must work together and that 'passing the buck' is not acceptable might help reduce the number of such tragic cases in the future. Communication breakdowns can be as a result of 'systematic failures' in that the established way of doing things is flawed, but they are often because individuals are careless about the quality and quantity of information that they acquire and give to other professionals.

Suggested further reading

Kidd, V. and Brazie, R., *Community Oriented Policing: Cop Talk* (San Francisco: Acada Books, 1999)

Useful websites

www.crimereduction.gov.uk
Communication strategy to help Crime and Disorder Partnerships

http://www.bichardinquiry.org.uk/
The Bichard Inquiry

http://www.victoria-climbie-inquiry.org.uk/
The Victoria Climbié Inquiry

http://www.homeoffice.gov.uk/rds/prgpdfs/fprs13.pdf
Historical research in the use of 'call grading'

Chapter 4

Study Skills

This chapter supports the following National Occupational Standards which describe the performance and competence required of a probationer officer.

Unit No.	Unit title
1A1	Use police actions in a fair and justified way.
1A2	Communicate effectively with members of communities.
1A4	Foster people's equality, diversity and rights.
1B9	Provide initial support to individuals affected by offending or anti-social behaviour and assess their needs for further support.
2A1	Gather and submit information that has the potential to support policing objectives.
2C2	Prepare for, and participate in, planned policing operations.
2C3	Arrest, detain or report individuals.
2C4	Minimise and deal with aggressive and abusive behaviour.
2G2	Conduct investigations.
2G4	Finalise investigations.
SH1	Interview victims and witnesses.
2H2	Interview suspects.
2I1	Search individuals.
2I2	Search vehicles, premises and land.
2J1	Prepare and submit case files.

▶

Unit No.	Unit title
2J2	Present evidence in court and at other hearings.
2K1	Escort detained persons.
2K2	Present detained persons to custody.
4C1	Develop your own knowledge and practice.
4G2	Ensure your own actions reduce risks to health and safety.

4.1 The study skills needed by probationer officers

'I had left school ten years ago and I was terrified that I wouldn't make the grade in my probation. But this was my second job and I knew I simply had to make a success of it. I found that I was in a class of probationers that contained people from a range of backgrounds. A few seemed to find it all relatively straightforward, others much harder than I did. By the time I did my first test my confidence had improved greatly and I didn't look back after that. Being a police officer is much more than having sufficient knowledge of the law. You have to behave in the right way and do some very practical things. My advice is to take being a learner and being a police officer seriously and listen – really listen – to the tutors and trainers – and then you will surprise yourself.'

Comments by a probationer police officer

Police officers are learning all the time, but the probationary period can seem particularly daunting. Most initial learning programmes now involve a greater range of different types of assessments than before and many are now linked to academic study in universities. The purpose of the following sections is to guide you through some of the study skills that you will require in order to 'survive'. These sections include report writing, essay writing and research skills.

Police officers who are studying require the same skills as other students in college and university. These include *self-motivation* (the ability to drive yourself to succeed), *self-reflection* (the willingness to review performance and improve), *time management* (an ability to organise your time effectively), the ability to *team-work* (a recognition that you sometimes have to work with others and gain help from others) and an ability to identify the core of academic and training material and see the material *in its proper context*. It is important to realise that your police force wants *every officer* to succeed. If you have passed the police selection process then it is very likely that you possess all the necessary qualities to succeed as a police officer, although everyone still needs to work hard to achieve very challenging targets.

Intelligence

The idea of intelligence (ability or cleverness) has preoccupied psychologists for many decades. But we can summarise two of the most important results of their work that are relevant to us.

The first is that there are different kinds of ability. Examples are the ability to read, to apply logic rules, to see in three dimensions, to play music or to catch a ball. Our everyday observations suggest that people have different strengths in each of these activities, but that we can all get better by practising. This can be generalised: we can get better at most of these tasks by repetition or through guidance.

The second is summarised by the phrase 'nature versus nurture'. Are our abilities genetic or are they the result of our environment or education? It seems most likely that environment is at least as important as our genes and this helps us in approaching any type of training – however late in life – because it allows us to acquire abilities which we did not seem to have possessed as young people. One feature of most probationer police officers is that they are strongly motivated, and experience suggests that this allows most officers to overcome any previous disadvantages of education or background. This can be simply summarised: 'others have done it and you can do it. Do not give up!'

4.2 Essay writing

All police officers – particularly aspiring managers – must be able to impress with the quality, brevity and accuracy of their written work.

Some basic essay-style tips: think before you write!

- Your essays should be written in a logical structure with correct spelling and punctuation. Do not imagine that good grammar and punctuation skills are achieved overnight. Like many things, these skills have to be continually improved upon – there is no 'quick fix'.

- Be careful when using spellcheckers on computers as some words are spelt differently in an American dictionary to those of an English counterpart, e.g. American, *'color'*; British, *'colour'*.

- Take care not to confuse similar words e.g. *principal* (as in 'principal partner') and *principle* (as in 'the principles of criminal investigation'). If in doubt, check your spelling in a dictionary!

- The format will usually be given out in advance, but if in doubt allow 1.5 line spacing and 'justify' your work. Use a TrueType font (e.g. Arial or Times New Roman) in regular style, size 12.

- If the essay is part of an assignment, always attach a relevant coursework sheet to the front of the essay.

- Staple your work together, and do not put your work in a plastic pocket sleeve unless fragile documents such as photographs or computer discs are included.

What is expected?

The reader of your essay will be looking for four distinct criteria when assessing your work. These are:

- *General understanding of the subject matter* – have you understood what the purpose of the essay is? Do you appreciate the breadth and complexity of the subject?

- *Structure of argument* – is what you say clear and understandable? Is your work accurate and is it comprehensive?

- *Level and logic of analysis* – have you understood what you are talking about and been critical enough? Have you just presented facts or have you talked about the strengths and weaknesses in arguments or in previous projects?

- *Level and use of research/literature* – have you correctly *referenced* a sufficient amount of work in accordance with the preferred system, taking into account the rules of plagiarism?

The 'four parts' of an essay

The essay should broadly contain four distinct component parts. These are:

- Introduction

- Main body

- Conclusion

- Reference list.

The introduction

- Clear statements at the outset are essential, both in terms of telling the reader about the content to be discussed and establishing an important impression. Provide 'a route map': a few lines that show the reader where you intend to go on the 'journey' (the essay) and what he/she will find out or be told on the way.

- This is your chance to explain the structure of your work and you also have the opportunity to justify the selection of your themes etc.

The main body

- Depending upon the essay question you may have to define key terms or concepts at the start. For example if you were writing an essay concerning 'the dark figure of crime', you would need to define that concept from the start, using an academic source (not just your notes).

- Read around the subject area and define your lines of argument through three or four main themes.

- Support each point you make with examples and illustrations from the literature and research in the area. You can now see why *referencing* is so important (see section below).

- Present your essay in a flowing and logical manner and also ensure that links are made between themes. For example, try to have each paragraph dealing with a particular issue/subject and use linking sentences such as *'at the same time ...'* or *'as well as ...'* to help the reader follow your arguments.

The conclusion

- The role of a conclusion is to present a final condensed version of the essay's main argument. It should take up no more than ten per cent of your essay.

- Here you can provide a summary of the main ideas or main features of the argument.

- You can also provide an answer to any question and can state any wider implications or trends and provide an overview of future considerations.

Remember, the ultimate goal is to construct and convey a sustained and objective argument which takes into account contrary evidence. A good essay undergoes several draft phases and it cannot be rushed.

4.3 Report writing

A report may be defined as a formal statement of the results of an investigation or of any matter on which definite information is required, made by some person or body instructed or required to do so. Reports may be written to record, inform and to recommend and they are regularly used by the police service to convey information about specific matters.

A report serves two main purposes:

1 Provides a permanent, comprehensive and coherent account of an investigation, study or piece of research.

2 Provides information which is required for decision making.

By perfecting the art of report writing you will be improving your performance as a potential manager, project leader, researcher or investigator.

The structure of the report

Rules are required to ensure all reports comply with the same corporate approach. This also assists everyone because of the use of a common style. The contents of a report should include the following main sections:

1 **Title** – includes the title, subtitle, the writer(s), the recipient and the date of the report.

2 **Summary or abstract** – Normally of one paragraph (50 to 100 words) or one page (300 to 400 words). It is a précis of the whole report (see example below).

3 **List of contents** – A list of chapters or sections as they appear in the report, giving the page on which each begins.

4 **Introduction** – This will include the events leading up to the request for the report, terms of reference, resources available to the writer, or acknowledgment of help from others.

5 **Body** – Under headings (see section below on headings).

6 **Conclusions** – Here the author looks back at the work and delivers the verdict. It may involve comparing different possibilities and it is here that the report may look more like an essay.

7 **Recommendations** – Recommendations should be kept short, crisp and to the point, avoiding overlaps with the conclusion.

8 **Appendices** – This may include a list of sources or a bibliography. It may also contain tables or diagrams, and sometimes – in technical reports – a glossary of terms used in the report.

Headings used in the body of the report

Some form of numbering in the main body of the report is essential for ease of reference. One of the most common forms is that called the Decimal Notation System. In this system, main sections within the body of the report are given single numbers (1, 2, 3, etc.) in numerical order. The first level of subsection under the major section will follow a decimal point (1.1) and the first subsection under that subsection will repeat the process. Usually three levels of numbering are sufficient. For example, if we were to organise a report on house insulation, then the contents may be organised as follows:

> 3. House Insulation (*the main section heading*)
>> 3.1 Walls (*the first subsection heading*)
>>> 3.1.1 Cavity Fillings (*1st subsection under 1st subsection*)
>>> 3.1.2 Dry Lining (*2nd subsection under 1st subsection*)
>>> 3.1.3 Pebble Dashing
>> 3.2 Loft (*the second subsection*)
>>> 3.2.1 Fibre Glass (*1st subsection under 2nd subsection*)
>>> 3.2.2 Polystyrene Tiles
>> 3.3 Windows
>>> 3.3.1 Double Glazing
>>> 3.3.2 Brick Over

4.4 Referencing

The act of providing links and acknowledgments to previous work is called *referencing*. Failing to reference is not only discourteous, it may also involve litigation against a charge of 'stealing someone's results'. Above all else, failing to reference is a matter of fairness; in academic circles passing off someone else's work as your own is called plagiarism and it is treated as a serious 'academic offence'.

The different ways of referencing in books and articles may appear confusing but it is important to remember that failing to reference is much more serious than failing to reference in the correct way! Here are a few examples:

The numeric system of referencing

Here the reference is indicated in the text using a number in a bracket or as a superscript. Suppose that an article contained the sentence:

> The importance of police culture has been previously examined[2].
> (The superscript method)

Or

> The importance of police culture has been previously examined (2).
> (The bracket method)

For both methods, the reference may appear at the foot of the page or at the end of the article or book chapter and would be shown as:

> (2) Smith GT, Zander P, 1999, *Improving the Police Service*, London, Atmore Publishers

The Harvard system of referencing

This involves giving the names of the researchers and the date of the publication being referenced in the text, e.g.:

> The importance of police culture has been previously examined (Smith and Zander (1999))

The reference may appear at the foot of the page or at the end of the article or book chapter as before, and would again be shown as:

> Smith GT, Zander P, 1999, *Improving the Police Service*, London, Atmore Publishers

Referencing a website

You must however be particularly careful that you complete the details of the website you are using correctly, as an examiner may wish to visit it him/herself. An example of referencing a website is given below.

> ... the number of dangerous driving offences recorded between 1989 and 2003 has been previously reported[13].

The reference may appear at the foot of the page or at the end of the article or book chapter and would be shown as:

> 13. Association of Chief Police Officers report on road traffic, http://www.acpo.police.uk accessed 21 July 2006

Referencing personal communication

Sometimes we rely on personal communication with an individual in order to complete our research. For example, your report might include the statement:

> It has been confirmed that Lancaster Police operate a substantial amount of community and race relations training[35].

In this case the reference would be:

> 35. Chief Constable of Lancaster Police, personal correspondence to author, dated 21 July 2006.

4.5 Research

In everyday language the word 'research' is often used to mean a study of any kind, but in the academic world research means an in-depth investigation of a subject which is carried out objectively and logically using accepted methods of data acquisition and data analysis and which reflects upon any previous and relevant work in this subject area.

If that definition sounds like a lot of hot air, consider a project to evaluate the effect of additional foot patrols in a city centre on the public's feeling of reassurance. We might decide to use questionnaires to find out the views of the public. There are many factors that need to be taken into account in such a study and they may be grouped into two classes:

Questions about the design of the information-gathering part of the project

- How do we define reassurance? How do we use questionnaires to measure it?

- How many questionnaires do we give out (i.e. what should be the 'sample size')?

- Where and when do we distribute them?

- Do we need to control the interviewee sample so as to contain representative numbers of young and old, rich and poor, minority ethnic and majority population?

- Is it possible to do a 'before and after' measurement of the public's reassurance?

Questions about the interpretation of the results

- Were the responses to the questions clear enough to be reliable measurements of reassurance?

- If respondents haven't seen the officers on patrol, do we ignore their comments?

- Are the results reliable?

- Are the results representative of the public as a whole?

- How do the results compare with any other similar research?

Running projects like this well relies heavily upon experience. For example, a particularly important part of this project is to ensure that respondents do not think they are being asked 'whether or not more patrolling police officers are a good idea', but that they are clear that they being asked 'do *you* feel reassured?'

We are confident that many members of the public will agree that more patrols are beneficial, but this project is focused on a particular city and on a particular investment in extra officers. It is important that managers in the police service are able to measure the benefits (or otherwise) of such initiatives. It is also important to see the results of this project against the results of previous studies in different cities which have been reported in the literature.

An example of police-related research: the 'TASC' project

The Tackling Alcohol-related Street Crime (TASC) project was a multi-agency partnership led by the police under the Home Office Targeted Policing-Initiative, with the aim of reducing alcohol-related crime and disorder in central Cardiff. Partners included the South Wales Police, Cardiff University, the local Licensees Forum, the local Accident and Emergency Department, the council and the probation service.

Traditionally, crime data is obtained from reports made by (or to) the police, but the TASC project also used anonymous information from the district hospital to provide a better measurement of the true scale and nature of alcohol-related crime. This meant that some crimes which were unreported to the police were, nevertheless, included in the data that was collected.

The resources required to manage the project included a project manager and alcohol licensing expert (both police officers), a data analyst, a nurse (for hospital liaison) and clerical support.

The method used in the study was carefully defined before the project began:

1 Data of alcohol-related crime would be collected from police and hospital sources.

2 The data would then be analysed to identify patterns and trends.

3 The analysis would be used to inform partners of any actions that could reduce alcohol-related crime. (This is often called 'intervention'.) Actions included better training of door staff in pubs and clubs and higher levels of advertising (particularly targeted against young people) promoting sensible drinking.

Hospital sources revealed 30 per cent more crimes than the police data. Some interesting patterns were identified. The 'hotspot' premises were not always the ones that patrol officers had identified. For example, the nuclei of disturbances included pubs as well as nightclubs. Additionally, pubs open 11:00 am to 11:00 pm and selling cheap drink were heavily implicated because they caused offenders to 'build up' alcohol levels so that they behaved violently later in the nightclubs. Five per cent of violent events involved underage drinkers.

The TASC project is a type of study called a 'before and after study': the effects of the actions taken by partners were assessed by comparing alcohol-related crime over a 12 month period with the 12 month period before

▶

the project began. There are many complex trends revealed in the project report but, overall, total alcohol-related crime fell slightly during the period (by 4%), but the benefits of the project may have been underestimated because the capacity of licensed premises increased by ten per cent during the project. 'Before and after studies' are most useful when underlying factors remain constant: we can then attribute changes in outcomes (here, reduced numbers of crimes) to those interventions that have taken place. But as the TASC project shows, factors may change over which we have no control and under these circumstances any interpretations of 'cause and effect' have to be very carefully justified.

An important part of any project is an evaluation of its 'value for money'. The total cost of the project was estimated to be £488,000 with project 'set-up' costs forming most of the costs. Nurse support cost £85,000, door-staff training £66,000 and the media campaign £54,000. Targeted policing (around 'hotspots', etc.) incurred additional costs of £40,000. Against these costs have to be balanced the costs of the NHS treating serious injuries incurred by assaults (typically over £100,000 for seriously wounded patients) and in savings on police time. However, the increase in the capacity of licensed premises over the timescale of the project made reliable financial estimates of the benefits of TASC impossible. This is not to say that the benefits didn't exist, but that that they could not be reliably estimated: this is an important feature of authoritative researchers – they will *not* make claims that they cannot support.

The project has also to be seen against the aims of the alcohol providers (which exist to make profits) and the 'magnet effect' of existing premises which causes new premises to be opened in a relatively small area of our major cities. It is inevitable that some alcohol providers will not wish to do anything that will reduce demand for the drinks they sell and that others will only wish to engage with the police service in limited ways. The concentration of premises in parts of our cities also causes conflict because of the limited numbers of taxis that are available when the night clubs close: the 'exit strategies' using coaches that are used for football supporters after major matches cannot be replicated in city centres in the early hours of the morning.

Exercise 4A

The definition of 'alcohol-related crime' is an important part of the planning of the project. Suggest a practical definition that one might use.

The definition adopted by the study was that it is violent crime committed in or close to licensed premises or violent crime in which the offenders were known to be drinking on the streets. Note that if subsequent studies used a different definition then we would not be comparing 'like with like'.

4.6 The use and abuse of statistics

Former prime minister Benjamin Disraeli is usually attributed with the famous statement 'there are three kinds of lies: lies, damned lies, and statistics'. Taken at face value, this is a very cynical view of statistics but it does warn us not to be too hasty in making conclusions from the figures that others provide. The 'golden rule' is that *you* have to be able to justify any conclusions that you make (in reports or verbally) which are based on statistics.

Exercise 4B

The use and abuse of statistical data

Discuss the validity of the following statements.

(a) 'Inspector Garett reported that car thefts had fallen by three per cent in the central ward during the last two years. This showed that the advice given by officers (e.g. to park cars in well-lit areas) was working.'

(b) 'The total number of abortions last year was 190,000, compared with 186,000 the previous year, a rise of two per cent probably caused by reduced funding in sex education in schools.'

(c) 'A police spokesperson said that there had been a decrease in drug use by 30 per cent during the last year and that this shows that our streets are safer.'

(d) 'The statistics showed a 40 per cent reduction in burglaries in the city over the last five years, a reduction which may be attributed to the improved working between partners and the police service.'

One would hope that the spokespersons would be able to support these statements with carefully-reasoned arguments and facts. Here are some responses which indicate weaknesses in attributing too much to these statistics. At the very least the responses indicate the follow-up questions that should be asked.

(a) Three per cent might be statistically insignificant. It might represent only a few extra thefts – perhaps due to one thief. For example, if there were only 100 thefts in the area during the two years, a reduction of only three thefts would reduce the total by three per cent. Other factors might be operating which have caused the slight decrease in theft, e.g. some 'problem families' leaving the main estate because they have been evicted by the council, a fall in population, different truancy policies in the school, etc.

(b) Has the child-bearing female population altered over the last year? Do immigration and demographic trends explain the increase? Don't be fooled by the word 'probably': you must still be able to justify any conclusions you make.

(c) We need more information! How many drug users are there? What does 'drug use' mean? Would an occasional user count as much as a habitual user? Does it mean the number of times people used drugs or does it mean the number of drug users? It would be valuable to know what kind of drug abuse has been responsible for the increase (some drugs are more harmful than others). Does the data include an increase in registered addicts on treatment programmes who might not pose a danger? How was the data collected? Can we be sure that it is accurate? Would respondents always tell the truth? What is the connection between drug use and 'unsafe streets'? Is there evidence that links the users with crime in most cases? Such evidence has not been presented. If statistics are being linked to other events, e.g. muggings, then this connection needs to be established statistically. That means more study!

(d) This might be partly or entirely true, but such a reduction might also represent the low resale value of goods (such as DVDs and televisions) which have traditionally formed a significant part of the burglar's 'haul'. A low resale value would mean that many burglaries would not be 'worth the risk'. Indeed, even a detailed study might not be able to disentangle all the factors involved. The key point is that you should be aware that claims of improved rates of detection or crime prevention are result of many influences, many of which do not lie within the control of the police service.

The words used by individuals drawing conclusions from statistics require careful examination. Consider (d) again. The words 'may be attributed' suggests that improved working practices *caused* the reduction. If instead of stating that the reduction *was caused* by improved working practices the reporter had said 'that the reduction was *consistent* with improved practices' we would have agreed with her unconditionally. The reduction is certainly consistent with improved practices in the sense that improved practices might reasonably be expected to reduce burglary. But the reduction is also consistent with improved home security, more visible patrols, fewer reported burglaries and (as we have noted above) with a reduced profit from stolen electronic goods. Nor is it likely that one factor alone has changed and the others have remained constant in their impact. Although one factor may dominate, the others will also be changing over the reporting period.

Sources of criminal statistics

There are, in general, three main sources of statistics used by the police when discussing crime. These are used to help the police respond to crime and to allocate resources. The three sources are:

1 **Official statistics** which are compiled each year from information supplied from police and court records. In the main these involve what is known as 'notifiable offences' such as burglary, theft and robbery amongst others. 'Notifiable' just means that they are crimes that the Home Office want to be notified about.

2 **Victimisation studies** which are surveys of people in general and are not connected to the official statistics. The most important of these types of surveys is known as the British Crime Survey (BCS). For this type of survey, people are chosen at random and are asked to give details of crimes in which they have been a victim in the previous 12 months. This information is often compared with the official statistics to see how accurate they are.

3 **Local surveys** which are carried out by Crime and Disorder Partnerships as part of their role in preparing a crime audit. This audit then helps to decide how the police and their partners should police communities at a local level.

4.7 Police-related journals

How do you find out what research is being done in policing? Below is a list of many of the police-related publications that are available in most university libraries. The Home Office website also contains electronic versions of sponsored research relating to crime and policing.

- *Police Review* – is a weekly journal which discusses many topical issues as well as having a large section explaining the law, etc.

- *Police Professional* – a journal which discusses many strategic and topical issues, particularly managing the police.

- *Police* – a magazine produced by the Police Federation and aimed at keeping police staff and police officers informed of current events within the police service.

- *Policing in Society* – a journal that covers many different police research activities from a sociological viewpoint and considers the role of police in society.

- *Police Research and Management* – a journal that comprises much research based on practical application in the workplace and aimed at practitioners.

Suggested further reading

Cottrell, S., *The Study Skills Handbook* Palgrave Study Guides (London: Macmillan, 2003)

Palmer, R., *Write in Style: a guide to good English* Routledge Study Guides (London: Routledge Falmer, 2002)

Maguire, M., Nettleton, H., *Home Office Research Study 265, Reducing alcohol-related violence and disorder: an evaluation of the 'TASC' project* (London: Home Office Research, Development and Statistics Directorate, 2003)

Huff, D., *How to Lie with Statistics* (London: Penguin, 1991)

Useful websites

www.learnhigher.org.uk
An excellent site for academic referencing and essay writing

PART 2

SUPPORTING POLICE WORK

Chapter 5

Ethical Policing Values

This chapter supports the following National Occupational Standards which describe the performance and competence required of a probationer officer.

Unit No.	Unit title
1A1	Use police actions in a fair and justified way.
1A2	Communicate effectively with members of communities.
1A4	Foster people's equality, diversity and rights.
1B9	Provide initial support to individuals affected by offending or anti-social behaviour and assess their needs for further support.
2A1	Gather and submit information that has the potential to support policing objectives.
2C2	Prepare for, and participate in, planned policing operations.
2C3	Arrest, detain or report individuals.
2C4	Minimise and deal with aggressive and abusive behaviour.
2G2	Conduct investigations.
2G4	Finalise investigations.
SH1	Interview victims and witnesses.
2H2	Interview suspects.
2I1	Search individuals.
2I2	Search vehicles, premises and land.
2J1	Prepare and submit case files.

▶

Unit No.	Unit title
2J2	Present evidence in court and at other hearings.
2K1	Escort detained persons.
2K2	Present detained persons to custody.
4C1	Develop your own knowledge and practice.
4G2	Ensure your own actions reduce risks to health and safety.

5.1 Introduction

Working in the police service presents many challenges. At some point in a police officer's working life they may find themselves in a dilemma over the activities of a colleague or a situation that has developed in the workplace. For example, an officer may have concerns over corruption, integrity or other unethical behaviour which they have witnessed or suspect a colleague of being involved in. They may have been subjected to, or witness, bullying, harassment or discrimination. One of the greatest demands made upon any police officer is one of always 'doing the right thing' in these kinds of situations.

5.2 Ethics

In recent years there has been increased attention given to ethics, integrity and corruption in policing. First we need to discuss just what we mean by the term 'ethics'. Ask your friends or family and attempt exercise 5A below.

Exercise 5A

Write down what you think ethics means.

A definition of ethics within a policing context has been provided by Neyroud and Buckley (2001) as 'how police officers and police leaders make the right judgements and do the right things for the right reasons'.

Ethics are important in policing because of the nature of police powers and privileges. People invest a considerable amount of power in police officers. They arm police. They give them powers to deprive a citizen of their liberty and the power to kill a citizen under extreme circumstances, although all of these actions have to be subsequently justified. It is therefore essential that such authority is used in a fair and non-arbitrary way. The public have a right to expect their police officers to behave in a manner that protects each individual's basic rights within the law. They expect help when they require it and fair treatment in their dealings with police officers and justice.

The study of police ethics is closely linked with the concept of 'integrity' which is commonly defined as being honest and trustworthy. Integrity in a policing context is concerned with being clear about what the police service stands for and acting in accordance with those values.

Exercise 5B

Consider to what extent these statements are true of your police service:

■ Police officers treat members of the public as they would wish their own family to be treated.

■ The police co-operate with other partners in the fight against crime.

■ The police can only work effectively if they hold the trust of the public.

The police service in the UK has no code of ethics. However, there are a number of ethical statements that inform the way that the police should behave. These are discussed below:

The Association of Chief Police Officers Statement of Common Purpose

This statement is very important in that it states the purpose of the police service. These are to:

■ Uphold the law fairly and firmly

■ Prevent crime

■ Pursue and bring to justice those who break the law

■ Keep the Queen's peace

■ Protect, help and reassure the community

■ Be seen to do all this with integrity, common sense and sound judgement.

It further stresses that officers must be compassionate, courteous and patient, acting without fear or favour or prejudice to the rights of others. The commitment of the police service to the Statement will only be demonstrated through the work of officers who behave with integrity. This means that an officer's behaviour must reflect the value that the service advocates, and officers must also support their colleagues' attempts to do likewise.

The Police Code of Conduct

This may be considered more of a discipline code than a statement of ethics as it exists to regulate the conduct of police officers. The public is entitled to expect the very highest standards of conduct from all members of the police service. In addition to this, the police service must be seen to discipline its own members when necessary. Areas covered by the Code include:

- Honesty and integrity
- Fairness and impartiality
- Politeness and tolerance
- Use of force and abuse of authority
- General conduct.

Sanctions for breaching the Code range from dismissal from the service or requirement to resign to reprimands or cautions.

The Council of Europe's Code of Police Ethics

From its earliest days, the Council of Europe has had police matters on its agenda. It has developed activities designed to promote human rights awareness within the police. The 'Code of Police Ethics' provides a framework for making clear the values and standards that are required of police in a modern, democratic society. It works to secure common policing standards across national boundaries to meet the expectations of increasingly mobile Europeans, who wish to be confident of uniform, fair and predictable treatment by police. The creation of this international code highlights the importance of the issue and demonstrates that police ethics are now regulated by national governments who take account of the increasingly diverse communities within Europe.

5.3 Conflict between organisational and personal ethics

Our own values are formed by our life experiences and influenced by people close to us such as family, friends, teachers, religious leaders, etc. Police officers may encounter situations that will cause conflict between these personal values or ethics and those of the organisation.

Consider how police officers respond to these ethical dilemmas by attempting exercise 5C below.

Exercise 5C

Consider the following scenarios and write down your thoughts about how you would react to them.

- What would your reaction be to a colleague who accepts a bribe?

- You discover that a person moving into your neighbourhood is a registered sex offender. Your neighbour has a child and you want to warn them.

- You are at a friend's party and other party-goers are clearly smoking cannabis.

Whilst all officers have a responsibility to report matters using the methods currently in place, we are all human and recognise that when faced with a dilemma, it is often easier working through it with an independent third party. To this end, many forces have launched a totally independent and confidential reporting service which could be contacted for advice if any of the above scenarios arose.

Recent research canvassed opinion on a number of similar scenarios and asked police officers to consider how serious they personally considered the behaviour portrayed.

These scenarios were divided into three categories:

1 **Acquisitive crime** – A police officer finds a wallet which contains money equivalent to a day's pay for the officer. The officer reports the wallet as lost property but keeps the money.

2 **Internal disciplinary infringements** – A police officer accepts free meals and other items of small value from shopkeepers on his beat.

3 **'Noble cause' rule breaking** – An on-duty police officer taking an off-duty officer home has been caught drink driving, without reporting the offence.

The survey revealed that the majority of officers who took part in the study regarded actions such as those involving the acquisition of goods or money as much worse than behaviour involving 'noble cause' rule-breaking in order to protect colleagues from criminal proceedings. It appears that a new recruit's commitment to the discipline code of police forces, which is instilled in them in the course of police training, may be abandoned when they are absorbed into the traditional police culture.

The survey suggests that there is evidence of a 'blue code' with a 'cop culture' that demands this solidarity and loyalty amongst officers. Without doubt, solidarity and loyalty to one another is a major feature of police officers. If someone makes a 'mistake' in the course of a policing operation, usually it can be talked about and settled. The problems arise when a 'mistake' becomes a premeditated act and, even more seriously, when a culture develops within a police organisation permitting or ignoring unethical behaviour. It is also suggested that there is a tension between this 'cop culture' and a police officer's personal integrity.

5.4 Impact of current changes upon UK police ethics and values

The changing context of policing in recent years has given renewed prominence to the ethics of the police service. A number of developments in policing have the central aim of delivering improved police performance and enhancing public reassurance. Some of these changes are covered below.

National Policing Plan

The 'right things' that the police should be doing have become increasingly nationally defined by an interventionist government. Each year the government and local authorities allocate billions of pounds to the police service. In 2003/2004 the total spent on policing was £11.3 billion. This money has to be spent in a way that will ensure that the service delivered to the public is what they want and is delivered efficiently. Exercise 5D below asks you to consider this problem.

Exercise 5D

Write down how you think the police decide what to spend money on.

One answer can be found in the **National Policing Plan**. The Police Reform Act 2002 requires the government to produce annually a National Policing Plan which sets out what the government has decided are the priorities, expectations, targets and developments for policing in England and Wales. Resources are then directed effectively at these priorities. The aim of the NPP is to deliver improved police performance and enhanced public reassurance. By having a plan that is published and available for scrutiny it makes the police more accountable to the public. The community served will know what they are entitled to expect from the police service.

Partnership policing

There is increasing emphasis on **'Policing in Partnership'**. The police are only one of the agencies with a remit to improve levels of safety and reassurance. Partnerships between forces and other bodies, particularly local authorities and community groups are vital aspects of policing. Section 17 of the Crime and Disorder Act 1998 imposes an obligation on every police authority, local authority and other specified bodies to consider crime and disorder reduction in the exercise of all their duties. Increasing participation in policing is seen as a potential way of improving police professional practice.

Public participation in policing

For policing to be ethical it must be negotiated with the public. Recent years have seen increasing emphasis on public participation in policing. British policing is firmly grounded in the concept of 'policing by consent' which involves dialogue about shared goals and a role of serving the community, not just enforcing the law. Policing by consent requires the support of the public, which can be developed only by learning about and trying to understand the problems of that public. For consent to be earned and sustained the public need to have absolute confidence in the police and the service provided to them. Public participation can be divided into three aspects:

- Consultation with local community groups

- Lay (independent) inspection which opens up policing to public scrutiny

- Active citizenship through Neighbourhood Watch and local patrolling schemes.

Public inquiries

In recent years there have been some significant public inquiries that have provided a catalyst in changing police ethics and values. Many of these public inquiries have criticised police culture and methods of working. They therefore have a greater chance of making a negative impact on public perceptions of the service and damaging the integrity of the police. These inquiries have consequently played a large part in forming and changing police policy, procedures, practices and legislation:

- The **Scarman Inquiry** was set up in 1981 to examine the strained relationship between police and some areas of the black community. Relations had deteriorated following the launching of operation 'Swamp 81'. The consequence of this operation was that a significant and disproportionate number of black youths were stopped and searched, intensifying the resentment of this group toward the police. Following the subsequent riots in Brixton, Lord Scarman's public inquiry made it clear that the riot was a result of an outburst of violence against the police. Some of the recommendations that came out of the Scarman report are:

– to eliminate prejudice from the force by improving police training

– reform of the complaints procedure to secure public confidence.

■ The report into the murder of Stephen Lawrence has been described as a 'landmark in the history of policing and race relations in this country'. The **McPherson Report** was published as a result of an inquiry into the investigation of the murder. There were a number of findings, most of which were highly critical of the police action at the scene of the murder and during the subsequent investigation. Recommendations were made as a result. Some of these recommendations had training implications, such as Recommendation 69 which states that 'all police officers and civilian staff should be trained in racism-awareness and valuing cultural diversity'.

■ The brutal murder of eight-year-old **Victoria Climbié** was one of the worst cases of child abuse Britain has ever seen. The subsequent report into her death identified that neither of the two constables who dealt with the investigation were trained detectives. The report stated that 'all police officers should, as a result of their initial training, be aware of the basic principles of effective investigation'. It was further recommended that the Home Office must devise and implement a national training curriculum for child protection officers.

The Human Rights Act 1998

The implications of a police officer not acting fairly, professionally, honestly and with integrity could be significant, given the scope of the police to infringe on the freedoms and rights of individuals. The **Human Rights Act 1998** has provided new avenues for the public to challenge unethical activities of public bodies. It has placed responsibility on all public bodies to ensure that their actions are compatible with the European Convention on Human Rights. It places a responsibility to safeguard citizens' rights and freedoms on every police officer in the UK.

5.5 Applying police ethics

Two concepts which may have an impact on officers' professional standards are the concepts of 'duty of care' and the exercise of 'police discretion'.

Duty of care

Police officers have a common law duty of care. There is no specific definition of 'duty of care' but it generally means that an officer must consider the health and safety of their colleagues and members of the public.

Here are some examples of what duty of care may include:

- Take reasonable steps to investigate crime with all reasonable diligence

- Take reasonable steps to protect, assist and support witnesses

- Take reasonable steps to ensure that officers do not behave in a racist manner towards members of the public.

The 2004/2005 British Crime Survey found, of incidents in the last 12 months where the witness had contact with the police, that 58 per cent were satisfied with the way the police handled the matter. This is positive, but what about the other 42 per cent of people? This is something that police officers need to change. How can police officers rely on the public to help them, if only just over half are satisfied with how the police handle matters?

Exercise of discretion

Doing the right thing does not amount to doing the same thing in all circumstances. Imagine the public outcry and attitude towards the police if every breach of the law, no matter how small or insignificant, were to be prosecuted. It is not an officer's duty to prosecute indiscriminately every person who commits an offence. Under the doctrine of 'policing by consent' police officers have an obligation to balance and, if possible, reconcile conflicting views in the interests of the community as a whole.

As long as officers are acting in good faith, it remains their perogative not to investigate complaints, but just to record them. This exercise of discretion is recognised as an essential policing skill.

Discretion can be understood as:

- freedom of judgement and action

- the authority to decide and choose

- selecting the best course of action, having recognised and considered all of the alternatives.

Where discretion is used in the operation of police powers the rights of an individual will be affected. By using discretion an officer will sometimes be making a decision not to act in circumstances where it may seem that their duty as a constable requires them to act. Failure to act could be interpreted as favouring or discriminating against certain individuals or groups, which can lead to accusations of neglect of duty, harassment or corruption. Therefore police officers must make sure that the decisions they make are fair. A key component of an officer's decision-making will be their personal and professional integrity.

There is a variety of ways that offenders may be dealt with following contact with a police officer. Officers must consider when each one might be appropriate. The different options available to the police when dealing with offenders are:

- Verbal advice and warning

- Formal warning

- Fixed penalty system

- Street bail

- Penalty notice for disorder

- Prosecution.

Exercise 5E

What factors do you think an officer may take into consideration in order to make a fair decision?

The following points are not comprehensive, but indicate the range of factors which might influence decisions:

- With whom am I dealing?

- What is their attitude to the incident?

- What is the physical or mental state of the person?

- What age is the offender?

- Have members of the public witnessed the incident?

- Might their behaviour be as a result of their culture or faith?

- Is there any harm to police/public relations by seemingly excessive enforcement?

A good way for an officer to make a decision is by following this simple method:

1 Identify the situation

2 Decide what needs to be achieved

3 Decide what factors need to be considered

4 Identify the various courses of action

5 Identify which is the best and why

6 Implement that course of action.

Following these objective principles of decision-making will assist the officer to make a fair decision by considering the needs of the individuals. By making fair decisions the officer is therefore able to maintain the public's confidence in the police service which is a key part in 'policing by consent'.

Case study

An 11-year-old youth is caught stealing sweets from a local convenience store. The attending officer identifies that an offence of theft has occurred.

The officer decides that he needs to address the youth's offending behaviour and also reassure the store owner that positive action will be taken.

The officer takes into account the offender's age and, by checking the Police National Computer, he confirms that the child has no previous history of offending. He also takes into account that the child is frightened and showing remorse for his behaviour.

The officer is aware that the child can be arrested for the offence of theft. Alternative options are also considered, such as reporting the child for the offence in the presence of his parents in order for a summons to court to be served.

The officer identifies that the best course of action is to take the child home to his parents and inform them of the incident. It is decided that the child has learnt from the experience and it would not be in the public interest for the child to be prosecuted. This course of action is discussed with and approved by the owner of the store.

The child is subsequently conveyed home and the matter is discussed with the child's parents.

5.6 Human Rights Act 1998 and the police service

Police officers are entrusted with many powers and privileges. Included amongst these are the powers to deprive a person of their right to liberty when arresting; the power to encroach on a person's right to a private life by entering and searching premises; and the power to use intrusive surveillance methods when investigating suspected offenders. The consideration of these human rights is a fundamental part of ethical policing as every time a police officer uses these powers it is inevitable that another person's human rights are affected.

Exercise 5F

Ask yourself, 'What do human rights mean to me?'

The basis of human rights – respect for each individual human life and human dignity – can be found in most of the world's religions and philosophies. Human rights mainly concern relationships between individuals and the state. They control and regulate the exercise of state power over individuals.

The Human Rights Act 1998 is one of the most significant pieces of legislation in relation to criminal justice for many years. The Act incorporated the rights and freedoms contained in the European Convention for the Protection of Human Rights and Fundamental Freedoms into UK law. The Convention is an international treaty agreed by governments in response to the atrocities of the Second World War.

Not only was the UK one of the first signatories, but it was also involved in the drafting of the Convention. However, it was not incorporated into UK domestic legislation because it was thought that the UK political and legal institutions adequately served to safeguard the rights of the individual. As a result of this, any breaches of the Convention could not be dealt with in our domestic courts, but in 1966 the UK gave individuals the right of petition to the institutions at Strasbourg directly.

Exercise 5G

Can you think of any UK cases that have been dealt with in the European Court at Strasbourg?

Some high profile cases might come to mind such as:

- *Thompson & Venables* v *UK* (1999) – where two juveniles were tried for the murder of Jamie Bulger in a Crown Court. The court found, amongst other issues, that it was unfair to try the two juveniles in an adult court.

- *Halford* v *UK* (1997) – the court found a violation of the right to privacy where the private telephone conversations of a senior police officer were intercepted.

Cases that were dealt with in the institutions in Strasbourg suffered from long delays and great expense. Section 2 of the Human Rights Act 1998 has made Convention issues more readily accessible to individuals as it requires UK courts to 'take into account' any decisions, judgements and opinions of the European institutions when Convention issues arise. Furthermore, Section 3 requires that current domestic legislation must be applied, as far as possible, so that it fits in with Convention rights. Consequently, all UK laws (past and future) must be compatible with the Convention and all UK domestic courts will be obliged to act in compliance with the Convention.

The impact of the Human Rights Act on public authorities

The Convention's provisions, set out in **Articles**, specify certain basic rights and freedoms which are protected from unjustified interference by the state. The Convention also imposes a positive obligation on the state to take measures to protect those rights. The Human Rights Act 1998 does not use the word 'state' but the phrase 'public authority', which is identified as any person or organisation that represents or performs the functions of a public nature. This definition is in wide terms and is intended to cover all agencies which exercise a public function.

All staff employed by the police service – whether they are civilian or police officers – are a 'public authority' and are bound to act compatibly with the Convention. Other obvious public authorities are the CPS, local authorities, councils and all courts and tribunals. Parliamentary activities are exempt from the definition of a public authority.

In most cases it will be obvious that an organisation is a public authority, but some bodies perform fixed functions. For example, when carrying out its functions relating to safety, Railtrack would qualify as a public authority, but when carrying out its functions as a private property developer, it would not so qualify. The same will apply to private security firms who will be 'public authorities' when managing contracted-out prison services, but would be acting privately when guarding private premises.

The public authority is liable for any Convention breaches by its individual employees. This does not affect the liability of employees with regard to any civil action or misconduct procedures. However, the Act exempts individuals from being classed as a public authority if the nature of their act is private. So an employee of an organisation with a public function is not classed as a public authority when they act privately. Take the example of a police officer, off duty, who gets involved in an argument and hits someone. This action would be a criminal assault, but it would not be a human rights violation.

Exercise 5H

Who are the only people who can bring proceedings under the Act against a public authority?

The simple answer is that only the person who is (or would be) the 'victim' of the unlawful act can bring proceedings. The word 'victim' is taken from the Convention itself and it includes:

- A person directly affected

- A person at risk (but not as yet affected)

- A person indirectly affected, such as family members where the victim cannot bring the case personally (cases of loss of life)

- A company or group.

Our domestic legal system provides remedies for those people who claim that human rights have been violated. Individuals who believe their Convention rights have been infringed can rely on their rights:

- As a defence in criminal proceedings (e.g. to challenge the admissibility of evidence)

- As a basis of an appeal or to seek judicial review

- To bring civil proceedings for damages.

The consequences in court of Convention rights being infringed without justification will depend on the facts of the case, but the powers of a court to quash a conviction, to stay proceedings, to allow a submission of no case to answer and to exclude evidence are of particular importance. If appropriate, compensation may also be awarded. It is only when all these possibilities have been exhausted at national level that a case may be brought to the European Court of Human Rights.

Exercise 5I

What human rights do you know about? Which of them do you think are relevant to policing?

The Articles

Below are the Convention rights listed by their Article number.

Article 2 – The right to life

Article 3 – Prohibition of torture

Article 4 – Prohibition of slavery and forced labour

Article 5 – The right to liberty and security

Article 6 – The right to a fair trial

Article 7 – No punishment without law

Article 8 – Right to respect for private and family life

Article 9 – Freedom of thought, conscience and religion

Article 10 – Freedom of expression

Article 11 – Freedom of assembly and association

Article 12 – Right to marry

Table 5.1	Articles created under the European Convention on Human Rights

These rights are to be enjoyed without discrimination on the grounds of sex, race, colour, language, religion, political or other opinion, national or social origin, association with a national minority, property, birth or other status.

Exercise 5J

Can you think of times when the above human rights can be violated for justifiable reasons?

Consider this case: A police officer is interrogating a terrorist who is suspected of planting a bomb. This bomb is hidden in an unknown place. The explosive effects of the bomb will cause substantial loss of life. The police officer knows that the suspect knows where the bomb is. Would it be acceptable to you if the officer slaps the suspect in the face in order to 'encourage' him to reveal the hiding place? How far should the officer go to find out where the bomb is hidden?

In this case it is understandable that the police officer will do anything to find out about the hiding place. You may be thinking that use of force, even lethal force, is not forbidden, provided the force used is proportionate to the threat posed and is absolutely necessary. You may feel that the use of force in this case is acceptable. However, if he beats the suspect up, it is still a human rights violation, even if to many people, it is an acceptable one. It does not help anyone (apart from the criminal) to see a conviction overturned because the investigating officer used illegal methods to obtain evidence. The prohibition of torture is total and absolute. On another level, the fear of physical pain may lead the suspect to tell the police officer anything he wants to hear. This is, of course, not necessarily the truth.

Restrictions on human rights

One of the key factors in the maintenance of a trusting relationship between the public and the police is the issue of safety. Preventing murders and investigating such crimes are vastly important police functions. Consequently, some human rights are limited to protect other rights or to assist the police in the preservation of social order or the prevention of crime.

Articles 2–7 are referred to as '**absolute rights**' which cannot be restricted or balanced with any general public interest. However, as with most things it is not quite as simple as this. Articles 5 and 6 are sometimes referred to as 'special rights' because of the extensive limitations which are placed within the Articles themselves. To illustrate this point, we can take the right to liberty (Article 5) – a basic and important right to which everyone is entitled. But it may be limited in certain cases. For example, the police are given powers to deprive a person of their liberty by arresting them if they are suspected of a crime, or to prevent them from committing a crime. It has to be remembered that some rights are not subject to any limitations; the right not to be tortured is absolute in all circumstances, even in time of war.

Articles 8–11 contain clauses which enable these rights to be restricted in the 'public interest'. These rights are called '**qualified rights**' and they can be breached only to the extent that the restriction in question:

- is 'prescribed by law'
- has a legitimate aim (listed in the Article)
- is 'necessary in a democratic society'.

What does this mean for the police? It means that police officers can only justify interference with an individual's qualified rights to the extent allowed by UK domestic law, for one of the interests specifically listed and only if it is 'absolutely necessary in a democratic society'.

For example, if it was felt necessary to tap a drug dealer's phone, interfering with their right to privacy under Article 8, then it could only be done if:

- there is a law that provides the power (Interception of Communications Act 1985) and
- only for one of the interests described in Article 8 (to prevent crime) and
- it was necessary in a democratic society (to gain sufficient evidence).

Interpretation of the above three qualifications by the court in Strasbourg has led to the development of the three principles of legality, necessity and proportionality.

Legality? – The first thing a police officer needs to consider when interfering with individuals' rights is 'Is the interference "lawful"?'

Necessity? – The questions the European Court would ask in addition to whether it is lawful are, 'Is there a social need for the state to infringe the Convention right in question?'

Proportionality? – When a situation arises where a public authority finds it necessary to interfere with a person's Convention right, there is always a range of actions that can be taken going from minimal to extreme. Of the options available to the officer, any restriction must be proportionate to the lawful aim pursued. Another way of explaining it is to ask, 'Would the action be using a sledgehammer to crack a nut?' Or 'Is there a less restrictive alternative?' Even though there may be a power to make an immediate arrest, this may not be proportionate to the problem. Verbal advice may be all that is necessary if it achieves the aim of stopping the threatening behaviour.

By means of the principle of proportionality, the Convention is seeking to achieve a fair balance between the conflicting rights of the community and those of the individual.

Respecting human rights sometimes appears to conflict with effective policing. This can be frustrating, but it is not an excuse to violate human rights. In the long term, not respecting human rights can actually decrease the effectiveness of police work. Consider the case where the suspect confesses a crime to stop the violence being used against him. If the manner in which the confession was obtained is revealed at the trial, the case will be dismissed and nothing will have been achieved. It is worth remembering that these principles of protecting rights are nothing new for the police service, as best practice in policing has always been to follow the same process. The overwhelming majority of UK legislation is compatible with the Convention and in some cases exceeds it. For example, the treatment of detained persons under PACE 1984 not only respects most aspects of the Convention, but offers protection that goes beyond what it demands.

Suggested further reading

Westmarland, L., 'Police Ethics and Integrity: Breaking the Blue Code of Silence' in *Policing and Society* Vol 15:2, 145–65

Wadham, J., Mountfield, H., *Blackstone's Guide to the Human Rights Act 1998* (London: Blackstone Press Ltd., 1999)

Neyroud & Beckley, *Policing, Ethics and Human Rights* (Cullompton: Willan, 2001)

Useful websites

www.ethicsinpolicing.com
A useful website that considers ethical policing

www.echr.coe.int
The European Court of Human Rights website

Chapter 6

Race, Diversity and Equal Opportunities

This chapter supports the following National Occupational Standards which describe the performance and competence required of a probationer officer.

Unit No.	Unit title
1A1	Use police actions in a fair and justified way.
1A2	Communicate effectively with members of communities.
1A4	Foster people's equality, diversity and rights.
2A1	Gather and submit information that has the potential to support policing objectives.
2C2	Prepare for, and participate in, planned policing operations.
2G2	Conduct investigations.
SH1	Interview victims and witnesses.
2H2	Interview suspects.
2J1	Prepare and submit case files.
2J2	Present evidence in court and at other hearings.
4C1	Develop your own knowledge and practice.

6.1 Introduction

In 1963 Martin Luther King delivered his famous 'I Have a Dream' speech:

'I have a dream that my four little children will one day live in a nation where they will not be judged by the colour of their skin but by the content of their character'.

One hundred and thirty four years earlier, across the Atlantic, these sentiments formed the basis of the guiding principles for the newly formed Metropolitan Police Force. These guidelines emphasised that all individuals should be equal before the law and judged only according to their actual behaviour:

'The police seek and preserve public favour, not by catering to public opinion, but by constantly demonstrating absolute impartial service to the law ... by ready offering of individual service and friendship to all members of society without regard to their wealth or social standing.'

Despite these noble guiding principles, in our society today there are still people who face prejudice and discrimination every day simply because they happen to be different in some way from the majority. This may be because of their religious belief, the colour of their skin, their gender or sexuality, their age or because they have a disability. So far as the police are concerned, equality and diversity are among some of the most important and sensitive issues.

6.2 The complexity and diversity of communities

British society is broken down into communities and these communities may themselves be broken down into smaller groups. These communities or groups are not exclusive as it is possible for an individual to be a member of various communities and/or various groups. Some of these sections in society may be identified as vulnerable with particular needs. In addition, there may be tensions that exist between certain groups and some of them will have different perceptions of the police. It is important to realise that the attitude and behaviour of one individual police officer may enhance or diminish community trust. Exercise 6A below helps you to understand this information by thinking about yourself and answering the questions.

Police officers, like all people, have a 'frame of reference' or 'way of seeing the world' which is influenced by many factors, including the community or groups to which they belong. Other factors that impact on an individual's 'frame of reference' could include their education, religion, family and upbringing or cultural background. These factors are responsible for developing a person's values and their prejudices. Police training encourages new police

---

Exercise 6A

(a) Make a list of the identifiable groups within the community in which you work.

(b) From this list, identify which of these groups is the most vulnerable and for what reasons.

(c) What community(ies) do you belong to?

(d) Within your community, what group(s) do you belong to?

---

recruits to identify the source of their values, recognise their personal prejudices and then challenge their perceptions of any unfamiliar or minority groups in their community. More importantly, police officers are encouraged to think about how their own values affect their attitudes and behaviour and then consider the impact that these attitudes and behaviour might have on others. Try completing exercise 6B and see if you can identify where some of your values and attitudes have come from and how they may influence your views of people or groups.

Exercise 6B

Consider your attitude to a subject like fox hunting or a group such as travellers. Can you understand where that attitude came from and how it is related to your values?

6.3 Prejudice

Prejudice can be defined as making negative pre-judgements about other people or other groups. In law a person is 'innocent until proven guilty'. Prejudices tend to work in the opposite direction as the individual who holds the prejudice may continue to hold the negative images until they are proven false. Prejudice may be suppressed, but it may often come out in our underlying attitudes, opinions and beliefs. Most people join the police service with some prejudice, of which they may or may not be aware. Our prejudices often stem from relying on our 'frame of reference' to fill in the gaps in our knowledge of other groups in society. This is where stereotyping comes in to play. Stereotyping is about making sweeping generalisations about groups of people, where you believe that just because people are members of a particular group, they must share particular traits which you think are characteristic of that group. Try to complete exercise 6C and reflect upon your views and assumptions. Police officers are often encouraged to be reflective practitioners and this requires honesty about oneself.

The above exercise may be a difficult personal journey for some people to undertake. However, it is important that police officers are able to honestly reflect on the way they think about and behave towards other people who are different from them, then question whether such views and behaviour are justifiable and fair. If a person is aware of their prejudices they can start to challenge their validity. By questioning why you think like that, you can work on changing your views and attitudes.

In 1953 Gordon Allport, an American psychologist, published a book entitled *The Nature of Prejudice* in which he identified five levels of prejudice. Allport related his scale particularly to the experience of the Jews in Nazi Germany but it can be equally applied to contemporary society. The scale used by Allport is shown in Figure 6.1 and the various stages of prejudice people experience are discussed below.

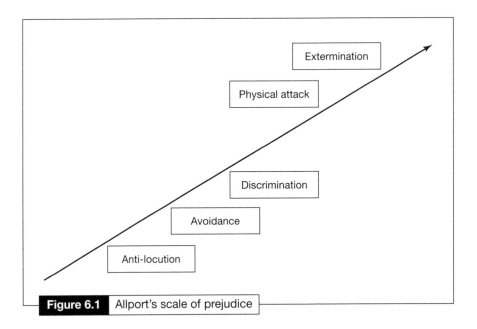

Figure 6.1 Allport's scale of prejudice

Gordon Allport explained that prejudice can follow a discernable pattern and that if not challenged an individual can experience each level which gets progressively worse over time. The various stages are explained below.

Anti-locution – Could be demonstrated by using phrases of colour which equate whiteness with purity and blackness to bad or evil. Other examples are using stereotypical language or ethnic jokes.

Avoidance – Quite simply this means to avoid another individual or group.

Discrimination – Means unequal treatment. This unequal treatment reinforces the power of the dominant group and disadvantages the minority group. Discrimination on the grounds of religion, gender, sexual orientation, disability and age are unlawful. The processes of discrimination can include denying employment or the provision of a less professional service.

Physical attacks – These may range from attacks on the property of the individuals to direct physical attacks.

Extermination – This is the ultimate violent expression of a prejudice. On an extreme level this could be demonstrated by the ethnic cleansing of a whole community. Within an organisation this could be interpreted as forcing someone to leave an employment position, or forcing a family to move out of a particular estate or area.

6.4 Discrimination

Another word used alongside prejudice is *discrimination*. When an individual has power, such as a police officer, and prejudice they are in a position to discriminate. Discrimination is demonstrated when we act more favourably towards one group of people than another and that favouritism is based on prejudice and without justification.

Discrimination may come about in four ways:

1 **Direct discrimination** occurs when a person (including a company or public authority), treats one person or a group of people less favourably than another person or group in similar circumstances. Examples include:

   – Refusing to search individuals from an ethnic minority group

   – Ignoring sexual harassment of employees

   – Assuming that all black prisoners are aggressive and therefore applying handcuffs to all black individuals who are arrested.

2 **Indirect discrimination** means selection criteria, policies, benefits, employment rules or any other practices which, although they are applied to all employees, have the effect of putting some individuals at a disadvantage. For example, an employer who imposes a requirement that all employees must have short hair may put people of a certain religious belief at a disadvantage

when compared with other employees. This type of discrimination is unlawful whether it is intentional or not.

3 **Positive discrimination** is also unlawful. For example, a position becomes available for a dog handler in a particular police force. A white female and an Asian male apply. The supervisor selects the Asian male as he wishes to have more ethnic minority officers within the department despite the fact that he is less well qualified for the position than the female. This is positive discrimination for the Asian male but is negative discrimination against the female. Opposed to this, there may be a situation where there is a need for 'positive action'. 'Positive action' means doing something to prevent or compensate for disadvantages experienced by individuals in a certain group. This is allowed in two areas:

– Access to training and educational facilities; or

– To encourage people to take up employment opportunities.

This means employers are able to target their recruitment advertising at individuals from minority groups, as long as the position itself is open to all.

4 **Victimisation** is a type of discrimination whereby a person is discriminated against because they have made allegations of discrimination under the employment legislation outlined below. The legislation is aimed at protecting a person who has made a complaint or brought a case under this legislation or any person who has given evidence or information in connection with proceedings. Such victimisation is often aimed at dissuading the person from pursuing their grievance. An example could be found where an employee is refused promotion after giving evidence on behalf of a colleague who has complained of discrimination.

It is important to understand how individuals respond to discriminatory behaviour and why they respond in a particular way. The trauma individuals suffer because of discrimination is, at best, unpleasant, while for some it is devastating, affecting their long-term mental and physical well-being. As we have discussed, reflection upon practice and performance is an important skill and by doing so, it can help improve performance and how we treat others. Bearing this in mind, complete exercise 6D.

Exercise 6D

Spend a few minutes reflecting on how you might feel if you were the victim, witness or suspect and were subjected to discrimination by the person investigating the incident. Record your thoughts on a separate sheet of paper.

You may have included some of the following:

- Guilt as a victim that it was your fault

- Mistrust of the police

- Anger at being treated differently

- Humiliation and distress

- Isolation

- Feeling of further victimisation.

6.5 Anti-discrimination law

There are a number of Acts of Parliament which fall under the heading of employment law. These laws exist to prohibit discrimination and protect the rights of various groups, both within the workplace and in society as a whole. All police service employees must play their part to ensure that their colleagues work in an atmosphere that is free from discrimination. Equally, every person working for the police service has a duty to ensure that those affected by crime, or have any other contact with the police, receive an non-discriminatory service. It is important that all police staff are aware of this aspect of law and that they are aware of the obligations it places upon police forces.

The provisions of the **Sex Discrimination Act 1975** make it illegal to treat a woman or a man less favourably on the grounds of their sex or marital status in the areas of employment, training and education and the provision of goods, facilities and services to members of the public. The Act also makes sexual harassment unlawful. Sexual harassment is unwanted, unreciprocated and offensive conduct imposed on another person because of his or her sex. Ask your friends or family to help you complete exercise 6E below.

Exercise 6E

Write down types of behaviour you may consider to be sexual harassment.

Examples of behaviour that could amount to sexual harassment can involve physical contact ranging from unnecessary touching through to more serious types of physical assault. It can also be verbal with suggestive remarks, 'jokes', sexual propositions, unwanted comments or any verbal abuse of a sexual nature. It could also include wolf whistles or displaying or circulating sexually explicit material. It is important to note that the offending behaviour may not be targeted at an individual but could consist of a general culture which, for instance, appears to tolerate sexist jokes.

The **Race Relations Act 1976** played an important role in changing public attitudes towards racism. This Act made it unlawful to discriminate against others on the grounds of race in relation to certain areas, namely employment, training and education and the provision of goods, facilities and services. Under the 1976 Act chief officers were held not to be vicariously liable for the discriminatory behaviour of their officers. This situation was amended with the **2000 Race Relations Act**.

This new Act extended the 1976 Act to the police service and the rest of the public. The 2000 Act therefore prohibits the police from discriminating – directly, indirectly or by victimisation – in carrying out their public functions.

The 2000 Act also created a duty on all public authorities to promote equality of opportunity and good relations between persons of different racial groups. Every public authority has to put in place means to ensure that their internal organisation is fair to ethnic minorities and that in the delivery of their services they pay attention to race issues. The expression 'public authority' follows the definition used in the Human Rights Act 1998 and clearly includes the police. Police services are required to publish a Race Equality Scheme every three years which sets out how it will meet its general duties to eliminate unlawful discrimination, promote equality of opportunity and promote good relations between people of different racial groups.

The **Disability Discrimination Act 1995** introduced a relatively new area of discrimination, that of disability. The Act introduces a statutory right not to be discriminated against on grounds of disability. Employers are placed under a duty to make 'reasonable adjustments' to working conditions or physical features within the workplace where these would place a disabled person at a 'substantial disadvantage'. Examples of the duty to make reasonable adjustments would include adapting keyboards or providing laptop computers and adapting access points to buildings. These rights will be infringed where an employer treats a disabled person less favourably than it treats or would treat other people, unless there are justifiable grounds. Given the complexity of the role of a police officer and the various physical and mental demands made on police officers, the defence of justification can cover a range of tasks and duties. The **Disability Discrimination Act 2005** both extended and amended the 1995 Act. There is now a duty on public authorities to ensure better performance in relation to eliminating disability discrimination. New groups were added who can now also benefit from the Act's protection, including those who have cancer, HIV infection or multiple sclerosis.

October 2006 saw the introduction of a new piece of legislation, the **Employment Equality (Age) Regulations 2006**. This legislation ensures that employers can no longer discriminate against employees on the grounds of age unless it can be objectively justified. An example of age discrimination could occur when a young police recruit is continuously told that they are 'straight out of the pram' and they find this behaviour humiliating and distressing. There may be certain circumstances when employers can justify discriminating on the grounds of age, but they have to prove that it is a proportionate way of achieving a legitimate aim. Proportionate means that what the employer is doing has to be appropriate and necessary. An employer might argue that it was appropriate and necessary to refuse to recruit people over 60 where there is a long and expensive training period before starting the job. In this case, the legitimate aim would be the need for a person to be in a job for a reasonable period before they retire, and for the employer to see a return on the investment they have put into training the employee. The employer would have to show that there was no less discriminatory way of achieving the aim.

There are other pieces of legislation which are aimed at discriminatory behaviour by anyone under certain circumstances. The **Crime and Disorder Act 1998** reflects the government's determination to eradicate racial crime. The Act introduced a number of new offences which carry harsher penalties where the offence is racially or religiously aggravated, that is, if at the time of committing the offence or immediately before or after committing the offence, the offender demonstrates towards the victim hostility based on the victim's membership (or presumed membership) of a racial or religious group. The offence may also be racially or religiously aggravated if the offence is motivated (wholly or partially) by hostility towards members of a racial or religious group based on their membership of that group. This aggravating element can be applied to offences of assault, criminal damage, public order and harassment.

It is also worth noting that Article 14 of the European Convention on Human Rights gives individuals a right not to be discriminated against on certain grounds.

6.6 Institutional racism

There is a degree of mistrust of the police service amongst certain sectors of the community following a number of indefensible failures in recent policing history. The Scarman report following the Brixton riots of 1981 highlighted a loss of confidence in the police and policing methods. It was during Lord Scarman's inquiry that the issue of 'institutional racism' was first raised. The Scarman Inquiry was set up to examine the strained relationship between police and some members of the black community. Relations had deteriorated when, following a significant increase in street crime in Lambeth, operation 'Swamp 81' was launched. The consequences were that a disproportionate number of black youths were stopped and searched, intensifying the resentment of this group. Violence broke out with 299 police officers injured and at least 65 civilians. Petrol bombs were thrown for the first time in mainland Britain and 82 arrests were made. As a result of these riots the Home Secretary appointed Lord Scarman to hold a public inquiry. Scarman identified evidence of 'racial prejudice' in the behaviour of certain officers who acted out their personal prejudices.

Some of the recommendations for policing that came out of the Scarman report were:

- Make efforts to recruit more black police officers

- Eliminate racially prejudiced individuals from the police service

- Improve police training to ensure that officers are able to support the whole of the community in the performance of their work

- Rationalise the 'stop and search' law.

Despite these recommendations, over ten years later the McPherson inquiry into the investigation of the murder of the black teenager Stephen Lawrence again revealed officers with unacceptable attitudes. On 22 April 1993 Stephen Lawrence was murdered in a racist incident in London. In a 1997 inquest Mrs Lawrence publicly accused the police of handling the initial investigation badly, stereotyping Stephen as a criminal and treating the family insensitively. The inquiry into his death and the subsequent, flawed police investigation was led by Sir William McPherson.

The 1999 McPherson Report has been described as 'a landmark in the history of policing and race relations in this country'. There were a number of findings, most of which were highly critical of police action. The McPherson Report sought to explain the incompetent police investigation into Stephen Lawrence's murder by the existence of 'institutional racism' in the Metropolitan Police Service. During the inquiry it became apparent that a form of racism was being displayed by some investigating officers who failed to recognise the attack as 'racist' from the start and this inevitably hampered the investigation. This failure was attributed to 'unwitting' racism which is defined as making certain assumptions about individuals on the basis of generalised information, or usually misinformation.

A number of recommendations were made as a result of the McPherson Inquiry. Recommendation 69 stated that 'all police officers and civilian staff should be trained in racism awareness and valuing cultural diversity'. Further recommendations were also made in relation to recruitment and retention with the proposal that policing plans include targets for recruitment, retention and progression of ethnic minority staff. Most importantly the inquiry provided a definition of 'institutional racism'. Institutional racism was defined as:

'The collective failure of an organisation to provide an appropriate and professional service to people because of their colour, culture or ethnic origin. It can be seen or detected in processes, attitudes and behaviour which amount to discrimination through unwitting prejudice, ignorance, thoughtlessness and racist stereotyping which disadvantage minority ethnic people.'

In simple terms 'institutional racism' is about stereotyping ... it is about ignorance: it is about not listening to or trying to understand those from minority communities.

The use of the phrase 'unwitting' highlighted that there had been unintended disadvantage to ethnic minorities. The concept of institutional racism recognises that an organisation may not *intend* to act in a racist way, but that its structures or its culture means that patterns of recruitment, promotion or service delivery may result in people from racial minorities being disadvantaged.

It is important to note that institutional racism is not unique to the police. Society as a whole faces these challenges and every individual and institution has a responsibility to examine their behaviour and prejudices.

6.7 Identifying a racist or homophobic incident

The ACPO guide *Identifying and Combating Hate Crime* was published in 2000. It defines hate crime as 'any crime where the perpetrator's prejudice against any identifiable group of people is a factor in determining who is victimised'. Therefore, a victim of hate crime does not have to be a member of a minority or someone who is generally considered to be 'vulnerable'. Effectively anyone can be the victim of a hate crime incident.

The McPherson report earlier defined a racist incident as 'any incident which is perceived to be racist by the victim or any other person'. The recording of racist incidents is therefore now based on the perception by *any* person that the incident is racist. 'Racist' does not simply relate to colour, but also to race, nationality, ethnic, religious or national origins.

Similarly a homophobic incident is 'any incident which as perceived to be homophobic by the victim or any other person'. 'Homophobic' does not only relate to lesbian women, gay men, bisexuals, transgender or transsexual people, but to any person perceived to be so by the perpetrator. As with racist incidents, the recording of homophobic incidents is based on the perception by any person that the incident is homophobic. The person making the report does not need to have any evidence to show that the incident was racist or homophobic. If any person believes that the incident was so motivated, it must be recorded as such.

National research has shown that under-reporting remains a common feature of all hate crimes as victims may be reluctant to report the incident to the police. It has also been found that many victims have suffered repeated problems before they contact the police. It is important to understand the reasons why victims are reluctant to contact the police so try exercise 6E below to see if you can think of some.

Exercise 6E

Write down some reasons why the victim of a racist/homophobic incident may be reluctant to report the incident to the police.

The impact of a hate crime can be more traumatic on the victim due to the realisation that a normally impersonal crime is actually a personal attack. As well as affecting the individual, hate crime has been described by the ACPO guide as a 'powerful poison to society' as it 'breeds suspicion, mistrust, alienation and fear'. Racists frequently exploit periods of raised anxiety following the recent terrorist attacks, such as currently exist and therefore there needs to be a heightened state of alert for hate crime with prompt action against racial harassment and strong support and reassurance for victims.

6.8 Conclusion

Now that you have read through this chapter you should have a better understanding of some of the more important legislation designed to promote equal opportunities and an awareness of some of the concepts surrounding equal opportunities.

The way that the country is policed has changed significantly in the past decade and it will continue to do so. Britain is a multi-racial society and most of us enjoy the benefits of diversity because it makes our country a richer place. Our culture is becoming much more international and more open to global influences. It is imperative that the police service continues to evolve as an organisation in order to meet the diverse needs of the communities it serves. Many of us have grown up with the opinion that we should treat people as we would want to be treated ourselves. People often say 'I am fair because I treat everyone the same'. But if the police treat everyone the same, are they providing the actual service that the individual requires? Is it fair to treat all members of the community the same when they may have different needs? Equal opportunity is about treating people fairly but not necessarily the same.

As the police service enters this period of unprecedented activity in counter terrorism, the potential for conflict with minority communities is higher than ever. Neighbourhood policing provides enormous potential to strengthen trust and develop the building of mutual respect between the police service and the communities they serve.

Suggested further reading

McPherson, W., *Report of the Stephen Lawrence Inquiry* (London: HMSO, 1999)

Allport, G.W., *The Nature of Prejudice* (New York: Perseus Books, 1954)

Clements, P., Spinks, T., *The Equal Opportunities Guide* (London: Kogan Page, 1996)

Chapter 7

The Basic Command Unit

This chapter supports the following National Occupational Standards which describe the performance and competence required of a probationer officer.

Unit No.	Unit title
1A2	Communicate effectively with members of communities.
2A1	Gather and submit information that has the potential to support policing objectives.
2C2	Prepare for, and participate in, planned policing operations.
2C3	Arrest, detain or report individuals.
2G2	Conduct investigations.
2K1	Escort detained persons.
2K2	Present detained persons to custody.
4C1	Develop your own knowledge and practice.
4G2	Ensure your own actions reduce risks to health and safety.

7.1 Introduction

The purpose of this chapter is to introduce the Basic Command Unit (BCU) and review its component parts. The chapter will then examine the role of the BCU, its structure, personnel and its performance.

Although it would be inaccurate to describe it as a 'mini police force', the BCU is the part of a police force that people know most about and care most about. The BCU is the unit of policing that is small enough to impact directly on its local communities, whilst being large enough to provide response policing, neighbourhood policing, protective services, community safety and the resilience to deal with both major events and the management of critical incidents.

There are currently about 250 BCUs in England and Wales. Normally the boundaries of a BCU are aligned to one or more Local Authorities (LAs) in order to ensure delivery of services by the police and other agencies is effective. Together, BCUs and LAs form the basis for the local Crime and Disorder Reduction Partnerships (CDRP) in England and the Community Safety Partnerships (CSP) in Wales.

Since most police officers are not involved in specialist departments at force headquarters, most police officers in England and Wales are attached to a BCU. In this chapter we look more closely at the structure of a BCU and the functions. We will be particularly interested in the diverse range of its staff, a mix designed to best deliver on government and force targets and to meet the demands of the community.

7.2 The purpose of the BCU

The BCU is a term widely used both in police and government circles and it represents a change from the older military terminology of 'police divisions'.

Everyone living in England and Wales is covered by a BCU and its component stations. Many people are not aware of what a BCU or local station is responsible for, how large an area they cover or which police services they supply. The BCU is in reality a geographical area that will have a BCU headquarters building, a number of out-stations, garages for vehicles, cell accommodation (in at least one station in the BCU) and a scenes of crime facility. Its service will be delivered by police officers, PCSOs, traffic wardens, special constables and police staff.

Try exercise 7A to see how much you know about your local BCU. Check your answers by looking at the website of your local force.

Exercise 7A

(a) What BCU covers the area where you live?

(b) Where are its headquarters?

(c) Where is your nearest police station?

How a BCU is structured depends upon the level of devolution of responsibilities within its parent police force. Currently each of the 43 forces in England and Wales have to meet national UK standards, but they also have the freedom to deliver services in a way that is efficient and effective for their particular area.

Perhaps the easiest way to sort out the functions of the personnel within a BCU is to separate those who provide a frontline police service to the public from those who work in a supportive role assisting those staff to deliver the service, as in the following sections. However, it is important to understand that all the personnel play a part in the success or failure of the BCU and the most successful BCU commanders are those who emphasise the importance of 'team BCU'. This is also a reflection of the highly inter-related role of personnel in BCUs. The part-time enquiry officer may be the person who receives, for example, information from a passer-by that drugs are being sold outside the local secondary school, information which causes a specialist operation to be set up which obtains video evidence of drugs being sold. Many other staff, including catering and custody staff, are involved after the arrest of suspects. The 'bust' is good news for the CID officers but there is also a feeling of overall success on the behalf of the community which is felt by all the officers and staff of the BCU.

7.3 Structure

The BCU commander has local accountability and is normally of chief superintendent or superintendent rank. The BCU commander is responsible for the overall performance of the BCU, and the actions of his or her staff in delivering the service to the community. The commander is answerable to the chief constable for police performance. The commander will normally have a deputy of superintendent rank, and a Senior Management Team (SMT) to assist in the delivery of this service. The SMT will consist of both senior ranking police officers and police staff. The size of the command team will depend on the size of the BCU and the services devolved by the force HQ.

The BCU is organised in ways which reflect both geography and function. Geographically, the BCU will be divided into a number of areas based upon defined local communities. These areas are headed by an operational commander of either superintendent or chief inspector rank.

In turn, each chief inspector will be responsible for small areas called 'sectors' headed by an inspector; these are in turn broken down into 'beats' for response and 'wards' for community policing purposes.

In addition the BCU has its own CID to deal with serious offences; this may be headed by a detective chief inspector who may, for some BCUs, also have responsibility for public protection. Public protection includes such offences as domestic violence, child protection and the management of dangerous offenders when they have been released from prison.

In line with the National Intelligence Model, the proactive arm of crime investigation is separated from the divisional intelligence unit, a small group charged with the gathering, analysing and disseminating of intelligence.

BCUs have responsibilities for making partnerships with local authorities and other agencies. These partnerships are sometimes called Community Safety or Crime and Disorder Reduction units. The units contain officers and staff who assist with operational and strategic planning, crime and disorder recording, and liaison with partner agencies and voluntary bodies.

7.4 Uniformed police staff

The term 'uniformed staff' covers a number of areas of policing and includes those officers who respond quickly to urgent incidents ('response officers') and those ('community officers') who follow up incidents or otherwise liaise with the public in small geographical areas. Community-based officers are normally part of Neighbourhood Policing Teams (NPTs).

In addition, uniform officers are found within the Roads Policing Units and in groups with special tasks such as search teams, armed response officers and public order. The degree of autonomy for the BCU will depend on local force procedures. In some forces the headquarters functions retain control of such resources whilst in others they are devolved.

An example of a typical BCU organisational structure can be seen in figure 7. 1.

You will notice the large number of functions and posts involved within the delivery of policing in this example.

7.5 Frontline services

Frontline police services include those uniform officers who provide response policing and the members of the Neighbourhood Policing Teams. (NPTs). The term should also cover those detectives who investigate serious crime, those involved in public protection and those officers working in a specialised role such as the drug squad.

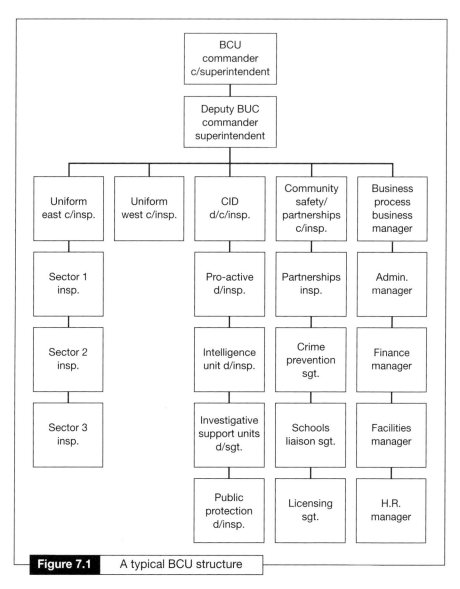

Figure 7.1	A typical BCU structure

Frontline services also include those members of police staff who provide a front line service, dealing directly with the public. These include police community support officers, traffic wardens and those who work in specialised units such as Scenes of Crime Officers (SOCO). This list is not extensive and as police reform and modernisation continues the BCU will probably see more police staff moving into front line policing roles.

7.6 Support services

Front line support includes both police officers and police staff. The BCU will have staff in a number of areas such as schools liaison, crime prevention, major planning, criminal justice, architectural liaison, community safety and investigative support such as scenes of crime work. BCUs follow the National Intelligence Model (NIM) and police staff work in acquiring intelligence and in evaluating information. Others will analyse crime and disorder, producing action plans for their front line colleagues to carry out their duties. In most BCUs, police staff will specialise in administration, finance and human resource management. The police staff manager will in effect be on an equal footing with senior ranking police officers as part of a unified command team.

7.7 Response policing

Response policing is concerned with those officers who respond to calls from the public. The nature of the response can range from 'immediate' – where the lives of persons are in danger – to a more considered or scheduled response where police officers can arrange with the caller to either attend sometime later or even to deal with the call over the phone.

Response policing has traditionally been aligned to specific geographical areas such as sectors or beats. Response officers are organised on a shift or relief basis and work to a set shift pattern, combining combinations of days, afternoons and night-time working. Shift patterns can vary from one police force to another. Response policing organised in this way has both strengths and weaknesses. A strong shift and local identity can be established and officers get to know local criminals and target persistent offenders. Perhaps the key to the effectiveness of the relief system is strong leadership at sergeant and inspector level.

The role of the response police officer is to attend and deal with calls from members of the public. Today, especially with the increase in the use of mobile phones, most of these calls are received via the telephone. These officers are required to attend calls and provide an effective service when they get there. Response policing has been termed 'fast time' or 'fire brigade policing' because of this.

This type of policing provides a 24-hour cover seven days of the week. Often based within particular areas, they are composed, in many BCUs, of the most inexperienced officers, often with less than two years' service. Whilst the officers have to respond to crime and disorder, they are increasingly seen as part of the NIM process. At briefings they are tasked to cover specific areas as a result of something called predictive analysis, which attempts to predict where crime and disorder will occur, yet this has to be balanced against an ever-increasing demand for their response capabilities.

7.8 Community policing teams

While many police forces state that 'community policing' is one of their most important priorities, there have been doubts expressed over whether community-based officers are sufficiently valued and supported. In this sense community policing has been called the 'Cinderella of the police service'.

The gap between statements of intent (such as 'community policing is at the heart of police service delivery and its professional ethos') and reality (too few community-based officers, officers abstracted for other 'more urgent' duties, etc.) is caused because many forces have found it difficult to maintain community officer numbers.

Exercise 7B

Why do you think community officers are drawn away to other duties? How can this be minimised?

The diversion of officers ('abstraction') from community-based work in this area is caused by competing demands such as response policing, policing big sports events, VIP visits (such as royalty), 'loaning' officers to other police forces, protective services and counter terrorism. The effect of such abstractions is made worse because it breaks down the continuity felt by the public in dealing with its local officers: if people in a small town see the same community officers about policing issues they are more confident that the officers will have more 'ownership' and be more interested in solving local issues.

Since funds are strictly limited, one solution is to make more use of PCSOs (which are cheaper than police officers to employ) in community work. This is not always seen as a good solution and it may be, at best, a help. More recently, there have been attempts to 'ring fence' community officers by reducing the time spent on issues (such as noisy neighbours) which can be dealt with by other agencies or by the complainant themselves.

7.9 Neighbourhood policing

In November 2004, the government produced the *Building Communities, Beating Crime* document on the development of neighbourhood policing. This was seen as a move towards ensuring that the police re-engaged with their communities and provided what the public constantly demanded; their own Community Beat Officer (CBO). The term community or neighbourhood policing encompasses far more than the appointment of a CBO, and it incorporates both the wider police family and the engagement of partner agencies in the solution to crime and disorder issues.

The neighbourhood policing team will include at least one CBO per electoral ward. Depending on the force policy, and levels of crime and anti-social behaviour, additional resources may be needed. This will include additional police officers, the use of PCSOs and officers from the special constabulary. Finally, some forces will look to incorporate volunteers from the community to assist in the policing of their local area. A typical neighbourhood policing team might look like that shown in figure 7.2.

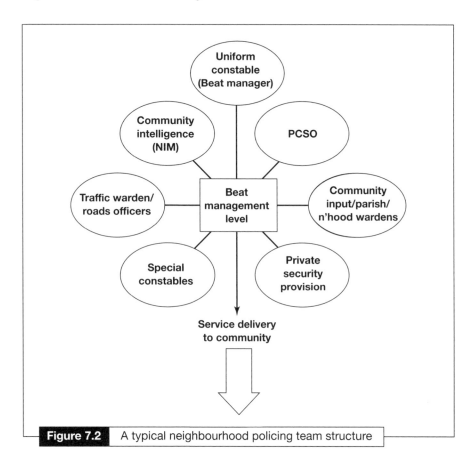

Figure 7.2 A typical neighbourhood policing team structure

The neighbourhood policing team is seen as one part of a multi-agency approach to crime and disorder reduction. The team will work with the partner agencies such as the local authority and housing associations, to address issues in the community it covers. 'Community engagement' is crucial to the success of such teams. The neighbourhood policing team must work with the community to address their concerns as failure to do so will see policing initiatives fail due to a lack of local support.

Figure 7.2 shows the central role of the police constable as the 'team manager'. This represents a new level of responsibility for constables.

7.10 Community consultation

The *National Community Safety Plan, 2006–2009*, together with *Building Communities, Beating Crime*, established the government's intention to ensure that communities are fully engaged in crime reduction. This is a vital role for the BCU. The programmes will also, for the first time, hold agencies accountable to their communities for service delivery. The process will see Partners and Community Together (PACT) meetings being held in each community. The police and local authority will be required to attend to address issues raised by the community. The development of PACT meetings will focus the police and local authority on what the community identifies as their priorities. The PACT meetings take place in each community. The definition of a community can be a recognised geographical area such as a political ward or village situated within the BCU boundary.

The process involves a representative community group setting out for the partners the priorities for improving the quality of life for the community. The partner agencies will then work to combat the problems with the community, reporting back the following month on the progress or problems encountered in tackling the issues. For community or neighbourhood policing to succeed there will need to be a commitment to reduce the removal of staff involved in policing communities to a minimum in order to allow officers time to get to know, and be known by, their communities. The use of information technology will allow the community access to the team, and the BCU needs to supply sufficient resources in order to resolve problems highlighted in the PACT meetings.

The Crime and Disorder Reduction Partnership (CDRP) and National Policing Plans will have to incorporate the information gleaned from PACT meetings and a mechanism will need to be constructed to cater for the sometimes competing demands of national, force, BCU and community targets. The BCU commander needs to balance a number of competing demands and must avoid promising a service that they may not be able to deliver.

Neighbourhood policing will become a police specialist role and one of the career pathways for future police officers and staff. In redistributing staff into this policing area, forces must work to break the constant time demand on officers, allowing resources to address community concerns and individuals in the community.

7.11 Police staff

Police staff are an integral part of the BCU and they also have their own command structure. Police staff will be of different grades depending on their role, responsibility or function within the BCU. It should also be remembered that in the modern police service this difference can be and often is blurred as, on occasions, police staff managers can supervise police officers and vice versa. Many members of police staff bring into the police service their professional expertise, particularly in such areas as finance, information technology and human resource management. The term police staff is taken to mean those members of the police force who are not sworn police officers. The BCU will include a large number of police staff performing a variety of roles, both front line service delivery and support. Before going any further, try and complete exercise 7C.

Exercise 7C

List the individuals who may be termed police staff.

You may have thought about some of the following in your answers.

- Scenes of Crime Officers (SOCO)

- Front desk personnel

- Jailers

- Photographers

- Prisoner escort

- Administration personnel

- Police community support officers.

The term police staff has often been replaced by the term 'civvies', a derogatory and inaccurate description of people working within a police service. Often police staff have been treated as second class. Hopefully, with the modernisation of the police service, attitudes will change and police staff will be seen for what they are, an integral part of a diverse policing service. Police staff within the BCU normally have their own rank structure. Headed by a business manager who sits on the BCU senior command team, police staff are in the main either divided into a number of support teams or integrated into departments alongside their police officer colleagues. Police staff are subject to a variety of terms and conditions which are set down nationally and they have the right to join trade unions and to strike. Today a large percentage of a BCU's staff consists of police staff members.

7.12 Other police support services

Police staff serve in a number of front line roles within the BCU. In a visible uniform role they work as traffic wardens and police community support officers. In addition to high visibility they also enforce the law in a number of areas. Some PCSOs will also have the power to intervene and detain suspects until the arrival of a sworn officer. Front line police staff also serve as station enquiry clerks and scenes of crime examiners. They can be found assisting in the custody unit, with interviews of suspects and preparing cases for court. In a support role within the BCU, police staff provide administrative back up, clerical support and a variety of specialised functions. In areas such as health and safety and finance and human resources, members of police staff ensure the BCU meets both its professional and legal obligations to its staff and community. Police staff are increasingly being employed in roles previously performed by police officers, thus releasing staff for front line duty. Within crime and disorder management, police staff provide an essential analytical role within the NIM process.

7.13 Criminal Investigation Department

The Criminal Investigation Department (CID), as the name implies, was established to investigate and detect criminal offences. Those officers working within this area of policing are termed 'detectives' and operate out of uniform. The BCU will allocate detectives to investigate the more serious type of offence in line with the force and BCU plans. The BCU will have a plan or protocol for the nature and type of offence to be dealt with by its detectives. For example, if a serious sexual offence should occur, a plan would exist regarding what should be done by detectives regarding the interviewing of witnesses and, possibly, the role of social services.

The physical location of the detectives working within a BCU will be dictated by force and BCU policy, but in the main they can be found either in sector stations or stations covering a cluster of sectors. The more senior ranks within the CID are charged with directing the investigation of these more serious offences. They are termed Senior Investigative Officers (SIO) and are highly trained and accredited to perform these important roles.

Whilst the BCU CID may be organised on a geographical basis it can also have staff allocated to specialised teams within the BCU. These specialised teams are designed to deal with particular areas of concern, such as the production or distribution of Class A drugs, or the theft of vehicles.

The problem for the BCU is that, once established, a squad may be difficult to disband. This can lead to further removal of front line uniform officers and the CID, which can be made worse if other detectives are assigned to major crimes or protracted enquiries.

7.14 Public protection

This is an area of policing that may be devolved to the BCU to deal with on a local basis. Here police officers deal with domestic violence, the management of dangerous offenders and the issues raised by child protection. These officers are specially trained to deal with their specific tasks, particularly the management of victims and witnesses to such offences. These officers may also carry out the arrest and interview of offenders, or this role may be passed on to other officers to action.

7.15 Criminal justice

The BCU has a responsibility, along with its partner agencies, to bring increasing numbers of offenders to justice, a process termed 'narrowing the justice gap'. This involves the BCU and its partner agencies within the criminal justice system looking to increase the number of positive outcomes in the system. For the police and Crown Prosecution Service (CPS), this primarily means an improvement in the 'sanctioned detection rate'. A sanctioned detection means an offence that has ended in a person being charged with the offence, having the offence Taken Into Consideration (TIC) when sentenced for another offence, been summonsed for the offence, or a person who has been cautioned, reprimanded or handed a final warning. Finally, a sanctioned detection can also be recorded by the issue of a fixed penalty notice for disorder.

The Crown Prosecution Service can now be found working alongside their police colleagues within BCUs in joint Criminal Justice Units (CJUs). The CPS now has responsibility for overseeing the charging process and it works to determine whether the charging standard for the offence has been met and, if it has, whether it is in the public interest to charge with the offence.

7.16 Crime and Disorder Partnerships

The BCU will be engaged in working with both partners and the community to combat not only the issues of crime and disorder but also the fear of such issues. The BCU will work alongside the local authority in a Crime and Disorder Reduction Partnership (CDRP), an arrangement in Wales termed a Community Safety Partnership (CSP). You can read more on Crime and Disorder Reduction Partnerships in Chapter 8.

In some CDRP and CSP structures staff from all agencies working within community safety are located within the same building. This leads to a more joined-up approach to crime and disorder reduction, and more effective partnership arrangements.

7.17 National Intelligence Model

The National Intelligence Model (NIM) is the recognised model for policing across all forces in England and Wales. The NIM encompasses crime, disorder and antisocial behaviour. The NIM is now being rolled out to partner agencies for incorporation into CDRP and CSP processes. A simple schematic of how the NIM system works can be seen in figure 7.3.

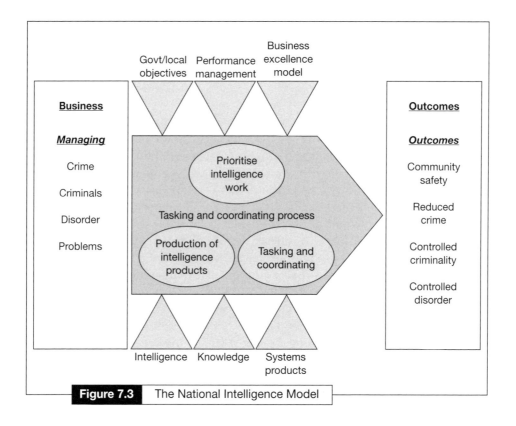

| Figure 7.3 | The National Intelligence Model |

The NIM is a business process. The intention behind it is to provide focus on operational policing and to achieve a disproportionately greater impact from resources applied to any problem. It is dependent upon a clear framework of analysis of information and intelligence, allowing a problem-solving approach to law enforcement and crime-prevention techniques. The expected outcomes are improved community safety, reduced crime and the control of criminality and disorder, leading to greater public reassurance and confidence. You can read more about this in Chapter 8.

7.18 Finance

Policing services are financed from central government funding and the local authority council precept. The BCU will be allocated funds to cover both capital and revenue expenditure. 'Capital expenditure' means money spent on physical items such as buildings, furniture equipment, etc. whilst 'revenue expenditure' relates to running costs such as salaries, rent, rates, telephones and so on. The degree of autonomy for the BCU will depend on the particular force policy.

In many cases, the BCU will have funds allocated for the maintenance of its buildings, its transport fleet and its general administration. Staffing costs – the bulk of all police force expenditure – is often subject to central control. The BCU may find that it is allocated funds for overtime, police staff cover and specific government initiatives. The BCU may be expected to bid for further funding in line with the control strategy of the force or other government initiative. Increasingly, the BCU is encouraged to bid for these funds alongside partners as part of a multi-agency approach to crime and disorder reduction.

7.19 Performance measurement

No examination of the structures of the BCU would be complete without a discussion of the performance targets in the modern day police service. Before going further, attempt the question in exercise 7D.

Exercise 7D

1 What do you think is meant by a performance target?

2 Write down some areas on which you think the police could be measured.

Like most publicly-funded organisations, the police are accountable to the public for what they spend their money on. People want to know what they get for their money, so one way of measuring this is to ask the police to reach specific targets. These targets are reached by the police performing their job better than before and hence they are known as 'performance targets'. The targets that each BCU has to reach are agreed as a result of a consultation process. BCUs are measured against other BCUs based on similar crime and other factors such as population, urban or rural and social deprivation.

The BCU along with the local authority publishes a three-year programme for the reduction of crime and disorder within its area. The plan is published and the CDRP are held to account for the joint performance. In addition, the

BCU will publish an annual policing plan, a document which incorporates targets from both CDRP and force annual plans. The BCU is subjected to scrutiny from a number of internal and external agencies.

Internally, the BCU commander will be subject to something called a 'compstat process'. This process involves an analysis of statistics such as burglary rates or auto-crime rates, to hold the BCU commander to account for the BCU's actual performance against its projected targets. In turn, the various sector and departmental heads will themselves be subject to the same compstat process. In some BCUs both individual officers and teams are subject to an evaluation of their performance in terms of sanctioned detections, arrests and submission of intelligence logs.

Externally, a number of agencies are at work in examining the effectiveness of the BCU. Her Majesty's Inspectorate of Constabulary (HMIC) has for a number of years carried out a baseline assessment of police forces. The aim of this is to reflect the performance of the force within the current working environment established by the Police Reform Act 2002 and the Policing Performance Assessment Framework (PPAF).

The HMIC inspection has now moved from a force-wide to a BCU-focused process. This means that they will focus on the performance of individual BCUs rather than the whole force. The resultant reports are published on the HMIC website for public consumption. The emphasis is on how well the BCU works with the local authority and other community safety partners to address local crime and disorder reduction. Its published aims are to:

- Promote effective leadership

- Disseminate good practice

- Identify inefficiencies

- Provide pointers to enhance performance

- Strengthen the capacity for self-improvement

- Leave behind a BCU management team that has learnt about itself and is committed to self-improvement.

The BCU will be assessed across a number of areas and will be assessed as being excellent, good, fair or poor. In addition, a trend line will state whether the service is improving, stable or deteriorating. The process is intensive and the BCU will be revisited to ensure that improvements have been made and any deficiencies addressed.

The Police Standards Unit (PSU) was established in 2001 to oversee the development of police reform. Working independently of HMIC, the unit is focused on:

- The measurement and comparison of police performance

- Understanding the underlying causes of performance variation

- Working with forces in need of assistance

- Identifying and disseminating good practice.

A BCU that fails to meet its targets and falls into the bottom quarter within its BCU family will come under close scrutiny. On occasion the PSU will come into the BCU and assist the command team in reaching its set targets.

The BCU is also subject as part of the police service to scrutiny under the Race Relations Amendment Act 2000. The BCU will be examined to see how it is performing in relation to the recruitment of staff from ethnic minorities and in relation to their retention and development within the organisation, both in terms of promotion and specialised departments.

Diversity is usually described as the 'golden thread' that runs throughout the BCU so that the organisation reflects the community it serves. The BCU must focus on:

- Eliminating unlawful racial discrimination

- Promoting equality of opportunity

- Promoting good race relations between people of different racial groups.

Finally, from being measured at a national, regional and force level, the BCU is also held to account on a local level. The introduction of the Partners and Community Together (PACT) meeting now holds the police accountable on a local community basis. Each month the community will give the police and partner agencies up to four priorities for the month. The agencies will then have to deliver or explain any failure to do so on a monthly basis.

7.20 The National Policing Improvement Agency

The National Policing Improvement Agency (NPIA) was set up to support the police service in England and Wales by providing expertise in a number of key areas, including information and communications technology, support to information and intelligence sharing, core police processes, managing change, and recruitment and national training. NPIA became operational on 1 April 2007, replacing several other agencies (such as Centrex and the PITO, the Police Information Technology Organisation). With a core focus on policing improvement in England and Wales, NPIA is likely to be highly influential in the direction policing takes in the future.

7.21 Conclusion

The BCU is the main organisational body responsible for local policing. It contains a number of differing roles and departments that are responsible for delivering services following a consultation process with the community itself. Furthermore it is held accountable not only to the community itself, but also to its force and at a national level through the inspection process invoked by Her Majesty's Inspectorate of Constabulary, ACPO and the Police Standards unit along with the National Policing Improvement Agency (NPIA).

Suggested further reading

Joyce, P., *Criminal Justice, An Introduction to Crime and the Criminal Justice System* (Cullompton: Willan, 2006) particularly Chapter 3: Policing Structure and Organisation

Roger, C., *Crime Reduction Partnerships* (Oxford: Oxford University Press, 2006)

Home Office, *Building Communities, Beating Crime* (London: Home Office, 2004)

Home Office, *National Community Safety Plan, 2006–2009* (London: Home Office, 2006)

Useful websites

www.homeoffice.gov.uk
The Home Office

inspectorates.homeoffice.gov.uk
Her Majesty's Inspector of Constabulary

www.acpo.police.uk
Association of Chief Police Officers

www.police.uk
UK police service

www.crimereduction.gov.uk
Crime reduction

npia.police.uk
Police.homeoffice.gov.uk/national-policing-improvement
National Policing Improvement Agency

Chapter 8

Crime and Disorder Reduction Partnerships

This chapter supports the following National Occupational Standards which describe the performance and competence required of a probationer officer.

Unit No.	Unit title
1A1	Use police actions in a fair and justified way.
1A2	Communicate effectively with members of communities.
1A4	Foster people's equality, diversity and rights.
1B9	Provide initial support to individuals affected by offending or anti-social behaviour and assess their needs for further support.
2A1	Gather and submit information that has the potential to support policing objectives.
2C2	Prepare for, and participate in, planned policing operations.
2G2	Conduct investigations.
2J1	Prepare and submit case files.
2J2	Present evidence in court and at other hearings.
4C1	Develop your own knowledge and practice.
4G2	Ensure your own actions reduce risks to health and safety.

8.1 Crime and Disorder Reduction Partnerships

Policing is changing rapidly. It is moving away from old principles of policing where the police were required and undertook to deal with crime and disorder largely on their own and left to their own devices. The police have always sought the co-operation of the public and witnesses as a source of information, but that relationship was always more informal than legalistic.

Since the introduction of the **Crime and Disorder Act 1998** the relationship between the police and the public has been put on a new footing. There is now a more interactive relationship between the police and many other agencies when it comes to tackling crime and disorder, with the police realising that they can no longer address these problems alone. Further, other agencies such as local authorities now realise they have a part to play as well. This means that partnerships are a key element when it comes to forming policies and strategies used to tackle crime and disorder.

The Crime and Disorder Act 1998 provides a framework for local people, local authorities, the police and other key partners to have new responsibilities for the reduction of crime and disorder.

Exercise 8A

Think about two examples that show where crime reduction partnerships are playing an increasing role.

Partnerships are not an option for the police, but have become a statutory requirement in which the police and local authorities are the lead agents. This means they must engage in partnership activity in reducing crime and disorder. However, there are numerous other agencies that might work alongside the police in the reduction of crime and disorder at a local level. Using the exercise below, consider some of these.

Exercise 8B

What agencies do you think may work alongside the police in crime and disorder reduction activities?

You may have considered some of the following amongst others:

- Probation service

- Housing department

- Education authority

- Social services department

- Crown Prosecution Service

- Fire and emergency rescue services

- Drug action teams

- Magistrates' courts

- National Health Service trusts

- Leisure centres

- Private sector organisations and businesses.

All of the above have a role to play in crime and disorder reduction and all should be included in the consultation process designed to make partnerships more effective.

8.2 Consultation

Partnerships are required to undertake a full audit of their area taking into account crime and disorder data. Another factor to be considered is what the community feels about crime and disorder. This is where the consultation process is so important as local people have a chance to have their say on how they are policed. As a result of this process a three-year plan is produced to address local issues of crime and disorder. However, there are some members of the community who, for a number of different reasons, may not be able or willing to take part in the consultation process. These are sometimes referred to as 'hard to reach groups'.

Exercise 8C

Create a list of groups that you may consider to be 'hard to reach'.

Those groups you may have considered could include the following;

- Young people

- Gay and lesbian communities

- Homeless people

- Victims of domestic abuse and violence

- Children

- Old people

- Travellers.

Having decided which groups appear to be hard to reach, we need to consider how we might consult with them. This area of consultation is important for crime and disorder reduction partnerships. You may have considered some of the following ways in which hard to reach groups could be contacted:

- Holding public meetings in places where such groups meet (for example gay clubs and bars)

- Enlisting the help of established groups such Race Equality Councils

- Advertising in minority languages

- Advertising in specialist media (for example, *The Big Issue*)

- Holding focus groups.

Whatever way you consider, it is important to understand that the consultation process should involve as many people as possible to ensure that long-term strategies and ideas aimed at reducing crime and disorder are broadly representative of the community.

8.3 Developing a crime-reduction strategy

When the strategic type of approach is considered, it includes a wide range of measures to deal with crime, criminality and anti-social behaviour. It includes many of the ideas we have discussed already but can be divided into four types or classifications of approach. These are:

- Enforcement

- Situational prevention

- Community/social prevention

- Rehabilitation.

Figure 8.1 below illustrates a typical approach that is used to make up a strategy and shows what each agency does.

	Police	Partnership	Non Police
Enforcement	Routine patrol. Intelligence-led operations linked to the National Intelligence Model. Police community support officers	Local wardens. Security guards.	Trading standards officers, noise legislation, licensing.
Situational prevention	Targeted patrol by neighbourhood policing teams.	CCTV schemes, preventing repeat victimisation, design of buildings to prevent crime. Neighbourhood watches.	Improved security in private car parks, guidance in planning for new houses, the use of land for any purpose.
Community/ Social	Police-orientated youth clubs and other types of activities.	Youth work, drugs education, school liaison.	Mediation schemes, diversion schemes, citizen schemes.
Rehabilitation	Cautioning of offenders, attendance centre, pre-court diversion schemes.	Arrest referral schemes.	Probation supervision, drug treatment, mentoring schemes.

Figure 8.1 Local crime reduction strategy – who does what?

Using the above as a guide, read the scenario below and consider how you would tackle the problem highlighted.

Exercise 8D

You have been informed that a local school has been the subject of burglaries when it is closed, and criminal damage may be taking place at the same time as the burglaries.

8.4 What exactly do we mean by crime and disorder reduction?

Start by completing exercise 8E.

Exercise 8E

Write down three examples of the ways in which crime reduction can be achieved. Ask your friends or relatives what they think the term means. You can then compare these responses with the information provided in this chapter.

The simplest and most obvious definition of crime reduction is that it is a reduction in the number of crimes or in the level or seriousness of recorded crimes. The reduction is made for many reasons, but primarily police and partnership strategies and operations achieve it.

Strategies are the plans that are designed to bring about crime reduction. These are quite broad in scope and will cover such things as targets that may include the expected reduction in numbers of crimes over a specified period of time

Operations are the tactics used at street level to achieve the strategies such as targeted operations against known drug dealers, the introduction of neighbourhood policing teams into an area with high crime and anti social problems or the use of police community support officers for high visibility patrols to reassure communities.

Crime reduction has several important characteristics. These are:

1 It is *interventionist*. Police officers are interested in achieving crime reduction by design. Strictly speaking even the positioning of a police officer in a busy shopping centre acts as a deterrent to crime and is an example of crime reduction, although the most interesting reductions are those which occur long term.

2 Such interventions *may be in the present* (so as to frustrate the commission of a crime, as with the deterrent of an officer in uniform on patrol) or involve reducing the likelihood and seriousness of criminal and disorderly events by intervention in their causes. In other words, the focus in crime reduction is on the crime and the causes of crime.

3 Crime reduction *does not just involve the police service*. For example, a local authority may achieve crime reduction if it improves street lighting or provides activities for young people to enjoy in their spare time.

Let's have a look at an example of crime reduction. Figure 8.2 below contains an example of a strategy and an operation in relation to a particular crime problem.

Crime/incident	Strategy	Operation
Mugging in shopping centres.	Increase the probability of detection using plain-clothes officers.	Officers in teams, linked by radio, working in partnership with shopping centre staff, mingle with customers in the shopping centre.

Figure 8.2 Strategy and operation applied to a particular crime problem

How might the above be applied to the following?

■ Burglary by criminals posing as gas board officials.

■ Theft of cars from a car park.

■ Disorderly conduct outside a shopping area by youths in the evening.

You will notice that the third incident is an example of disorderly behaviour by youths. This highlights the point that the term 'crime' when used in this sense also refers to instances of public disorder (including violence caused by drunkenness) or high volume crime (such as burglary). For this reason, crime reduction is sometimes called 'crime and disorder reduction'.

8.5 The opportunity to commit crime and disorder

The opportunity to commit crime and disorder often means that a number of conditions come together whereby the offender believes it is safe to commit a crime, or that he or she does not feel threatened. This is known as the 'conjunction of criminal opportunity'. Take a few moments to think about conditions that may encourage or discourage a person to commit a crime.

You may have thought of some of these:

■ Discourage an offender

  – The presence of a uniformed police officer/PCSO

  – A burglar alarm fitted to a house about to be burgled

  – The presence of CCTV.

- Encourage an offender

  – No witnesses around to see the criminal act

  – The offender considers that the rewards from committing the crime out-weigh the chances of getting caught

  – Another offender encourages him/her in the commission of the offence.

By looking at some of these factors and the way in which they combine to create a criminal event, we can formulate ways in which criminal opportunities can be disrupted by removing or upsetting any element in an effort to tip the scales away from offending. Now try exercise 8F below.

Exercise 8F

Having seen the information above consider some ways in which criminal opportunities can be removed or disrupted.

You may have thought of several ways to intervene in crime and anti-social behaviour and these may well have included social and educational ideas and increased security making it harder to commit these types of offences. The increased security measures are often termed 'target hardening' because they make the potential target of crime much harder to access.

Social and educational interventions

These types of interventions include:

- Increased opportunities for youth employment through partnerships between private sector businesses and crime reduction partnerships

- Schools and colleges working together in partnership to teach students about the risks and effects of offending

- Ensuring greater understanding of the prevention of crime through talks to community groups and schools, crime prevention booklets and the raising of awareness through high-visibility activities.

Target hardening techniques

These interventions can be seen in the form of:

- CCTV

- Communal door entry systems

- Alarms, locks and security lights

- Improved lighting in streets, parks and other public spaces.

Figure 8.3 shows a gate used in an initiative to reduce the number of domestic burglaries and anti-social behaviour. This scheme, known as alley gating, has been very successful in many parts of England and Wales and is a good example of situational crime prevention and target hardening techniques. It allows residents and utility/emergency services to have access to these alleys and has proved to be very successful.

Figure 8.3   A typical alley-gate used in crime reduction

Source: Author's collection.

8.6 The motivated offender

A technique known as 'routine activity theory' states that there are three elements that must coincide for a crime or anti-social event to take place.
    These are:

- **A motivated offender**. This means that there must be a person who has sufficient drive to want to commit an offence.

- **A suitable victim**. This means that there is a victim who has not taken sufficient care to reduce the opportunity for a crime to occur.

■ **The absence of a capable guardian**. This refers to the fact that there is no one around who can witness the event taking place. This includes of course non-human technology such as CCTV.

The idea is that if any one of these three can be affected or altered in some way, the criminal or anti-social event can be removed. For example, the presence of CCTV cameras in a public car park may mean that a potential thief (a motivated offender or someone who is looking to steal a car) is deterred from committing offences. Similarly, if the owners of the cars install anti-theft devices on their vehicles then they reduce their chances of being a victim (no longer suitable victims).

Exercise 8G

Try to apply this approach to the problem of reducing domestic burglaries. How can you influence a motivated offender, suitable victim or provide a capable guardian?

8.7 Repeat victimisation

Much work carried out by crime and disorder reduction partnerships revolves around something called 'repeat victimisation'. However, before looking at some of the techniques used in this area, we need to understand what is meant by that term. One definition is: 'Repeat victimisation occurs when the same person or place suffers from more than one incident over a specified period of time.'

It is quite a simple definition, and one which can easily be remembered. Patterns of repeat victimisation have been used to help identify domestic and commercial burglary, racist attacks and domestic violence. It is believed, for example, that a house that has been burgled is up to four times more likely to be burgled than a house that has not.

The importance of using repeat victimisation information is that it can be used as a preventative tool because it tells police and partners where and how they should focus their efforts. It can also help target offenders as we know where they are likely to return.

There are certain trends that patterns of re-victimisation suggest. These are that repeat victimisation is predictable, rapid and highest in high crime areas. The following illustrates these points:

Predictable   Once victimised, a person or place is more
                     likely to be victimised again. This increases
                     the more a place or person becomes victim
                     to crime.

Rapid	The second and subsequent offences tend to occur quite rapidly after the first offence.
Highest in high crime areas	Some areas have high crime rates – not because of separate crime incidents, but because of repeat victimisation.

8.8 The Problem Analysis Triangle

The Problem Analysis Triangle (PAT) is a tool that is often used to analyse a particular incident of crime or disorder. Its main aim is to help understand the problem and point towards a possible solution. Each side of the triangle encourages you to think about the specific aspect of a problem and to note important information about it. These aspects are:

- The features of the location

- The features of the caller and or the victim

- The features of the offender and/or the source of the problem.

The PAT can be seen in the figure 8.4 below.

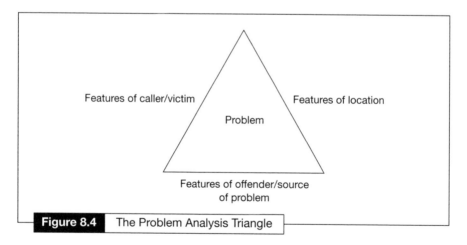

Features of caller/victim

Features of location

Problem

Features of offender/source
of problem

Figure 8.4 | The Problem Analysis Triangle

By thinking about each of these features, you should have some idea of how to intervene in the problem. One way of intervening is by trying to find out who the offender is and arresting him/her. However, that is just one way. Intervening in other features such as environmental aspects of the location – for example, improved lighting – can also lead to long-term management and resolution of the problem. Now try to apply this information to the information in exercise 8H.

Exercise 8H

An elderly lady is walking home late one evening along a poorly-lit path leading to a housing estate. A young male runs up to her, grabs her handbag and runs off. Try to apply the Problem Analysis Triangle to this simple example.

You may have considered some of the following in your ideas.

- **Victim**

  Victim support

  Witness statement and description of suspect

  Support and counselling

  Crime prevention advice of offender

- **Location**

  Improved lighting requirement

  Removal of overhanging foliage

  Design features

  Surveillance by nearby occupants of houses

  Access and egress

  Weather at the time

- **Offender**

  Description

  Access and egress directions

  Escape routes

  Possible disposal of property

Another useful aspect of using the PAT is the way it moves you into automatically involving other agencies in helping to address the problem. In the above case, we have thought about victim support and counselling for the victim provided by such services as the Victim Support Service, and also lighting issues which may be the province of the local authority. Use of this approach is not confined to crime and disorder alone. Many events that the police are called to are repeat events which take up a lot of police time and resources, yet can be solved quite simply. This is demonstrated in the case study below.

Case study

Friday night in Anytown

It is late on a Friday night in a busy town. There are limited police resources avail-able. An emergency call is received from an elderly lady that a man has broken into her house through the chimney and is stealing the furniture. Two double-crewed cars attend the scene as well as the single-crewed supervisor. At the scene it is discovered the elderly lady suffers from delusions and the call is a well-intentioned one but false. The officers spend a considerable amount of time at the scene reassuring the lady and arranging for a neighbour to look after her. One of the police officers present states that it was the third time that week she had received a call from this lady.

The supervisor, when he returns to the station, checks the address on the computer system and finds that in total, some 60 hours of police time in the pre-vious three months had been spent at the address dealing with unfounded complaints from the lady. A phone call, followed by an official letter, to the local health authority and welfare department meant the lady being hospitalised and treated for her complaint. The police received no more calls to the address and the lady received help. By applying and analysing the situation using the problem analysis triangle considerable police time and resources were saved.

The problem-solving approach to crime and disorder reduction is a useful tool for anyone engaged in this activity. It is particularly useful in the delivery of policing services with the introduction of neighbourhood policing teams.

8.9 Neighbourhood policing teams

The concept of neighbourhood team policing appears quite straightforward. It is about dealing with crime and disorder more intelligently and building new relationships between the police and the public. This relationship should be one built on cooperation rather than mere consent. It relies upon local people being part of the solution to local problems of crime and disorder. Firstly, how-ever, we need to understand what a neighbourhood means. The answer is that for the purposes of neighbourhood policing teams it depends upon many fac-tors. These include:

- Crime statistics

- Housing information

- Employment information

and many other social factors – not just a political ward or group of houses.

To a person living in an inner city, the idea of neighbourhood may seem different from someone living in a country village. A whole council may appear to be a neighbourhood in one instance, whilst in some areas it can mean a political ward.

The government, in pursuing this initiative, have suggested that the definition of neighbourhood should be left up to local communities, police forces and authorities and their partners. Therefore what comprises a neighbourhood for policing teams will differ in different parts of the country.

Now that we realise that a neighbourhood is not quite as simple as we thought, we need to consider who will make up the neighbourhood policing team.

Well, the police, of course, but who else do you think might be part of this new team approach to local community and problem-solving approach? In exercise 8I below, who you think may be part of the team?

Exercise 8I

Police officers		Community representatives	
Police community support officers		Volunteers	
Police specials		Neighbourhood watch	
Private security guards		Parish or neighbourhood wardens	
Community intelligence		Traffic wardens/road officers	

The answer is all of the above will be a part of the new neighbourhood policing teams, which will target specific problems identified by close liaison with communities throughout the country.

The way the team may operate can be seen in figure 7.2 in the previous chapter.

The idea of neighbourhood policing teams tackling crime and anti-social behaviour has been seen in several parts of the country already, for example in Merseyside and Leicester as can be seen in the box opposite.

Neighbourhood policing

Merseyside police operate in 43 'neighbourhoods', which equate to two to three council wards each. Teams are headed by an inspector who has responsibility for a number of sergeants and constables, supported by community support officers, special constables and volunteers. In consultation with the community they tackle issues that really affect people. Local surveys indicate that crime has been reduced and public satisfaction increased since their introduction.

In Leicester, officers are given small areas or 'micro beats' to patrol and oversee. These can be a small number of streets, an estate or a hotspot. Officers are considered as guardians for their area, solving problems and listening to local people. In one area alone, crime has fallen by 20 per cent as a result of this initiative.

This approach should be much more than just high visibility reassurance policing. It uses local knowledge and intelligence from local people to target crime hotspots and disorder issues causing most concern to local communities. The government has stated that the latest technology will support the initiative, including the issue of mobile telephone numbers to individuals within neighbourhoods so that they can contact the local beat manager directly.

Neighbourhood policing teams mean that people will:

- Know who their local police officers are and how to contact them
- Have a real say in local policing issues and setting local priorities
- Know how well their police are doing locally in tackling crime and antisocial behaviour.

Neighbourhood teams are an excellent example of delivering police services through a variety of different people, not just sworn police officers. The group of people engaged in this activity are often referred to as the extended policing family.

8.10 The extended policing family

We have seen from the Police Reform Act 2002 (Home Office 2002) that substantial change is in store for the police service and it is this Act that enables us, with some accuracy, to predict the future delivery of policing. The introduction of police community support officers, coupled with the use of neighbourhood watch and local warden schemes, will introduce a more flexible method of dealing with community problems, even if at this stage they may lack sufficient powers to carry out their full role. The extended police family, responsible for ensuring the tackling of day-to-day policing of crime and disorder, is worthy of exploration.

Uniformed constable

The role of the uniformed constable is crucial in that he/she will act as the 'manager' of the co-ordinated service delivery. This enables the constable to perform a more proactive role in consultation, coordinating delivery through the various officers available and, where necessary, being available to use the full powers available to a police constable. The role dramatically alters the idea of constable from one of enforcer of laws only to that of facilitator and leader. This will require a more professional approach and therefore, perhaps, a more highly-qualified individual to perform the role. The constable, it is envisaged, will be directly accountable to his/her line supervisor, the sergeant, who will have responsibility for two or more of the policing teams.

Police specials

The powers held by police specials, who are volunteers, are exactly the same as for regular officers. They receive the same amount and level of training as regular officers, wear the same uniforms, and provide invaluable support in many situations. As volunteers, they are able to offer only a certain amount of their time. Despite this fact, they should, if their availability is intelligently managed, provide useful, high-visibility patrols, backed up with the lawful authority to use force if necessary, just like regular sworn police officers.

Police community support officer

The Police Community Support Officer (PCSO), working with the other members of the delivery team, will be used not only to provide reassurance through visible patrolling at relevant times, but also through use of his/her powers to resolve low level community problems. They will provide the beat manager with invaluable assistance in dealing with minor instances of public disorder and anti-social problems.

Traffic wardens

With the idea of traffic wardens not only enforcing road traffic offences, but also being able to issue fixed-penalty notices for certain other offences, this role becomes a vital part of the integrated policing system. They can further operate as a means of obtaining information for the policing team, supplying criminal and community intelligence through their visible presence on the street. They will be available to deal with local traffic problems as well as being involved in maintaining safety on the roads.

Parish or neighbourhood warden schemes

Whilst originally conceived as an 'eyes and ears' approach for the police, coupled with concierge and reassurance functions, these warden schemes may well be able to issue fixed penalties for various offences such as minor criminal damage (graffiti) and the dropping of litter. The increase in surveillance and reassurance by high visibility patrolling that these schemes provide will be an invaluable asset to the beat manager.

Private security provision

It is possible that within neighbourhood teams use could be made of private security officers to enhance the policing capability. Whilst the main function of the private security industry has, in the past, been the protection of private property, there has been an increase in their use for such roles as prisoner escort, as well as other custody duties assisting sworn officers. The Private Security Industry Act 2001, which regulates the industry, will have wide repercussions for the use of private security in the public domain of policing. The main areas of current activity include the roles of wheel clamping, guarding premises, and as security consultants. Section 40 of the Police Reform Act 2002 introduces the community safety accreditation scheme, which is designed to extend limited police powers to persons already engaged in community safety duties. These include local authority wardens as well as security guards within private security industry.

Volunteers

A clear theme of the current government agenda for reform and modernisation of the public services is the development of new ways of involving local communities in shaping the priorities and outputs of public service delivery. This involves identifying new and less formalised methods of communication between the public services and service users to make delivery of services more responsive to the needs of local people. Generally speaking the police service in England and Wales has a modest record in the involvement of volunteers in its activities. The special constabulary has been the principal initiative and significant effort has been put into recruitment, retention and empirical evaluation of the business and community benefits of using these volunteers.

The following case study illustrates how neighbourhood policing teams can be used.

Case study

Neighbourhood policing teams in West Yorkshire

Neighbourhood policing teams should be at the centre of policing communities. They should be able to work together, be contactable and listen to the needs of the community. In Bradford South, West Yorkshire, neighbourhood policing teams now comprise more community support officers than community police officers. The full teams comprise an inspector, two sergeants, 18 police constables and 22 community support officers. CSOs conduct uniform patrols, not in an unstructured manner, but are focused on particular problems that have been identified within the previous 24 hours. The whole idea of the local policing team is supported by the use of good local knowledge and the unit has been very successful in combating vehicle crime and burglaries because of this. CSOs are encouraged by the local commander to visit people, enter their homes and have a cup of tea, thereby gaining their trust and confidence. CSOs have assisted regular officers in arresting an individual for a large number of burglaries, pooling their local knowledge to discover his hiding place. The neighbourhood team has built up many contacts in the area, such as schools and the community centre, and this personal involvement means the community believe the teams are working for and with them.

8.11 Conclusion

There is now an understanding that crime and disorder reduction cannot be achieved by the police service alone and this has meant the introduction of many changes. Most visible policing in England and Wales is carried out in partnership with someone else. This makes the police service more effective in tackling problems as they are able to utilise the expertise of other agencies, such as licensing departments of local authorities. It has also introduced a more effective way of policing by engaging in wide consultation with the community and hard-to-reach groups to identify local problems. It seeks to address them through a problem-solving approach using the new neighbourhood policing teams, the extended policing family, partnerships and the wider community.

Suggested further reading

Clarke, R.V. (ed), *Situational Crime Prevention: Successful Case Studies*, (2nd ed.) (New York: Harrow and Heston, 1997)

Felson, M. and Clarke, R.V., *Opportunity Makes the Thief: Practical Theory for Crime Prevention* Police Research Series No. 98, Policing and Reducing Crime Unit (London: Home Office, 1998)

Goldstein, H., *Problem Oriented Policing* (London: McGraw Hill, 1990)

Leigh, A., Read, T. and Tilley, N., *Brit Pop II: Problem Oriented Policing in Practice* Police Research Group Crime Detection and Prevention Series Paper 64 (London: Home Office, 1997)

Rogers, C., *Crime Reduction Partnerships* (Oxford: Oxford University Press, 2006)

Useful websites

http://www.communityengagement.police.uk/
Community engagement

http://www.audit-commission.gov.uk/
Audit Commission

http://www.lga.gov.uk/
Local Government Association

http://www.homeoffice.gov.uk/
Home Office

http://www.bbc.co.uk/crime/prevention/index.shtml
BBC crime prevention website

http://www.crimereduction.gov.uk/
Government crime reduction page

http://www.neighbourhood.gov.uk/
Neighbourhood regeneration

http://www.securedbydesign.com/
Secured by Design

http://www.jdi.ucl.ac.uk/index.php
Jill Dando Institute for Crime Science

http://www.drugs.gov.uk/
Drugs prevention

www.crimereduction.gov.uk/streetcrime
Street Crime Initiative

Chapter 9

Forensic Support in Law Enforcement

This chapter supports the following National Occupational Standards which describe the performance and competence required of a probationer officer.

Unit No.	Unit title
1A1	Use police actions in a fair and justified way.
1A2	Communicate effectively with members of communities.
1A4	Foster people's equality, diversity and rights.
1B9	Provide initial support to individuals affected by offending or anti-social behaviour and assess their needs for further support.
2A1	Gather and submit information that has the potential to support policing objectives.
2C2	Prepare for, and participate in, planned policing operations.
2C3	Arrest, detain or report individuals.
2G2	Conduct investigations.
2G4	Finalise investigations.
SH1	Interview victims and witnesses.
2H2	Interview suspects.
2I1	Search individuals.
2I2	Search vehicles, premises and land.
2J1	Prepare and submit case files.
2J2	Present evidence in court and at other hearings.
4C1	Develop your own knowledge and practice.
4G2	Ensure your own actions reduce risks to health and safety.

9.1 Introduction

Twenty years ago, the archetypal police officer would be one who was computer illiterate and had little or no knowledge or interest in science and technology. Now science and technology are at the heart of criminal investigation and police officers must be both computer literate and scientifically aware. Police officers are not all expected to be technical experts, but they are required to understand how scientific support and technology can help their work and the work of their colleagues. The purpose of this chapter is to introduce the new police officer to some of the principles of scientific investigation, to increase awareness of forensic science and the role of technology in police work and to provide some examples of the police officer's role in collecting evidence. The chapter ends by considering cyber crime and how this increasingly challenges the way that police work and how they are trained.

9.2 Range of scientific and technical support available to the police service

The development of forensic science and allied professions is about 100 years old. In the early 1900s a blood stain could not be identified as animal or human in origin. The identification of fibres as belonging to an individual person was impossible. Fingerprints were used by crime investigators in the late 1800s but a rapidly searchable UK-wide database for fingerprints and DNA samples awaited the availability of computers and so are relatively recent additions to the investigators' armoury. Although the application of science to serious crime (particularly murders) is well known, the use of scientific techniques has revolutionised the investigation of 'high-volume crime' (such as car theft and burglary).

Forensic science is the application of science to the investigation of crime. It includes the analysis of drugs, fibres, fingerprints, ballistics, documents, photographs and of DNA-containing fragments. Much of the collection of potentially-useful evidence at the scene is carried out by Crime Scene Investigators (CSIs) (who were formerly known as Scenes of Crime Officers [SOCOs]) or by police officers themselves. Potentially valuable pieces of evidence are further examined by laboratory-based scientists. Allied to forensic science are forensic pathology and toxicology. The interrogation of computer hard disks (particularly in fraud and pornography investigations) is a relatively new branch of forensic investigation. The use of technology in mapping crime (part of 'Crime Analysis') is an important support for the National Intelligence Model (NIM). Nor is the use of science or technology restricted to crime investigation. For example:

- 'Airwave' is the commercial name for a secure digital radio network project which, although costing £2.9 billion, has greatly improved the geographical coverage and quality of police radio communication through the UK.

- The use of technology in measuring alcohol levels in blood and breath is a crucial part of attempts to deter drink-drivers. At least 500 people die from drink-related accidents in the UK each year.

- Accident investigation uses scientific principles to establish the causes of serious road traffic collisions.

- Non-lethal weapons (such as TASERS) and protective body armour have been developed for use by police officers.

The development of fast computers (which we now take for granted) has revolutionised much police work because it permits very rapid comparison of crime, vehicle and personal data (e.g. fingerprints, DNA profiles, disqualified drivers, serial offender behaviour) against centralised databases that serve all police forces. As time goes on, the databases are getting larger and so the opportunities for successful searches are greater, but the value of such databases is crucially dependent upon the quality and accuracy of the data they contain.

Although police forces employ staff with considerable scientific expertise and carry out scientific tests themselves (particularly in fingerprints and photography), specialist analysis is carried out by external agencies and companies such as the Forensic Science Service and Forensic Alliance in which the police force is the 'customer'. It is important that the best value for money is obtained in such work, and each police force has nominated individuals who will decide whether the costs of an investigation are justified by the potential gains.

The Police National Computer

The most important database available to the police service is the Police National Computer (PNC). The PNC is an on-line intelligence tool managed by the Police Information Technology Organisation (PITO), but individual police forces are responsible for the entry and maintenance of information relating to arrests and court results. Information is stored under the headings of *names*, *vehicles* and *property* and data can be accessed in seconds from any of the 30,000 PNC terminals across the UK. For example, an officer at the scene of an accident and in radio contact can almost immediately check whether the cars involved are stolen and whether or not the drivers are disqualified. The PNC has links to fingerprint and DNA databases and is linked to the Schengen Information System (SIS) which shares information Europe-wide.

A person's name is added to the PNC for a wide range of reasons including where they have been:

- Arrested on suspicion of a recordable offence
- Reported missing or as having deserted from the armed forces

- Added to the firearms register

- Sought as a witness to an incident

- Disqualified from driving

- Reported as having failed to appear at court.

To ensure data protection, every request for information on the PNC is logged. A code of practice for the use of the PNC has legal force under the Police Acts of 1996 and 1997. PNC information is confidential and the disclosure of information (such as previous convictions) to unauthorised individuals is a criminal offence. There are also restrictions on the use of some of the information held on the PNC. For example, a motor insurance database (provided by the insurance companies) has now been added to the vehicles part of the PNC database. The motor insurance database is used to check that vehicles are insured (so deterring uninsured drivers) and to inform insurance companies of the location of stolen or abandoned vehicles recovered by the police service, but it is illegal to use this database for intelligence gathering or for crime investigation.

    The use of PNC is increasing as new systems such as Automatic Number Plate Recognition (ANPR, which quickly scans and checks a car number plate against records of stolen and 'untaxed' vehicles) are used more widely. About 5,000 checks in the PNC are made each week through the 'jurors' link, which allows courts to check whether a proposed juror has a criminal record. During January 2006, the PNC hit a 'new high' of 10,870,276 transactions.

9.3 Scientific evidence

The use of science in crime investigation follows some simple rules which are generally accepted by the scientific community. These include:

- The scientist can only give evidence on work carried out personally or under his/her direct supervision. However, an 'expert witness' can interpret factual evidence given by another witness under oath.

- Scientific examinations used in court should be based on established scientific principles, validated, and preferably published so that they can be scrutinised by the scientific community at large (in the USA this is called the 'Frye Test').

- Where the scientific findings require interpretation, the basis of the interpretation should be available to the scientific community.

- The responsibilities of the scientist are personal and not corporate. In other words, scientists (like police officers) cannot evade their ethical responsibilities.

It is important to distinguish between 'methodological error' and 'practitioner error' in forensic techniques. Methodological error is an error in the principles or written procedures. Practitioner error arises from individual mistakes or negligence (which can be avoided) or from inbuilt uncertainties in measurements (which cannot be avoided). We can illustrate the distinction by looking at fingerprints in more detail.

Fingerprints

The surface of our fingers has raised skin ridges which nature has designed to improve friction so that we grasp objects more firmly. The skin ridges, when covered with ink and rolled on paper, produce an impression called a fingerprint. No two individuals (even identical twins) have the same fingerprints. There are well-tested methods for extracting and developing fingerprint impressions (known as *finger marks*) at the scene of a crime. The task is to compare a *finger mark* with the *fingerprints* of individuals who are known to the police. The initial identification of a finger mark is often achieved using a computer search of the national database operated through the National Automated Fingerprint Identification System (NAFIS). A final identification is then carried out by an expert fingerprint officer.

At first sight the comparison of a finger mark with a fingerprint might be seem a perfect and infallible way of linking a person to the crime scene. However, finger marks found at the scene of a crime are frequently badly smudged or incomplete. In a tiny number of high profile cases, fingerprint officers have made mistakes in the identification, and innocent people have been convicted of crimes they did not commit. But this is not a methodological error – there is nothing wrong with the principle of the technique or the method – it is an individual or practitioner error and, since it remains true that more cases are solved by fingerprints than by any other single forensic technique, we must endeavour to improve the way that individuals work rather than jettison the technique as 'fatally flawed'.

Table 9.1 gives one way in which physical evidence is classified.

It is important to understand that forensic scientists and CSIs cannot influence the way in which the evidence has accumulated at the crime scene. In a traditional scientific experiment, scientists can usually select the variables and repeat experiments using fresh samples of chemicals or biological materials. But forensic evidence is often far from ideal. A footprint in a garden might be eroding as you observe it under a deluge of rain, and a finger mark at the scene might be so fragmentary that it cannot be searched against the national database.

The idea of 'experimental controls' (comparisons) is well known in scientific experiments and this idea is equally applicable to forensic science. For example, in the case of fingerprints, the finger mark is compared with the 'control' (the fingerprint). Exercise 9A contains another example.

Category	Examples
Chemicals	(a) Unidentified powders at the scene of a suspected drug factory are analysed in order to establish if they are controlled drugs.
	(b) Alcohol analysis in the breath of a suspected drink-driver.
Trace (microscopic evidence)	(a) Glass shards are found on the clothing of an individual who denied that he was present at the scene of assault using a beer glass.
	(b) Hair fibres belonging to a victim are found in the accused person's car.
Biological	(a) DNA extracted from the victim of a sexual assault.
	(b) A poison is extracted from the body parts of a victim.
Pattern	(a) Fingerprint identification at the scene of a burglary.
	(b) Document examination of a cheque to aid a suspected fraud investigation.

Table 9.1 The main categories of physical evidence

Exercise 9A

CSIs find red seat cover fibres from a suspect's car on the clothes of a victim. What control should be used by the SOCO in this case?

The control would be that we must thoroughly check whether or not the red fibres originate from another innocent source, e.g. from the victim's own car. Therefore, several fibres will be examined from a range of sources. Investigators will also have to ensure that the fibres did not originate from contamination from the examining officer. This is done by adopting scrupulous 'hygiene' practices through the collection of evidence. This is the reason why investigators often wear disposable 'snow suits'.

Exercise 9B invites us to consider the limitations of some kinds of forensic evidence.

Exercise 9B

A hair follicle found at the scene of an assault in a flat is shown to contain DNA which matches that of the chief suspect. What does this prove?

Without thinking too deeply, we might think that this evidence proves that the suspect assaulted the victim. But it does not. It does not even prove that the suspect has been in the flat. All we can say with near certainty is that a hair fibre of the suspect was found in the flat! This might not appear very useful, but it illustrates the limitations of forensic science. Forensic science is very rarely capable of achieving convictions on its own, but taken together with other evidence (such as statements to the police by the suspect or reports from witnesses) forensic evidence can be very powerful. In this example, if the suspect denied that he had ever entered the flat, the DNA evidence might be viewed as highly influential in a successful prosecution case because (contrary to the suspect's statement) it *links the suspect to the scene.*

Exercise 9C

A house burns down and a body is found in the embers. A forensic scientist takes swabs from the hands of the deceased and sends them off to the lab with the instruction to 'test for any hydrocarbons (fuels) in the swabs'. The swabs are found to be hydrocarbon-free. Does this rule out arson?

In the absence of other information, the answer is 'no'. The deceased might have been attempting to light a fire with fuel (such as that contained in a fire-lighter) when the fire got out of control. Hydrocarbons evaporate easily and in the high temperatures of a fire all the hydrocarbons might have been driven out or burned. The absence of hydrocarbons on the deceased is consistent with an accident, but does not prove that it was an accident. We must be careful not to make unjustified conclusions from the absence of evidence. This is summarised by the adage 'Absence of evidence is not evidence of absence'.

9.4 Police officers as gatherers and preservers of forensic evidence

Forensic exhibits, like all evidence, must be properly protected, secured and accounted for from the collection at the crime scene, to the laboratory, store room and ultimately to court. This is known as the 'continuity of evidence'. The police must be able to show to the court that the piece of evidence has been properly stored and labelled and that only named individuals have had access to the evidence. If jurors suspect that potential evidence has been mishandled, contaminated or erased it becomes worthless.

One particular concern is that a crime scene may become damaged or contaminated and this places particular responsibility on the First Officer Attending (FOA) the scene.

> **Exercise 9D**
>
> State three actions that the FOA should take on arrival at the scene of a large-scale burglary at a carpet factory.

Your answers might include:

- A call for assistance from colleagues to protect the scene and a message to the CSI to attend as soon as possible
- Notify the key holder (normally the manager of the factory)
- Preservation of the scene (from passers-by, etc.).

9.5 Police science and technology strategy

The scale of scientific and technological development in the world at large is huge. Only some developments will prove useful to police investigations and forces are not usually able to fund the development of new crime investigation techniques themselves. With few exceptions (such as the Video Identification Parade Electronic Recording: VIPER) the task of identifying and developing 'forensically useful' science is left to the government and its agencies. The government has written a strategy (*Police Science and Technology Strategy 2004–2009*) with the purpose of equipping the police service to exploit the opportunities that new developments present. This involves:

- Anticipating future opportunities
- Prioritising future science and technology applications
- Co-ordinating the use and development of such applications across relevant organisations.

The strategy feeds into national policing plans. Three main organisations provide the police with advice on equipment and services: the Home Office Scientific and Development Branch, the Forensic Science Service, and the Police Information Technology Organisation.

The Home Office Scientific and Development Branch (HOSDB) provides impartial advice on equipment and technology, much of which is provided by the private sector. A detailed operational requirement is agreed with the police force (as customer) before the HOSDB can recommend an appropriate technology solution.

The Forensic Science Service, as well as being the biggest provider of forensic science services to the police service, also provides independent advice to the Home Office and Crown Prosecution Service.

The Police Information Technology Organisation (PITO) manages the national information and communications technology. Examples of the project include the National Automated Fingerprint Identification System (NAFIS, a database of fingerprints), Vehicle on-line descriptive searches for the police national computer, the Violent and Sexual Offenders Register (ViSOR) and Airwave (the system which has replaced the older VHF and UHF personal police radios). The National Policing Improvement Agency (NPIA) is a new body that will support forces to improve the way they work across many areas of policing. PITO will form part of the National Policing Improvement Agency from 2007.

DNA profiling

DNA (deoxyribonucleic acid) is a molecule that is found in almost every cell of the human body and varies sufficiently between individuals (except identical twins) to form a unique genetic pattern that can be extracted (and subsequently processed in the laboratory) from a sample of semen, blood, saliva or skin.

Over 3 million DNA 'fingerprints' are stored in the National DNA Database (NDNAD). The database is run by the Forensic Science Service. Samples are contributed to NDNAD from two sources: (a) criminal justice samples, consisting of saliva taken by mouth swab from anyone charged, cautioned or reported by the police for a recordable offence and (b) evidence recovered at the crime scene (cigarette butts, blood swabs, etc.). A 'DNA hit' occurs when the DNA profile from the crime scene is searched against NDNAD and found to be identical with that of a criminal justice DNA profile. This allows the police to identify a suspect even if the crime occurred many years ago. However, DNA evidence in itself is not regarded as proof of guilt and it is up to the police to build a case for the prosecution and test any alibi that the suspect may have. Even medium-sized police forces have DNA budgets (to pay for searches and analyses) of over £1million.

In 2003 DNA evidence proved crucial in solving the murder of Lynette White in Cardiff in 1988. DNA material collected at the original crime scene was analysed using the new SGM+ method (giving a so-called 10-point DNA profile) in 2002 and the profile searched against NDNAD. The search gave a partial match with the profile of 14-year old boy who (although not a suspect himself) was known to be related to Jeffrey Gafoor. Since relatives possess similar DNA profiles, police investigated Gafoor, who subsequently admitted the 1988 murder.

9.6 Crime analysis

The term 'crime analysis' includes the use of crime-mapping and of offender and offence profiling analysis. COMPSTAT uses statistics produced by crime analysis.

Local crime data may be analysed to produce the following classes of information:

- Crime patterns – the type, number and location of crimes

- Crime trends – changes in crime within an area over time

- Crime clusters – crimes linked by common features, e.g. the use of firearms

- Crime series – different crimes involving the same offenders.

Exercise 9E

1 Classify the following as crime patterns, crime trends, crime clusters or crime series.

   (a) Data showing the number and location of muggings in a city suburb over a month.

   (b) Data showing the different crimes committed by members of a gang over the last ten years.

   (c) Data showing the number of detected shop thefts averaged over different days of the week.

   (d) Data showing the number of thefts by criminals posing as 'gas safety engineers' in a county.

2 You suspect that shoplifting is greatest during school half-terms. What kind of analysis would you request in order to confirm this?

The answers to (1) are: (a) crime patterns, (b) crime series, (c) crime trends and (d) crime clusters. In (2), a crime pattern would be requested, perhaps over half-terms over the last three years.

Crime-mapping has become more sophisticated because of the availability of databases linked to Geographical Information Systems (GIS). The analysis of patterns of criminal behaviour is used to direct police resources most effectively and efficiently. For example, burglaries in a city over a three-year period may be mapped electronically according to geography as well as day and time so that any 'hotspots' can be identified. This not only directs the use of deterrent action (such as visible patrolling or CCTV), it also helps intelligence officers to link criminal activity with data on housing, age of population, type of housing, social deprivation, etc. This has been of particular value to Crime and Disorder Reduction Partnerships between the police service, local authorities and other agencies which can then jointly agree activities that will reduce the reoccurrences of crime. Crime-mapping provides information that is essential to the 'intelligence products' of the National Intelligence Model (NIM). For example, the mapping might include where drugs are supplied, how often they are supplied and where they are suspected of being purchased.

Offender profiling is known as Behavioural Investigative Analysis (BIA). Offender and offence profiling involves an analysis of criminal behaviour and the mode of operation by the criminal. Such profiling is practised by specialist advisory units such as the Serious Crime Analysis Section (SCAS) of the National Centre for Policing Excellence. Crime cases are referred to SCAS from intelligence officers in police forces with the aim of identifying serial murders, serial rapists and potential murders and rapists. The elements of an attack (e.g. the age of victims, and the location of the crime) are logged and stored on a database. Details of a new offence are searched against the database with the intention of finding out whether or not the offender has previously offended.

An example of the use of crime analysis in Crime and Disorder Reduction Partnerships: CADDIE

CADDIE (Crime and Disorder Data Information Exchange) has been used by partners (including the emergency services, councils and community organisations) in Sussex, Hampshire and South Wales. CADDIE links together crime and disorder information from partners to provide an accurate picture of what is happening in areas within Sussex, so helping to reduce crime and to reduce the fear of crime.

CADDIE works at three levels:

Level 1: Public online access at *www.caddie.gov.uk* allows the general public to examine crime and disorder data-mapped to individual wards. (There is lots of useful information on this site).

Level 2: Partner access: community partners can access more detailed information held on the CADDIE system. This is not available to the general public.

Level 3: Partnership analyst. The third access level to CADDIE is provided by the partnership analyst, who can provide precise details of offences and acts of disorder, and generate crime trends, patterns and clusters, supplying detailed analysis including crime patterns, trends, clusters and series.

9.7 Use of HOLMES in major investigations

The Yorkshire Ripper case of the 1980s illustrated the difficulties of analysing and cross-referencing huge amounts of information using a manual 'card system'. Eventually, this led to a computer-based system which has become a national database for major police investigations. The system was named the Home Office Large Major Enquiry System, HOLMES. The latest version (named HOLMES 2) permits links to be made with the Police National Computer and includes a 'casualty bureau' for managing information following major incidents.

9.8 Cyber crime

Cyber crime is crime that involves the use of computer networks. Examples include:

- The deliberate release of computer viruses with the intention of damaging computer systems

- The transmission of child pornography using the internet

- Identity theft (e.g. obtaining the bank account details of individuals)

- Illegal software piracy

- The use of e-mails to send hate mail or to 'remotely stalk' or threaten vulnerable individuals

- 'Hacking in' to private bank accounts (often called 'cyber trespass').

Exercise 9F

Cyber crime

List three of the special challenges of combating and investigating cyber crime.

Cyber crime is a 'whole new ball game' and the challenges are very different from conventional crime investigations. Some of the reasons for this include:

- Cyber crime is often international in nature and may require difficult and time-consuming liaison with police forces in other countries. Cyber crime is often information-based and not property-based. The transmission of data and software across the World Wide Web is so easy that even small groups of criminals can carry out their activities across national boundaries.

- Cyber crime requires technical expertise. It requires police officers to work very closely with computer experts.

- Computer hard disks can store huge masses of data and analysis of hard disks is very time-consuming.

- The World Wide Web allows similarly-minded individuals to communicate and share ideas. This can often be a constructive activity, but it also provides a ready-made communication channel for extremists and terrorists.

- The priority of law enforcement agencies and the availability of specialist legislation vary across different countries. For example, many child pornography sites are based in Russia, which appears to have fewer laws relating to such activities.

Although many non-police agencies (particularly parents and internet service providers) play an important role in regulating websites and the access children have to them, investigating cyber crime is not a community-based police activity. Specialist teams are required to investigate cyber crime and these are likely to be based within one office within the police force. By definition, the actions of such investigations are remote from the public: the police are using computers to probe for computer-related crime and such actions are invisible to most members of the public. Nevertheless, some police operations have gained considerable public attention. Perhaps the most famous to date has been 'Operation Ore', in which 390,000 subscribers to child pornography sites throughout the world were traced through their credit cards.

In the UK, legislation has targeted computer-based crime by passing the Computer Misuse Act 1990, which makes it an offence to attempt to gain unauthorised access to a computer. Further amendments to the law have been made within the Police and Justice Act 2006.

The scale of cyber crime is very difficult to measure. Statistics on cyber crime are notoriously unreliable and it is very easy for specialist police units to become bogged down with the sheer amount of information relating to potential offences that may be generated from an operation. Prioritisation is doubly important in investigating cyber crime, but not everyone will agree with the priorities that are given to certain crimes. The development of a UK national strategy on e-crime and the creation of the Serious Organised Crime Agency (SOCA), with responsibility for much high-tech crime, will accelerate the law enforcement response to cyber crime in the UK. This is just as well: cyber crime is likely to become even more important, and the consequences of such crime to individuals and organisations can be very great indeed. Individual police officers cannot afford to dismiss cyber crime as abstract and unimportant. It is very likely that cyber crime will cause the police service dramatically to alter the way that it organises and trains its officers to deal with such crime. In particular, the computer literacy skills of all future police officers must be greatly improved and the student officer is strongly advised to anticipate such demands and improve their own computer knowledge as much as possible.

9.9 The future

No one can predict with confidence how technology and science will influence policing and crime investigation in the future. There are many influences at work and we will briefly discuss three of them.

The first is the rapid development of science and technology, driven by academic and commercial institutions, which have added many more products to the market place. Just as the adoption of new scientific treatments in the National Health Service is fuelled by large multi-nationals willing to invest in research and development in order to generate long-term profits, so the IT and scientific industries are identifying new opportunities in both private and public law enforcement and security. This has created a bigger range of commercial products (e.g. communication and database systems, CCTV, body armour and surveillance cameras) than has ever been available in the past (see table 9.2).

The second is the nature of crime itself. Higher-level criminality is becoming more concerned with selling services or products and routing profits into purchases than with physically stealing objects. Fraud and cashless transactions are often difficult to detect and are not restricted to regional or even national boundaries. In the future, we may use less cash (even in everyday transactions) and so identity theft will become more important. This will mean that the use of biometric data (such as iris recognition) by financial institutions becomes more widespread. The changing nature of crime will dictate the nature of the police response, but technology will play a massive part in the strategies that are adopted.

The third is that the Home Office and its agencies, such as PITO, are playing the dominant role in selecting and approving new technology and in funding massive IT projects, such as those using national databases. The technology used by the police service will ultimately be that which reflects the priorities of the government itself.

The rationale for using science and technology is to make police work and police forces more effective and more efficient. For example, the advantages of being able to confirm individual identity on the street (using a portable fingerprint scanner linked by radio to national databases) are immediate: officers do not need to arrest individuals because they fear that false names have been provided: they can instead report those individuals for subsequent processing in the criminal justice system. On the other hand, the increasing use of surveillance and the pursuit of cyber crime 'behind closed doors' raise public concerns about police accountability and visibility.

An objective assessment about the 'value for money' of the use of technology is notoriously difficult to achieve. The police officer who uses an image from a very expensive and controversial CCTV system in a shopping centre to solve a serious assault may well regard the technology as 'having proved its worth', yet the assault might have been deterred if the money had been spent in other ways. The trainee police officer will perhaps be more concerned about using technology rather than evaluating it, but such arguments are certain to resurface later on in their career.

Technology	Current or future application
Radio frequency identification devices	'Chipping' valuable goods
Face recognition systems	Tracking of individuals under surveillance
X-ray and mass spectrometry	Detection of explosives in luggage
Hand-held fingerprint scanners linked to national databases	Authentication of identity 'on the street'
Biometric technology	Iris identification of individuals attempting to gain access to buildings or computers
Thermal imaging systems	Location of bodies trapped in accidents

Table 9.2 Some examples of current technologies in use by the police and security agencies

Suggested further reading

Gaule, M., *The Basic Guide to Forensic Awareness* (Goole: The New Police Bookshop, 2004) (Very readable guide to the work of the Scenes of Crime Officer).

Jackson, A.R.W., and Jackson, J.M., *Forensic Science* (Harlow: Pearson Prentice Hall, 2004) (A more advanced introduction)

Newburn, T., *Handbook on Policing* (Cullompton: Willan, 2003) (Chapters 14, 20 and 26 are particularly relevant)

Useful websites

http://www.homeoffice.gov.uk/documents/PoliceST_S2_part11.pdf
Police science and technology strategy 2004-2009

http://www.homeoffice.gov.uk/science-research/police-science-tech/?version=1
General information on police science and technology

http://www.airwaveservice.co.uk/airwave5.asp
Airwave communication radio system

http://police.homeoffice.gov.uk/news-and-publications/publication/operational-policing/Police_nat_comp.pdf
Code of Practice for the Police National Computer

http://www.forensic-access.co.uk/forensic-access-publications/benchmark-newsletter/fire-investigation.htm
Some examples of forensic cases from the company Forensic Access

http://www.michaelspecter.com/ny/2002/2002_05_27_fingerprint.html
A reporter's article on the validity of fingerprints. Not to be considered in isolation, but an interesting discussion

http://news.bbc.co.uk/hi/english/static/in_depth/uk/2001/life_of_crime/cybercrime.stm
Introductory site on cyber crime produced by the BBC

http://www.cybercrime.gov/
US Department of Justice site on computer crime

http://www.soca.gov.uk/assessPublications/downloads/threat_assess_unclass_250706.pdf
An analysis of the threats by serious and organised crime by SOCA. It contains several references to types of cyber crime

http://en.wikipedia.org/wiki/Cybercrime
Wikipedia's excellent article on cyber crime with links to related legislation

http://www.crimereduction.gov.uk/internet02.htm?n46
The Home Office E-crime Strategy

http://www.parliament.uk/documents/upload/postpn258.pdf
An excellent summary of the DNA database and of the legislation allowing the acquisition and retention of DNA samples

http://www.centrex.police.uk/cps/rde/xchg/centrex/root.xsl/scas.html
The Serious Crime Analysis Section (Centrex)

http://www.holmes2.com/holmes2/whatish2/
Information on HOLMES 2

PART 3

Practical Police Work

Chapter 10

Criminal Investigations

This chapter supports the following National Occupational Standards which describe the performance and competence required of a probationer officer.

Unit No.	Unit title
1A1	Use police actions in a fair and justified way.
1A2	Communicate effectively with members of communities.
1A4	Foster people's equality, diversity and rights.
1B9	Provide initial support to individuals affected by offending or anti-social behaviour and assess their needs for further support.
2A1	Gather and submit information that has the potential to support policing objectives.
2C2	Prepare for, and participate in, planned policing operations.
2C3	Arrest, detain or report individuals.
2G2	Conduct investigations.
2G4	Finalise investigations.
SH1	Interview victims and witnesses.
2H2	Interview suspects.
2I1	Search individuals.
2I2	Search vehicles, premises and land.
2J1	Prepare and submit case files.
2J2	Present evidence in court and at other hearings.
2K2	Present detained persons to custody.
4C1	Develop your own knowledge and practice.
4G2	Ensure your own actions reduce risks to health and safety.

10.1 Introduction

One of the main functions of the police is to investigate crimes and criminal activity. Their performance in this area is continually under examination by the government, the criminal justice system and the media. There is always a need to ensure criminal investigations are improving so as to make criminal investigations more professional. This chapter will consider the main areas being introduced to ensure that people who investigate crime do so professionally, with integrity and in an accountable manner.

One reason why this should be so lies in the changing nature of crime. Since the 1960s, society has seen increased affluence, consumerism, changes in moral attitudes and technological developments. There has been a rise in activities such as fraud, counterfeiting of goods, pornography, etc. Gun-related crime has become quite prevalent and is sometimes linked to other forms of crime such as illegal drug dealing or human trafficking. These modern forms of criminal activities require new forms of response, which are organised at a local, national and international level.

10.2 Why should the police investigate professionally?

This may seem at first, a strange question to ask. You may think that the answer is obvious. If that is the case, write down what you think.

You may have come up with answers such as:

- The police are the professionals in dealing with crime

- They are paid to do it

- The public expect them to.

In a sense all of the above are true. However, there are also many other benefits for the police in carrying out professional criminal investigations. Apart from being something called the 'core' business of the police service (which just means it is one of the main functions), criminal investigations should not be separated from other police activities. Conducting good quality investigations can generate information that can be fed into the National Intelligence Model process. This can then be used to brief and deploy uniform patrols and identify intelligence-led initiatives designed to reassure communities and reduce offending and anti-social behaviour. Further, when conducting criminal investigations, the police invariably have direct contact with a member of the public. This can have a substantial impact upon the quality of information provided by witnesses and victims and can help their understanding of the criminal justice system as a whole.

10.3 What is an investigation?

Firstly, let's consider the question 'what is a criminal investigation?' At first glance this may seem quite straightforward. You may think that everything a police officer investigates is a criminal investigation. To some extent you are right. However, a criminal investigation is defined under Part II of the Criminal Procedure and Investigations Act 1996 (CPIA) code of practice as:

'An investigation conducted by police officers with a view to it being ascertained whether a person should be charged with an offence, or whether a person charged with an offence is guilty of it.'

This will include:

- Investigations into crimes that have been committed

- Investigations whose purpose is to find out whether a crime has been committed, with a view to the possible introduction of criminal proceedings

- Investigations which begin in the belief that a crime may be committed, for example when an individual or premises is kept under surveillance, with a view to possibly commencing criminal proceedings

- Charging a person with an offence which includes prosecution by way of a summons.

As we can see, the definition of a criminal investigation is quite wide ranging. What it covers is:

- Where a crime is known to have been committed, e.g. burglary or assault that is reported to the police

- Where it is suspected that a crime may have been committed, e.g. where valuable diamonds are recovered at a car boot sale

- Where it is believed that, through the use of informants/intelligence, a crime will be committed, e.g. a planned armed robbery.

10.4 The role of the criminal investigator

Firstly, try and complete exercise 10A below.

Exercise 10A

What does a criminal investigator do?

Perhaps you have decided that a criminal investigator is simply a person who investigates crime. Well, you are not far from the definition, although it is slightly more complicated than this. The CPIA Code of Practice under Part II of the Act clearly defines who an investigator is and what their role is when investigating. This is shown below.

Definition of the role of an investigator

An investigator is any police officer involved in the conduct of a criminal investigation. All investigators have a responsibility for carrying out the duties imposed on them under this code including, in particular, recording information and retaining records of information and other material.

An important point to note from this definition is that it is essential that during an investigation information and material gathered as a result of the inquiry must be recorded and retained. This means that as the investigation proceeds, the investigator will compile a list of information and material that can be referred back to.

Whilst the code specifically states police officer, you must remember that investigations can be conducted by persons other than police officers with investigative powers. With this in mind, try exercise 10B below.

Exercise 10B

Speak to your friends or family and compile a list of people who may have investigative powers apart from the police.

This may not be as easy as you first thought of, but there are a number of agencies that have similar investigative powers to the police, and sometimes work closely with the police on investigations. These include:

- Serious Fraud Office (SFO)

- Independent Police Complaints Commission (IPCC)

- Department for Trade and Industry (DTI)

- Department for Transport (DfT)

- Post Office Investigations.

There are many others, but one thing they all have in common is that they must obey the rules and legislation regarding criminal investigations.

Ethical investigations

What you have to remember is that criminal investigations must be carried out in an ethical manner. You can read more about ethical policing in Chapter 5. However, don't forget that investigators have a wide range of powers and can deprive people of their liberty, can use reasonable force to do so, as well as being able to enter someone's house to gain access to information, and also deploy covert surveillance equipment on occasions. The use of these powers and the discretion available to investigators places a responsibility on the investigator to act in a professional and ethical manner at all times.

10.5 What legislation covers criminal investigations?

There are, of course, a large number of Acts of Parliament that set out what a crime is, when it is committed and the punishments attached to the crime. This section will concentrate on those major Acts of Parliament that have a direct influence on how criminal investigations should be carried out.

1 The Police and Criminal Evidence Act 1984 (PACE)

This Act, along with its Codes of Practice, is one of the key elements in the framework of legislation, providing powers the police need to investigate crime. It tries to balance the rights of individuals and the powers of the police, by being based on the principles of fairness and openness. It covers such areas as search, detention in custody, interviewing and many other police powers.

2 Prosecutions of Offences Act 1985

This Act created the Crown Prosecution Service (CPS) under the direction of the Director of Public Prosecutions (DPP), which has the responsibility for public prosecutions in England and Wales. By creating the CPS, all existing police prosecution departments were incorporated into it, thereby removing the authority for the police to conduct public prosecutions. The CPS now offers advice regarding serious criminal investigations as well as being available for consultation in other criminal investigations. They are sometimes found working within police stations to guide and advise police officers, which means they work with the police to improve performance in criminal investigations and bring more offenders to justice. This Act also introduced a code for crown prosecutors covering such issues as:

- evidential tests, which means the prosecutor must be satisfied there is a realistic prospect of conviction

- the Public Interest Test for Prosecutions, which means each case must reach given criteria such as the evidence available at the time, the impact of the expected evidence, etc.

- charging standards, which looks at which charges should be preferred in each case.

3 Criminal Procedure and Investigations Act 1996 (CPIA)

This Act sets the standard for criminal investigations and covers the important issue of disclosure of material and information to both the prosecution and defence teams in a criminal trial. It also establishes the role of the disclosure officer who is a person responsible for examining material retained by the police during the investigation, revealing material to prosecutors and certifying that this has been done.

4 The Human Rights Act 1998

Whilst this Act has been discussed elsewhere, it is important to acknowledge its influence on criminal investigations. It applies to all public bodies and it makes it unlawful for the police to violate the rights contained in the European Convention of Human Rights (ECHR). When conducting criminal investigations therefore, the police should remember that all their actions involved in carrying out the investigation should be justified, authorised, proportional, accountable and necessary.

5 Regulation of Investigatory Powers Act 2000 (RIPA)

Prior to the introduction of this Act, covert police investigations were governed on a non-statutory basis. However, to ensure that compliance with the directives of the European Court of Human Rights (ECHR), RIPA was introduced to provide a statutory framework for the use of covert techniques. The Act provides for criminal investigations to use the following techniques in the interests of national security, to prevent or detect crime and to safeguard the economic well-being of the UK:

- Interception of communications such as post and telecommunications

- Surveillance and covert human intelligence sources, which involve, for example, the use of technology for listening to conversations and the use of undercover personnel to gain information as a result of their relationship with criminals.

It must be remembered, though, that the use of the provisions of this Act needs quite a high authority and must be for legitimate and lawful purposes.

10.6 The Professionalising Investigation Programme (PIP)

The Professionalising Investigation Programme or PIP is an Association of Chief Police Officers (ACPO) project commissioned by the Home Office in partnership with the National Centre for Policing Excellence (NCPE) to examine, develop and make recommendations regarding professionalising investigations. The PIP programme identifies four levels of investigators and includes details of who should operate at each level and what types of crime are typically investigated at each level. Consequently, the level of investigation an individual operates at depends upon the level of training the individual has received. Examples of the different roles and levels can be seen in the following table.

Investigative level	Example of role	Typical investigative activity
Level 1	Patrol constable/police staff/supervisors	Volume crime
Level 2	Dedicated investigator, e.g. CID officer	More serious crime and includes road deaths
Specialist investigative role	Child protection, major crime	Family liaison, etc.
Level 4	SIO (Senior Investigating Officer)	Lead investigator in murders, rapes etc.

Table 10.1   The PIP level of investigation

10.7 The Serious Organised Crime Agency

The Serious Organised Crime Agency (SOCA) is a new law enforcement agency created to tackle people who cause harm to communities within the UK by serious organised crime. It incorporated the functions of the National Crime Squad (NCS), the National Criminal Intelligence Service (NCIS) and also some of the functions of the UK Immigration service (UKIS) in dealing with drug trafficking, related organised criminal finance and organised immigration crime.

SOCA has five main aims. These are:

- To build knowledge and understanding of serious organised crime, the harm it causes and of its effectiveness of different responses

- To increase the amount of criminal assets recovered and increase the proportion of cases where the proceeds of crime are pursued

- To increase the risk to serious organised criminals operating in the UK, through proven as well as innovative investigation capabilities

- To collaborate with partners in the UK and internationally to maximise efforts to reduce harm

- To provide agreed levels of high quality support to SOCA's operational partners and, as appropriate, to seek their support in return.

Clearly, SOCA is an important criminal investigation agency that operates at a national (and international) level to deal with high-level, organised crime. Even so, it must carry out its criminal investigations within the rules laid down by Acts of Parliament and in an ethical manner.

10.8 Reactive and proactive criminal investigation

There are two methods of criminal investigation: reactive and proactive. The proactive method is sometimes referred to as intelligence-led or covert-type investigations. However, the two approaches should not be considered as entirely separate from each other as they sometimes overlap in a criminal investigation.

The reactive method starts with the discovery of a crime and seeks to bring offenders to justice by uncovering material that identifies suspects and provides sufficient evidence to enable a court to determine their guilt. In the main this process depends upon interviewing victims and witnesses, on the examination of the crime scene and on establishing forensic links to suspects.

The proactive method generally starts with information and intelligence that an individual is, or group of people are, about to engage in criminal activity. This is often organised crime such as drug dealing or human trafficking. This approach is often used to deal with suspected terrorists. Investigators generally use a range of covert surveillance techniques which are used to link offenders to the criminal act. These investigations are often complemented by financial and forensic science investigation techniques.

10.9 Covert investigations

This type of criminal investigation involves the use of techniques designed to ensure that the operation and sources of information it uses remain concealed. Covert methods of policing can be used in both reactive and proactive investigations and the methods used include:

- Static surveillance

- Mobile surveillance

- Technical options

- The use of a covert human intelligence source (an undercover officer)

- Covert financial applications

- Undercover test purchases (used when investigating sales of illegal drugs. etc.).

The type of covert technique used during a criminal investigation is normally decided by the intelligence or covert team. However, there are a number of important points that have to be considered before covert methods are used – investigators need to:

- have a good understanding of the intelligence process and of the National Intelligence Model

- ensure that the amount of covert policing used is proportionate to the overall objectives of the investigation

- have a thorough understanding of the RIPA (Regulation of Investigatory Powers Act 2000) and other relevant legislation

- maintain operation security

- consult the CPS at the earliest possible opportunity in the investigation.

Surveillance logs

A surveillance log is a record of events, actions and movements witnessed by a surveillance officer. These must be kept by the covert team during the course of any covert operation and apply to events involving the surveillance subject.

10.10 The National Intelligence Model

The National Intelligence Model (NIM) is a major introduction in the context of police reform. NIM is a model that ensures information is fully researched and analysed to provide intelligence that senior police managers can use to inform strategic direction, make tactical decisions about resourcing and operational policing; it also helps to manage risk. One important point to note is that the model is not just about intelligence: it can be used for most areas of policing. For example, it sets the requirements for the contribution of patrolling, reactive, proactive and intelligence staff.

The NIM is, as detailed in Chapter 7, a business process. Figure 7.3 on p 106 shows a simplified schematic of the National Intelligence Model. The NIM is so important you will read about it in several chapters throughout this book.

The NIM is the product of work carried out by the National Criminal Intelligence Service on behalf of the Crime Committee of ACPO. It is a method whereby more rigour can be introduced into the management decision-making process for both strategic and tactical purposes. Its introduction, it is believed, will greatly help 'joined up' law enforcement.

The model has been designed to have an impact at three levels of police activity; these levels are explained in figure 10.1.

Level 1 (daily tasking) – Local issues which are the crimes, criminals and other problems affecting a BCU. This area will encompass wide issues from low-level theft to murder, and it is anticipated that the handling of volume crime will be at this level.

Level 2 (force/regional tasking) – Cross border issues that affect more than one BCU. This may include problems that affect a group of BCUs or neighbouring forces, and may also involve support from the National Crime Squad, HM Customs and Excise, or the NCIS. Common problems, the exchange of data and provision of resources for the benefit of all concerned will be key issues at this level.

Level 3 (national tasking) – Serious and organised crime, which usually operates on a national and international scale, will be dealt with at this level.

Figure 10.1   Levels of activity in NIM

The NIM, therefore, drives the investigation process in many crime and disorder issues and is an invaluable tool for the investigator.

10.11 Features of crimes

In general terms, crime can be placed into three broad categories. These are:

- Property crimes, such as theft, or burglary

- Crimes against the person, such as assault or sexual offences

- Crimes against society (sometimes referred to as 'victimless crimes'), such as illegal drug use, prostitution, etc.

All of these include a wide variety in terms of the behaviours and types of victims, witnesses and offenders, methods used to commit crime and the degree of planning involved. Each criminal act is different and generates its own problems for investigators to solve. For example, shoplifting and commercial fraud are both property crimes, but they produce different types of exhibits and other material due to the different ways in which they are committed. These factors help guide decision-making in the criminal investigation process, so knowledge of them is important. One of the main factors that criminal investigators need to know about is the *modus operandi* (MO) or the ways things are done. Police officers often refer to the MO of a crime, which means the ways in which the offender carried out the criminal act. A detailed knowledge of the MOs used by offenders within a particular area helps investigators to:

- Understand how a crime has been committed, the type of information and material that may have been generated and how this material may be recovered

- Identify a linked series of crimes with the same MO

- Identify links between crimes and known offenders who use the same MO

- Predict future offending patterns which may enable preventative measures to be taken

- Predict future offences which may lead to the capturing of an offender in the act of committing the offence

- Identify likely disposal places for stolen property or other substances such as illegal drugs.

10.12 Material

Police officers and other people involved in criminal investigations often refer to the use or generation of 'material'. Understanding what material is, how it is generated during a criminal offence and how it can be located, gathered and used are all important points in the investigation of crime. The official definition of material is provided by the CPIA (Criminal Procedure and Investigations Act 1996) Code of Practice Part II and is shown below.

Definition of material

'Material is material of any kind, including information and objects, which is obtained in the course of a criminal investigation and which may be relevant to the investigation; material may be relevant to an investigation if it appears to an investigator or to the officer in charge of an investigation, or to the disclosure officer, that it has some bearing on any offence under investigation or any person being investigated, or on the surrounding circumstances of the case, unless it is incapable of having any impact on the case.'

Therefore, material can be anything that is created by the commission of a criminal act, and includes such things as DNA, witness statements, stolen property, CCTV footage, fingerprints, reports, weapons, etc.

Material therefore can be gathered from a number of different sources that the criminal investigator should be aware of. These include:

- Victims

- Witnesses

- Suspects

- Locations, including scenes of crime and the victim's or suspect's home

- Systems used to collate or record data automatically, such as credit card machines or telephone records

- Intelligence databases held by the police or other agencies.

However, it must be realised that not all material generated by a criminal offence will end up as material that is admissible in court. The total material generated by an offence depends on a number of factors, such as the amount of planning that went into it, the experience of the criminal and the number of people involved as witnesses or victims. Each crime has a unique mixture of material.

The material gathered by the police does not always include the total material generated by the criminal offence. Some physical material may be destroyed, some witnesses may not be located, some of the material will only be known to the offenders, etc. Further, the police may obtain material that would not pass the evidential test, e.g. hearsay evidence or evidence of opinion. However, the police should gather as much material as possible, regardless of whether it will eventually end up as admissible in a court of law.

Therefore, as any case progresses, the amount of material admissible in a court of law will be less than that gathered in total by the police. The CPS should always be consulted so that all material gathered can be examined and decisions made regarding its value and admissibility as evidence made. Material not used in evidence may be disclosed to the defence as part of the unused material in the investigation. Figure 10.2 illustrates the attrition of material in a criminal investigation.

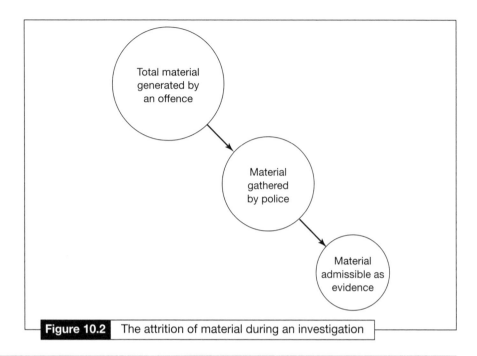

| Figure 10.2 | The attrition of material during an investigation |

10.13 The golden hour and the early stages

The golden hour is a term used for the period immediately following the commission of an offence when material is in plentiful supply and readily available to the investigator. Positive action by the police in this period reduces the attrition of material and greatly enhances the chances of securing admissible material for court purposes. Investigators need to consider some of the following during the golden hour:

- Victims – identify, support and preserve evidence in a sensitive manner
- Scenes – identify, preserve, assess and commence a log
- Suspects – identify, arrest and preserve
- Witnesses – identify, support and prioritise, recording first accounts
- Log – decisions and reasons for them
- Physical evidence – preserve scene and prevent contamination.

By engaging in such activities soon after a criminal event, the chances of a successful arrest and conviction are greatly improved.

10.14 Victims and witnesses

Traditionally, victims appear to have been regarded as not important in the investigation process. Much criminological theory, for example, concentrated on those who committed crime, and this was reflected throughout the criminal justice system. Indeed, the victim has been seen as the forgotten party in the criminal justice process. However, victims should be regarded as a fundamental part of any investigation. They can provide the investigator with important information such as:

■ Identification of culprit

■ Intelligence

■ Evidence.

Victims must have confidence in the police if the criminal justice system is to operate effectively. Therefore the needs and concerns of victims must be recognised and they should be provided with support, protection, reassurance and appropriate information to ensure that they have trust in the system. A number of important developments have brought the role of the victim to more prominence. These are:

■ **The Victims Charter** – originally published in 1990 and redrafted in 1996, this document makes all agencies within the criminal justice system more responsive to the needs of victims by setting out standards concerning how victims should be treated and what information they should be provided with at each stage of the investigation.

■ **The Victim Support Movement** – this developed out of different schemes in 1979 and by the mid 1990s covered the whole of England and Wales. It is now organised by the charity Victim Support and provides emotional and practical help to those who are victims of crime.

■ **The Crown Court Witness Service** – this scheme was extended to all crown courts during the mid 1990s and provides a full range of services to help victims of crime, including advice and information to help them through the stress of a court appearance.

■ **The Victim Personal Statement Scheme** – this scheme was introduced in 2001 and provided relatives of murder victims the opportunity to put on record the anguish caused to them by the crime. These statements are collected by the police when they take witness statements and are available to the courts.

■ **The Criminal Injuries Compensation Scheme** – provides compensation from public funds to innocent victims of violent crime. The scheme was enshrined in law by the 1995 Criminal Injuries Compensation Act.

Above all it must be remembered that a victim is also a witness and that a large number of offences can be linked with information provided by them. The manner in which the police approach witnesses from the first point of contact, during interviews and through to the conclusion of any prosecution case can have an important bearing on how witnesses view the police and other members of the criminal justice system. If the witness is dealt with in an inappropriate manner then this may hamper the investigation and delay or prevent any relevant information that might assist the criminal investigation.

10.15 Interviewing witnesses

Effective interviewing of witnesses requires a great deal of skill and ability on the part of the interviewer. The investigator must establish trust with the person being interviewed, as many people fear the consequences of providing information to the police. The police service uses a nationally-accepted model when interviewing victims, witnesses and suspects. It is known as the PEACE model. PEACE stands for:

Planning and preparation

Engage and explain

Account clarification and challenge

Closure

Evaluation.

The skills needed to use this model are as follows:

- **Planning and preparation** – assembling facts: knowledge of the location, circumstances of the offence, knowledge of the person being interviewed; being methodical and having the legal knowledge; considering the time, duration and location of the interview.

- **Establishing a rapport** – considering how to approach the person being interviewed; being aware of their needs, culture, background and language; approachability; not prejudging and avoiding personal bias.

- **Listening skills** – the ability to listen actively, displaying empathy, consideration and tolerance; using silence to obtain further information.

- **Questioning skills** – asking the right questions at the right time; use of appropriate language; perseverance.

Above all what must be remembered is that if a witness has confidence in the interviewer they are more likely to provide a full and accurate account of events. Witnesses should be listened to and receive fair treatment.

10.16 Investigative knowledge

Good investigators need to decide whether or not a criminal offence has been committed, what types of material have been generated during the offence and where this material is likely to be found. This information can be of great assistance in bringing offenders to justice. Try exercise 10C below.

Exercise 10C

Discuss amongst your friends the different types of knowledge you think a good investigator needs to have.

There are three main areas where a good investigator can get his/her knowledge from. These are:

- The law

- The crime itself

- National and local policy documents.

Let's have a brief look at each of these.

The law

Perhaps it seems obvious, but an investigator needs to know the law and this knowledge must be in-depth and up to date. It must include such things as legal definitions of offences, evidential points that have to be proved, potential defences from case and statute law, and relevant rules of evidence. Without this knowledge investigators could conduct their enquiries in a manner that is unlawful and gather evidence that will not be acceptable by the courts.

The crime itself

Crimes vary widely in terms of those responsible for committing them, the motives for committing them and the different ways in which they are committed. Different crimes determine the evidence and material available to the criminal investigator. An example is shown below.

Shoplifting and commercial fraud are both property crimes, as mentioned earlier in this chapter, although they generate different types of evidence and material due to the different ways in which these offences are committed. Evidence for the shoplifting offence may include witnesses such as a store detective, the property which the person stole, possible CCTV footage, etc. Commercial fraud may include witnesses, but also technical and computer records, and may not actually involve property in the usual sense, as money may be transferred between computer accounts.

Another important element about the crime is the way in which the offender committed it. This is known as 'modus operandi' or the ways of doing something and has been discussed in section 10.11 (see above).

National and local policy documents

Police forces are large and sometimes complex organisations and in order to carry out the necessarily large number of functions they use documents called policy documents. Policy documents are created by forces at a local level and by other agencies such as Her Majesty's Inspector of Constabulary (HMIC) for use and guidance at a national level. The reasons for using policy documents are:

- To ensure that the law is complied with

- To ensure good practice

- To improve the service for the customer

- To help manage and run inter-agency work

- To enable managers to manage resources effectively.

Many of theses policies will have a bearing on how investigations should be run and are a useful source of knowledge for the investigator. Examples of national policy documents include:

- The National Intelligence Model

- The ACPO Investigative Interviewing Strategy.

Local force policy documents could include:
- Force orders

- Electronic or verbal briefings

- Force intranet briefings and newspapers.

Suggested further reading

Clark. D., *The Investigation of Crime* (Oxford: Butterworths, 2004)

Doak, J. and McGourlay, C., *Criminal Evidence in Context* (Exeter: Law Matters Publishing, 2005)

Gibson, B. and Cavadino, P., *Introduction to the Criminal Justice Process* (Winchester: Waterside Press, 2002)

Innes, M., *Investigating Murder – Detective Work and the Police Response to Criminal Homicide* (Oxford: Oxford University Press, 2003)

Johnston, D. and Hutton, G., *Blackstones Police Manual 2007, Vol.2 – Evidence and Procedure* (Oxford: Oxford University Press, 2006)

Sampson, F., *Blackstones Police Manual 2007, Vol 1 – Crime* (Oxford: Oxford University Press, 2006)

Useful websites

http://www.cps.gov.uk/index.html
The Crown Prosecution Service website which has much interesting information regarding criminal investigations, proof, etc.

http://www.cicb.gov.on.ca/en/index.htm
The website of the Criminal Injuries Compensation Board which contains information on how to claim

http://www.opsi.gov.uk/acts.htm
A useful website that contains all the details about Acts of Parliament passed in this country

http://www.forensic.gov.uk/index.htm
The website of the Forensic Science Service

http://www.soca.gov.uk/
The Serious Organised Crime Agency website which explains the aims and objectives of this organisation

Chapter 11

Drug and Alcohol Related Crime

This chapter supports the following National Occupational Standards which describe the performance and competence required of a probationer officer.

Unit No.	Unit title
1A1	Use police actions in a fair and justified way.
1A2	Communicate effectively with members of communities.
1A4	Foster people's equality, diversity and rights.
1B9	Provide initial support to individuals affected by offending or anti-social behaviour and assess their needs for further support.
2A1	Gather and submit information that has the potential to support policing objectives.
2C2	Prepare for, and participate in, planned policing operations.
2C3	Arrest, detain or report individuals.
2C4	Minimise and deal with aggressive and abusive behaviour.
2G2	Conduct investigations.
2G4	Finalise investigations.
SH1	Interview victims and witnesses.
2H2	Interview suspects.
2I1	Search individuals.
2I2	Search vehicles, premises and land.
2J1	Prepare and submit case files.
2J2	Present evidence in court and at other hearings.
4C1	Develop your own knowledge and practice.
4G2	Ensure your own actions reduce risks to health and safety.

11.1 Introduction

'Alcoholic beverages' are those containing enough alcohol to create intoxication or to produce an incapacity to drive. 'Drugs' are substances controlled by the Misuse of Drugs Act 1971, such as cannabis, heroin, ecstasy, and amphetamines, although tobacco, alcohol and caffeine are also pharmacologically classified as drugs (see table 11.1). Most of the drugs discussed in this chapter are highly addictive: addicts maintain a steady (and in some case an increasing) demand for drugs and the suppliers of these drugs – whether legal or illegal – provide the drugs only because it is profitable to do so.

Drugs and alcohol may cause criminal offences to be committed by virtue of being traded or consumed (as when illegal drugs are imported or where a person assaults another while drunk), but they may also catalyse crime (such as theft) by individuals who are seeking to pay for the drugs or alcohol to which they have become addicted – so-called secondary crime.

Exercise 11A

Legislation

The misuse of alcohol and other drugs has been codified into law by governments all over the world. Why have governments done this? What are the advantages of enforcing such laws for society?

Governments have sought to legislate for 'the common good'. Specifically, alcohol and drug legislation is designed to outlaw or limit the use of these substances so as to protect individuals, their (often vulnerable) dependents and the public at large. The degree of prohibition in the UK varies: whilst there is an outright ban on LSD consumption (a Class A drug), there is no general ban on alcohol consumption. Vulnerable groups, particularly children, are often the subject of specific legislation. For example, the Licensing Act 2003 makes it an offence for under-16s to be unaccompanied in licensed premises, but it also prohibits the sale of alcohol to anyone (of any age) if they are drunk (since drunk individuals are themselves vulnerable). There are restrictions on the selling of tobacco to persons under 16 (Children and Young Persons Act 1933), but no restrictions on the sale or consumption of caffeine.

The arguments for legislation are complicated. Few individuals would question the outlawing of drugs or alcohol when workers are using heavy machinery or driving lorries or buses, but is it necessary to outlaw some drugs for recreational use? Again, the government has assumed the role of the 'knowing parent' in taking decisions on behalf of the public. The overall effect of widespread and uncontrolled drug abuse is taken to be very damaging for current and future generations and many people in society support that view. It would be very difficult to enforce drugs and alcohol legislation if the balance changed and most people were hostile to the legislation.

Government legislation against drugs is historically relatively recent, but drug and alcohol abuse is very old. Drunks have been dealt with under tribal or common law for thousands of years. The fictional character Sherlock Holmes was addicted to cocaine and this was quite common in the upper reaches of Victorian society. The brilliant scientist, Sir Humphry Davy, was addicted to the stimulant nitrous oxide and this may have contributed to his death in 1829.

This chapter is organised into two main parts, one dealing with drugs other than alcohol, and the other dealing with alcohol. Although alcohol and drugs both fuel acquisitive crime, alcohol differs in that it generates high levels of public disorder and domestic violence.

The student officer will see the effects of drugs and alcohol upon people and their behaviour in their everyday work. Tackling drug and alcohol abuse cannot be achieved by the police service alone and often it will appear that all the police are doing is (at best) 'keeping the lid on things'. Yet, in individual cases, the police officer often has a crucial part to play. The rational behind this chapter is that an informed officer – one armed with a background knowledge of drugs and alcohol – is better able to carry out their part in policing drug- and alcohol-related crime.

Drugs

11.2 Drugs and drug crime

Drug-related crime is found in every part of Britain. Drug use pervades all elements of our society, all classes and all professions. The effects of drugs upon the health of individuals, upon crime and upon the families of drug abusers have reached epidemic proportions in many areas and 'drug crime' is a politically important and recurrent issue.

Laws in which the possession or supply of drugs are prohibited create criminal offences which are necessarily *caused* by drugs: without drugs these offences do not take place and they could not be proven in court. However, the general question 'does drug misuse cause crime?' is more complicated than may appear at first sight. There is a strong statistical association between drug misuse and crime (as one goes up so does the other), but the causes for this association appear to be very varied and depend upon the type of drug involved (with heroin misuse being particularly strongly linked with burglary and robbery). To take a few examples, well-off cocaine drug users may not need to resort to crime to pay for their drugs and in such cases there will be no additional crimes over and above the serious offence of possessing a Class A drug. On the other hand, police officers will frequently encounter seriously ill and drug-addicted people, whose life is dominated by the need to acquire funds to purchase more

Drug	Where does it come from?	How is it taken into the body?	What does the drug do?
Amphetamines and methamphetamine	These drugs are synthetically manufactured – they do not occur naturally.	Tablets are swallowed.	Powerful stimulants producing a feeling of euphoria with subsequent fatigue.
Cocaine	Extracted from the coca plant in South America.	The hydrochloride form is snorted into the nostrils. Pure cocaine ('crack cocaine') is smoked.	Powerful stimulants which produce a feeling of exhilaration and energy for about 30 minutes, followed by fatigue.
Cannabis	Derived from the cannabis plant, grown in vast amounts in Asia.	Smoked in the form of dried leaves or as a dried dark resin (hashish).	Smoked cannabis produces a feeling of well-being. Although there are believed to be long-term harmful effects associated with cannabis consumption, no fatal dose in humans has ever been reported.
Heroin, morphine, opium resin and methadone	Known as opiate drugs. Most heroin comes from Afghanistan.	Injected or smoked.	Heroin is the commonest opiate. It can induce euphoria, but side effects include nausea.
Ecstasy (MDMA)	Synthetically manufactured.	Tablet form.	Produces a feeling of euphoria and energy for several hours, followed by tiredness and mild depression. Deaths have been associated with dehydration.
LSD	Manufactured, but related hallucinogens are found in 'magic mushrooms'.	Tablet form, or absorbed through the skin. LSD is so potent that it is sold in tiny quantities.	Produces powerful hallucinations, intensifying the appearance of colours and the perception of sounds.
Alcohol (Ethanol)	Manufactured by fermentation.	Alcohol drinks contain between 4–40% alcohol.	Small amounts produce a feeling of well-being.
Caffeine	Found in coffee, tea and in cocoa beans.	A cup of coffee contains about 150 milligrams of caffeine.	Moderate amounts increase alertness, but higher levels produce anxiety.
Tobacco	Found in leaves of tobacco plant.	Usually smoked but can be chewed or snorted as 'snuff'.	The active ingredient is nicotine. Nicotine is a mild stimulant at lower concentrations.

Table 11.1 Common drugs and their effects

Adapted from 'A concise guide to mind altering drugs', *New Scientist* 13 November 2004.

drugs. It is tempting to presume that such individuals became addicted to drugs before becoming criminals, but that may not have been the case: they may have been practising criminals anyway, or it might be that their drug addiction has amplified (but not induced) their criminality so that they now commit more crimes than before addiction. The police service, though, has to try and deal fairly and effectively with the criminal *effects* associated with drug and alcohol consumption, *whatever* the precise causes in individual cases.

There are vast amounts of statistics concerning drugs and drug misuse. Young people (below 29 years of age) show the highest level of drug misuse, with males misusing drugs more than females. At the extreme end of the damage caused by drugs are drug-related deaths – 1,427 in 2004. The drugs market in the UK is financially lucrative, and is valued at a minimum of £4 billion a year. Governments have responded by investing huge sums of money to rehabilitate drug offenders, with an increase of 50 per cent in the number of drugs workers since 2002. The national average waiting time for drug treatment is currently 2.4 weeks.

The seizures of drugs are recorded annually. In 2004 there were 107,360 drug seizures by police (including the National Crime Squad – now SOCA) and HM Revenue and Customs. The number of seizures by Revenue and Customs officers represents four per cent of the total. About 70 per cent of all seizures involved cannabis, nearly all of the remaining 30 per cent involving class A drugs: this amounted to 4.6 tonnes of cocaine, 2.1 tonnes of heroin, 4.6 million tablets of ecstasy, 1.2 tonnes of amphetamines and 83.5 tonnes of cannabis (which includes 88,000 cannabis plants). Twenty-seven per cent of all police seizures involved class A drugs whilst 70 per cent of all National Crime Squad seizures involved class A drugs. The seizures may be broadly indicative of demand, but less bulky drugs are harder to detect and so the figures will underestimate their market share.

Most of the heroin used in the UK originates from Afghanistan. Most of the cocaine is imported from South America (particularly Colombia). Ecstasy is believed to be manufactured mainly in illicit laboratories in the Netherlands and Belgium. Cannabis originates from Colombia, Jamaica and Africa. It is believed that the bulk of all drugs are imported in freight vehicles through the southern English ports. Seizing drugs before they enter the UK, whilst temporarily reducing supply, may be less effective than controlling demand since there are numerous importers willing to fill in any gaps in supply. It is arguable whether the police service has a large role in reducing the demand for drugs: demand originates in society and it is from society that long-term solutions will have to come.

11.3 Legislation and drugs

The legislation on illegal drugs has not been harmonised across Europe, with the UK occupying a middle position between Sweden (very tough drug policies) and the Netherlands (somewhat more lenient).

The Misuse of Drugs Act 1971 classifies drugs into Class A, B and C. All drugs so classified are referred to as 'controlled substances'. Courts impose higher penalties for offences involving Class A drugs. The opiates, cocaine, some amphetamines, LSD and fungus obtained from 'magic mushrooms' are all Class A drugs. Cannabis is a Class C drug.

Since the Medicines Act 1968 did not deal with the unlawful possession of drugs, the 1971 Misuse of Drugs Act made it an offence to unlawfully possess (with or without an intent to supply) controlled substances. The import or export of controlled substances ('trafficking offences') and the unlawful production of controlled substances are also covered by the Act. The Act gives police officers powers of entry, detention and search. Note that it is possible for an individual to be prescribed a drug (such as methadone) legally, but to use it illegally by consuming all the drug in one go or by administering it by injection rather than by swallowing.

The Customs and Excise Management Act 1979 deals specifically with illegal importation or exportation of drugs. The Road Traffic Act 1972 makes it an offence to drive under the influence of drugs as well as alcoholic drink. Subsequent legislation relating to drugs reflects the constant need of the government to combat increasingly sophisticated and informed suppliers and traffickers and to attack the infrastructure used by drug suppliers. The Drug Trafficking Act 1994 outlaws some drug-related equipment (such as cocaine-snorting kits) and it also allows the seizure of assets of someone who has been found guilty of trafficking, even if it cannot be proved that the assets have arisen from the trafficking. The Drugs Act 2005 reverses the burden of proof in cases where suspects are found to be in possession of larger quantities of controlled substances than would be expected for personal use. This means that the suspect has to prove that they were not intending to supply or sell the drugs. The Act also introduces compulsory drug-testing of arrested individuals (i.e. before any charging) where the police have reasonable grounds for believing that Class A drugs were involved in the commission of an offence. The Act also provides for an intervention order to be attached to Anti-Social Behaviour Orders (ASBOs) issued for adults whose anti-social behaviour is drug-related, requiring them to attend drug counselling.

Exercise 11B

The 'drugs industry' often occurs at three levels: user, street supplier and importer/producer. Which level should be the police be targeting? What are the difficulties in targeting that group?

Supply follows demand and criminal empires are fed by the proceeds of drug crime. Tackling the supplier/importer would therefore have the biggest impact in reducing drug-related harm and crime, *provided* that another importer/producer does not step in to fill the gap. In fact, some 'back filling' is likely to occur: the modern view of high-level criminal targets is that they are entrepreneurs – like businessmen – who will satisfy any demand with supply. This suggests that drug supply will often re-emerge after a successful police operation and that the police have constantly to maintain their operations to remain effective.

Drug-related crime is now associated with guns to a greater degree than was the case ten years ago and this poses particular problems for the police service, particularly when supplier gangs operate across regions.

Case study

The classification of drugs and re-classification of cannabis

Cannabis was reclassified as a Class C drug (from a Class B drug) in 2004. Subsequent and well-publicised concerns about the damaging effects of cannabis on mental health led to a reconsideration of the classification and the Home Secretary asked the Advisory Council on the Misuse of Drugs (ACMD) to consider any new evidence. Having listened to their recommendations, the Home Secretary decided that cannabis should remain a class C drug for the time being.

One consequence of the 'downgrading' of cannabis is that police intervention will increasingly be focused upon the most serious cases, e.g. access to the 'school market', rather upon the *use* of cannabis itself.

The reclassification has prompted discussions of the value of the 'A, B, C classification' of drugs, and whether or not the status of other drugs should be reviewed. One idea is that the classification should reflect the degree of harm caused by the substance and not the penalty associated with its use. A 'harm-based' classification would clearly signal to the public the relative harm caused by substances and, controversially, would place alcohol and tobacco (both addictive and very harmful) above ecstasy and LSD.

11.4 Policing drug-related crime

The government's 'drugs strategy' is intended to:

- Reduce the supply of illegal drugs

- Prevent young people from becoming drug misusers ('reducing demand')

- Reduce drug-related crime

- Reduce the use of drugs through greater participation in treatment programmes.

Most of these aims are reproduced by the local agencies, including police forces. Most police forces have dedicated crime squads which specialise in drug-related crime. Their strategies include:

- Acquiring intelligence about 'bigger players' from banks, informers and by surveillance (link with NIM).

- 'Street sweeping' – large-scale police operations in an area in which as many as 100 officers make mass arrests of users and suppliers.

- 'Disruptive policing' – which can occur at various levels. At the highest level, financial assets are confiscated and arrests are made. The lowest level is making drug dealers aware of the presence of patrolling police officers and, perhaps, forcing them to reorganise some of their operations. This also deters the casual user.

- Taking part in educational programmes (e.g. in schools) to discourage drug use.

- Working with partners to avoid duplication and to maximise effect.

There is surprisingly little research on the effectiveness of some of these strategies, but some observers remain pessimistic about their success, particularly when the demand for certain drugs, such as crack cocaine and heroin, remains so strong.

Exercise 11C

Tracking drug-related crime

What might indicate that an individual might be involved in drug-related crime as a seller, dealer or trafficker? What kind of investigations would you suggest be carried out?

The answer is simple: money, and the higher up the chain the individual is, the more money there is to spend, re-invest or launder to another country.

The development of 'intelligence-led' policing, together with better ways of tracking finance, has greatly assisted drug-related investigations. In particular, the ability of investigators to track finances has improved considerably as banks have allowed access to personal and corporate accounts. Legislation has also aided law enforcement. The Proceeds of Crime Act 2002 allows for the freezing of assets at the start of an enquiry so as to prevent the money being quickly transferred.

Amongst the numerous factors influencing the policing of drug-related crime, the following are particularly significant:

- The 'internationalisation' of drug production and importation has forced countries to organise their own national police responses more efficiently (as with SOCA) and to liaise more with law enforcement agencies within their borders in other countries. Nevertheless, deterring both local suppliers and users still requires vigilance and action by the local police forces and the public expects constant reassurance that 'drug use is being tackled'.

- Drug users are increasingly seen partly as victims rather than simple offenders, and probation and prison services are now seen as a major partners in organising attempts to reduce demand for drugs. Referral schemes at the point of arrest and after court are attempting to break the 'offender cycle' driven by addiction to drugs. Government figures suggest that treatment is cost effective: for every £1 spent on treatment, at least £9.50 is saved in crime and health costs.

- The Crime and Disorder Act 1998 creates partnerships which aim at producing local drug- and alcohol-reduction strategies.

11.5 Analysis of drugs: how do we know what drug it is?

Suppose you come across a pill, resin or powder. How can you find out whether or not it is a controlled drug? To some extent, police officers will have to rely upon 'reasonable suspicions' when dealing with suspected drugs offences and in deciding whether or not to make an arrest. Ultimately though, a successful prosecution relies upon unambiguous identification of the identity of a substance. Although Home Office approved test kits are available, the usual procedure is to submit unknown substances for analysis by a forensic science provider. Particular care must be exercised in sending hypodermic needles for analysis: they should always be sent in plastic tubes in order to protect all concerned from serious infection.

Many companies are concerned about the consequences of their employees working whilst under the influence of drugs. For example, a police officer might be called to investigate a few days after an accident has occurred in which a driver is thought to have been under the influence of drugs. The driver denies ever having taken drugs. The body rapidly loses the blood- or urine-borne drug metabolites that are tell-tale indicators of drug consumption and so an analysis of the blood or urine of the suspect is worthless. As figure 11.1 shows, blood only holds such metabolites for about one day. However, human hair retains trace amounts of such metabolites for longer. The tips of a person's hair give the 'drug history' of that individual over one or two years; the roots give information about drug history going back several months.

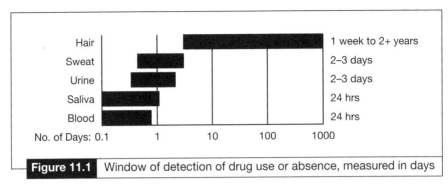

| **Figure 11.1** | Window of detection of drug use or absence, measured in days |

Courtesy of TrichoTech *www.tricho-tech.com*

Alcohol

11.6 Basic facts about drinking and its effects

The following facts illustrate the scale of alcohol misuse and its effects:

- About half of all violent crimes (some 1.2 million incidents) are related to alcohol misuse.

- About half of all facial injuries occur in violent circumstances and alcohol is associated with many of these incidents.

- About one-third of all domestic violence incidents (some 360,000) are alcohol-related.

- Over £100 million is spent annually on specialist alcohol treatment in the UK.

- 22,000 people die prematurely through alcohol misuse in the UK and there are about 1,000 suicides associated with alcohol misuse.

- 17 million working days are lost through alcohol-related absences.

- About one million children are affected by parental misuse of alcohol, with divorce being twice as likely.

- Heavy drinkers are much more likely to be involved in car accidents.

- Underage drinking is commonplace and regular drinkers aged 10–17 years are more likely to commit crime than those who are not regular drinkers.

- At peak times, up to 70 per cent of all admissions to accident and emergency units are alcohol-related.

A distinction is usually made between binge drinkers (young men and women who are at risk from alcohol poisoning and of committing violence or being violently attacked) and *chronic drinkers* (generally over 30 years of age and mainly men and for whom the greatest risks are health related).

The harm caused by excessive alcohol consumption is not always easy to quantify. Estimates have been made of the costs of dealing with alcohol-related disorder or violence through the criminal justice system and of the consequences of alcohol-related illnesses through the loss of days at work and the cost of treating people in hospitals, but the damage done to families and marriages (through, for example, increased chances of divorce, child abuse, domestic violence and car accidents) cannot adequately be expressed in pounds and pence.

The 'alcohol culture' of the UK is much more widespread than drug culture and has a longer history. Young people see adults drinking all the time and may associate drinking with maturity and even with fashion. And as with drugs, the police service cannot hope to tackle the consequences of the demand for alcohol unless it has the support of other agencies and of the public.

Exercise 11D

Give three reasons why violence is found in and around pubs and night clubs.

Alcohol reduces the inhibitions of individuals and makes violence more likely. Other reasons include:

- Pubs and night clubs may inherit drunken customers from establishments which open and close earlier

- Pub and nightclub culture has historically been associated with fighting (as seen in many films)

- Pubs and nightclubs may concentrate certain groups together (e.g. those for whom the exhibiting of aggression and violence are status symbols).

11.7 Legislation related to alcohol

Legislation related to alcohol is aimed at:

1 Reducing consumption by vulnerable groups (e.g. Licensing Act 2003)

2 Tackling public disorder (e.g. the offence of being 'Drunk and Disorderly', Criminal Justice Act 1967)

3   Eliminating drink-driving (e.g. Road Traffic Act 1988)

4   Reducing the fear of alcohol-related crime, disorder and anti-social behaviour (e.g. dispersal orders under the Anti-Social Behaviour Act 2003).

11.8 Drink and crime

Some legislation creates offences in which alcohol forms one of the elements which have to be proved. For example, drinking and driving, serving alcohol to minors and to already-drunk people are offences which are caused by alcohol in the sense that the offences are not proved unless alcohol is involved. But, in general, the connection between alcohol and crime is as complex as the relationship between drugs and crime. There is often a strong statistical association between alcohol and crime, but there may not be a causal link. Consider the following examples:

■ People may consume large quantities of alcohol because of family or financial problems. Here, alcohol is the symptom rather than a cause.

■ A drunk person in a city centre is more likely to be violent than a person who is sober, making it likely that such violence is at least partly *caused* by drink.

■ Whilst alcohol is associated with aggression, it is also associated with vulnerability. A person who is heavily intoxicated may have started a fight or they may have been the innocent victim of an assault by another drunk person. Alcohol is statistically associated with the injury, but we cannot always state the cause.

■ A person usually consumes alcohol before stealing, but would attempt to steal with or without alcohol. In this case, alcohol does not cause the theft. In other cases, a burglar may use alcohol for 'Dutch courage' and we would say that alcohol is then a contributing factor to the crime, without being the cause of the crime.

Exercise 11E

Risk factors

For the individual offender 'risk factors' have been identified which increase the likelihood of alcohol misuse leading to violent crime. Can you suggest three factors that are relevant here?

Research by M. McMurran gives a list of risk factors including family history (which includes poor example-setting by parents), childhood psychiatric disorders and mental illness, low intelligence, an aggressive disposition and a lifestyle of crime and substance misuse.

Research by A. Deehan suggests that there are also 'environmental risk factors' associated with licensed premises that make violent behaviour more likely. This includes restricted access to a bar, poorly maintained and unclean premises, loud music and insufficient seating. To this list we may add insufficient numbers of taxis around the exits of pubs and clubs.

11.9 Government strategy

The government has recognised that tackling the harmful effects of alcohol requires coordination from numerous departments, agencies and partners, including the National Health Service, education departments, courts, HM Customs and Excise, probation service, police service and the alcohol industry. (See also the TASC project page in Chapter 4.)

Although the government has recognised that the drinks industry has an important role in promoting responsible drinking, there is an obvious conflict between the profit motives of sellers and the imperative to reduce the misuse of alcohol.

The Alcohol Misuse Enforcement Campaign (AMEC)

AMEC 3 was a six-week police enforcement and poster campaign running over the Christmas period from 12 November 2005 to 24 December 2005. The Home Office provided £2.5 million of funding for the operation. Features of the operation included:

- The closure of 'problem premises' using the powers provided in the Licensing Act 2003

- Testing the implementation of licensing laws by major supermarkets using under-age agents

- Multi-agency cooperation and action against rogue retailers

- The use of CCTV to detect potential disorder and violence

- Issuing of fixed penalty notices for alcohol-related disorder.

During the operation, police and trading standards officers carried out over 6,000 test purchase operations, dealt with more than 30,000 offences, issued over 8,000 fixed penalty notices (mainly for the offence of being drunk and disorderly and for public order offences), issued 649 summonses (mainly against retailers selling alcohol to minors) and made over 25,000 arrests. 27,000 licensed and off-licence premises were visited. Violent crime was reported to have fallen by 11 per cent.

11.10 Drinking and driving

The physiological effect of alcohol upon human beings is well known. The concentration of alcohol in blood is measured in milligrams (mg) of alcohol per 100 millilitres (ml) of blood.

At a concentration of 50–100 mg/100 ml, a person loses some coordination and speech may be slurred. Between 100 and 200 mg/100 ml, the usual symptoms associated with drunkenness are observed, including swaggering and sickness. Above 200 mg/100 ml a person is increasingly likely to enter into a coma. Concentrations above 300 mg/100 ml are likely to lead to paralysis and death.

If these are the effects of alcohol upon individuals in a domestic or pub setting, what are the implications of higher alcohol concentrations on the ability to drive? Studies have confirmed that medium and higher levels of blood alcohol reduce the ability of the driver to drive safely, but the controversial question is what should the 'legal limit' for drivers be? The UK 'drink-driving limit' is 80 mg per 100 ml of blood, but many others countries define a lower limit.

Legislation has permitted two measurements of alcohol to be made of those suspected of 'driving above the limit'. The first is a 'screening measurement' at the scene using a hand-held instrument. If the screening measurement is at or above the limit, the law gives police officers the power of arrest and the suspect is taken to a police station for a second measurement using a more sophisticated instrument. The second measurement is known as an 'evidential measurement' because only this measurement may be used as the basis of a prosecution.

Both the screening and evidential instruments measure alcohol concentrations in the breath of the driver. Blood and alcohol concentrations are simply related, with a concentration of alcohol in breath of 35 micrograms (µg) per 100 ml of breath being equivalent to the legal limit of 80 mg of alcohol per 100 ml of blood.

Suggested further reading

Newburn, T (ed.), *Handbook of Policing* (Cullompton: Willan, 2003) (especially Chapter 17 by Lee and South)

Bean, P., *Drugs and Crime* (Cullompton: Willan, 2002)

Bennett, T. and Holloway, K., *Understanding drugs, alcohol and crime* (Maidenhead: Open University, 2005)

Useful websites

http://www.bbc.co.uk/crime/drugs/index.shtml
Information on drugs and their effects. Very useful quiz to test your knowledge

http://www.drugs.gov.uk/
The main government website connected with drug policies

http://www.homeoffice.gov.uk/rds/pdfs06/hosb0806.pdf
Home Office Statistical Bulletin on Seizures of Drugs, England and Wales, 2004 (published 25 May 2006)

http://www.drugscope.org.uk/
An informative website on drugs and independent of the government

http://en.wikipedia.org/wiki/Arguments_for_and_against_drug_prohibition
A summary of arguments for and against drug prohibition

http://www.alcoholconcern.org.uk/servlets/home
Home website of 'Alcohol Concern'. McMurran's and Deehan's work on 'risk factors' is also discussed

http://www.pm.gov.uk/files/pdf/al04SU.pdf
The Alcohol Harm Reduction Strategy for England 2004

http://www.homeoffice.gov.uk/rds/prgpdfs/crrs3.pdf
'Alcohol and Crime: taking stock' (1999). Still a useful background read

Chapter 12

Anti-social Behaviour

This chapter supports the following National Occupational Standards which describe the performance and competence required of a probationer officer.

Unit No.	Unit title
1A1	Use police actions in a fair and justified way.
1A2	Communicate effectively with members of communities.
1A4	Foster people's equality, diversity and rights.
1B9	Provide initial support to individuals affected by offending or anti-social behaviour and assess their needs for further support.
2A1	Gather and submit information that has the potential to support policing objectives.
2C3	Arrest, detain or report individuals.
2C4	Minimise and deal with aggressive and abusive behaviour.
2G2	Conduct investigations.
2G4	Finalise investigations.
SH1	Interview victims and witnesses.
2H2	Interview suspects.
2J1	Prepare and submit case files.
2J2	Present evidence in court and at other hearings.
4C1	Develop your own knowledge and practice.

12.1 Introduction

Both the police practitioner and partner agencies will find that a great deal of their work and effort revolves around dealing with activity classed as Anti-Social Behaviour (ASB). Whilst major events and critical incidents have an effect on people, it is the day-to-day experience of people living, working or visiting our communities that determine their quality of life and perception of the policing service of this country.

The largest part of police contact with the public concerns problems and issues relating to the activities of both individuals and groups who, by the nature of their behaviour, interfere with, harm or even destroy the quality of life of their fellow citizens. This chapter will help the police practitioner to define what is anti-social behaviour, look at how to quantify the problem, examine its causes and outline some of the techniques available to address this problematic issue.

The chapter will examine the role of the Crime and Disorder Reduction Partnerships (CDRP) (Community Safety Partnerships [CSP] in Wales) – the aim of all agencies being to work towards a more just and civil society where people can go about their daily business unhindered by the small anti-social element that can exist in all communities.

12.2 The impact of anti-social behaviour

The problems associated with anti-social behaviour are widespread. It can affect the individual, community, business and ultimately the economic wellbeing of an area. This, in turn, can further increase fear of crime, lead to outward migration and little inward economic investment, thus creating a spiral of increasing deprivation and the creation of 'sink estates'.

The problems of anti-social behaviour are, of course, not simply confined to the less affluent areas of the community. Increasingly, both town centres and suburbs in the more affluent areas of the country are suffering from such activity. However, the impact of anti-social behaviour appears to be more severe on those communities that suffer from high levels of social and economic deprivation. The tabloid press has been quick to seize on such areas as evidence of a decline in society, often linking such activity to a decline in moral values. The term 'sink estates' has been used to reinforce negatively stereotypical images of certain groups within our communities. Wherever it is found, it must be remembered that the level of such anti-social behaviour is attributable to a small minority of the population. It is the effects of the activities of such elements that the police and their partners need to address.

The challenge for the police and the community is to ensure that the balance between the individual's human rights and their public responsibilities are recognised by all, including those responsible for such anti-social behaviour. For the police, the response to anti-social behaviour must not only be effective, but also proportionate; when they respond it must be to build and retain the support of the community. The police and their partners' actions help the community to build a more cohesive society.

The impact of anti-social behaviour is widespread. It can manifest itself in many ways: people attending local shops or parks may feel intimidated and avoid public space; children and older people may feel threatened and unable to access community facilities; the local authority may find increasing levels of damage being caused to the physical infrastructure of the area.

Government statistics for 2003 revealed that, in a one day period, police and partners recorded 66,107 instances of anti-social behaviour, or one incident every two seconds. The cost to public services of dealing with this level of anti-social behaviour was estimated at £3.4 billion per annum. These costs are shared not only by the community but also by partner agencies, and it is here in a joint response that the answers can be found to deal with such anti-social behaviour.

12.3 Tackling anti-social behaviour

In 1998 the Government introduced the Crime and Disorder Act which created the Crime and Disorder Reduction Partnerships (CDRP) and Community Safety Partnerships (CSP) in Wales.

The CDRP and CSP are required to carry out a crime and disorder audit and through consultation determine the priorities as identified by the community in their area. Having carried out this process, the CDRP and CSP are required to develop effective strategies to tackle these issues. This strategy should include:

- An action plan outlining what is going to be undertaken to tackle the relevant issues

- The outcomes to be achieved

- The resources, both human and financial, which need to be allocated to achieve the stated outcomes.

The anti-social behaviour strategy must look at a number of areas:

- Prevention – including youth provision, supported housing

- Interventions – multi-agency case conferences, mediation, etc.

■ Enforcement – injunctions, ASBOs, FPND and possession proceedings, etc.

■ Victim and witness support – to ensure all available support is given, e.g. special measures at court.

The CDRP/CSP will be operating at the BCU/local authority level providing an overall strategy for the area. With the development of the Partners and Communities Together (PACT), the local practitioners will have to develop their own effective response to community issues. This will mean that at the local level, the neighbourhood policing team, working with its partners and the local community, needs to identify ASB issues, and then provide realistic practical answers to the problem.

When addressing such issues the police need to take into account the problem-orientated policing approach discussed in Chapter 8, Crime and Disorder Reduction Partnerships. In so doing they also need to understand the role of community intelligence within the NIM (discussed elsewhere throughout this book). Firstly, though, without consulting with anyone, attempt exercise 12A below.

Exercise 12A

What do you think the anti-social behaviour issues are in your area?

You may have thought of some of the following:

■ Graffiti

■ Noise

■ Youth annoyance

■ Dog owners allowing their dogs to foul the footpath.

Of course, all of the above are considered a form of anti-social behaviour. However, some people may have thought of lots of other behaviour which could be termed anti-social. This highlights a problem – what exactly constitutes anti-social behaviour?

12.4 Problems of defining anti-social behaviour

In order to be able to deal with anti-social behaviour we need to be able to define it, and this presents a difficulty. Working within a multi-agency framework can lead to confusion, as organisations and groups may seek to define problems in different ways. This can not only lead to confusion but also hinder the recording of information relating to ASB.

The term is also associated with problems relating to other areas of concern such as alcohol or drug abuse, child neglect, mental illness and family breakdown. The police practitioner needs to remind themselves that whilst many ASB problems are concerned with young people, they are often the victims of such behaviour themselves and any action must be proportionate and directed at the causes of ASB, not a particular group in general.

An additional note of caution has to be exercised in defining anti-social behaviour when dealing with the diverse community that exists in Britain today. We need to understand that what might be regarded as being anti-social by some is regarded as normal by others. An example of such changes relates to the inward migration of Eastern European migrants into the UK. Some of these groups see it as perfectly acceptable to congregate outside one another's homes, drinking alcohol and socialising. Other residents may see such activity as anti-social or even intimidating – the police practitioner must use common sense and good communication skills to build cohesive communities in such situations.

Anti-social behaviour has become a generic term to describe certain types of behaviour which the community in general finds unacceptable.

The following two examples illustrate the different types of behaviour regarded as anti-social.

A residential community reports that a number of prostitutes have come into the area and are standing in the street looking to attract paying customers for sex. A large number of men have been driving around the area and have been stopping and speaking not only to the prostitutes but also single women walking in the area. In addition, prostitutes are taking their customers into local parkland to ply their trade. Residents and parents feel under threat and are afraid to venture into the street and public areas of their community.

A new resident has moved into a block of flats that has a settled residential population. The new resident has begun to play loud music at all times of the day until the early hours of the morning. In addition, groups of youths have begun to congregate at the flat drinking, shouting and using abusive language. There are now reports of persons attending the premises and driving their cars at speed in the residents' car park; stolen vehicles have also been reported as being recovered in the immediate vicinity of the flats.

In both these scenarios we could say that the behaviour outlined would generally be termed to be anti-social, and we would expect the community to seek action from the police and partner agencies. Even though we can use examples to illustrate what we mean by behaviour that may be anti-social, the question still remains – how do we define anti-social behaviour?

12.5 Officially defining anti-social behaviour

The police and partner agencies may wish to use the definition as stated in the Crime and Disorder Act 1998. The definition is as follows:

'Acting in a manner that caused or was likely to cause, harassment, alarm or distress to one or more persons not of the same household as the defendant.'

The definition is wide enough to cover the problems encountered by both the community and practitioners in this area. At the same time the definition is not designed to deal with disputes and issues involving people of the same household. The list of the types of behaviour under ASB can include a variety of selfish or unacceptable behaviour that can and does blight the quality of life of either individuals or an entire community.

The Home Office website has listed some examples of such behaviour:

- Nuisance neighbours

- Rowdy and nuisance behaviour

- Yobbish behaviour and intimidating groups taking over public places

- Vandalism, graffiti and fly posting

- People dealing and buying drugs on the street

- People dumping rubbish and abandoning cars on the street

- Begging and anti-social drinking

- Misuse of fireworks.

This list is not exhaustive and many other examples of individual or group activity can be termed anti-social. What is interesting for the police practitioner is that the issues raised and, therefore, the solutions are not the sole responsibility of the police. We now see that in practice the term 'working in partnership' means something on the ground and not only at a strategic level. In the past the report of a noisy party or rubbish being dumped would be seen as a low priority for the police, one to ignore or to pass on to other agencies, many of whom were not structured to provide a timely, effective response.

Previously, some partner agencies chose to ignore anti-social behaviour believing it was the responsibility of the police or feeling powerless to deal with such issues. Legislation has forced all agencies to address the issue. The police and their partners now have a statutory duty and ability to share information. The public now have the ability to scrutinise these agencies' actions and demand results. Through choice or compulsion, people are now working in a more structured way. We increasingly see innovative solutions to such anti-social problems being introduced at a number of levels.

Through the Crime and Disorder Act 1998, these structures are now in place and are being developed with the growth of tasking centres and non-emergency numbers. These, coupled to a robust use of anti-social behaviour legislation, will allow agencies to tackle such behaviour, improve the quality of life and build cohesive communities.

12.6 Local definitions of anti-social behaviour

There is, of course, the capacity for CDRP to incorporate a local framework within this national definition, thus identifying particular issues within their community that they wish to class as ASB. This process has advantages which include:

- The definition is tailored to local ideas of the community, making it particularly relevant to that area

- Both the agencies and communities who agreed the definition will have ownership of it and ensure it is applied

- The same term used by all agencies will allow standardisation of recording and reporting of such issues. This will assist in data analysis and the evaluation of any ongoing problems.

12.7 Why do we have anti-social behaviour?

Having defined what we mean by anti-social behaviour, we will now examine four areas we need to address to reduce its effect. If we understand why anti-social behaviour may occur, we can move on to address the causes as well as the effect of such activity.

There are many factors that contribute to the increased risk of an individual engaging in anti-social behaviour. This does not necessarily mean that if they are present an individual will become so engaged, but their presence increases the likelihood of such engagement. The police practitioner needs an understanding of such factors to determine where and how intervention should take place, and how other agencies fit in to the overall programme.

The Home Office has used these four main areas to outline the risk factors impacting on the likelihood of an individual engaging in anti-social behaviour. They are as follows:

Family environment

The risk factors include:

- Poor parental discipline and supervision
- Family conflict (between parents or between parents and children)
- Family history of problem behaviour
- Parental involvement/attitudes condoning problem behaviour.

Schooling and educational attainment

The risk factors include:

- Aggressive behaviour (e.g. bullying)
- Lack of commitment to school
- School disorganisation
- School exclusion and truancy patterns
- Low achievement at school.

Community life/accommodation/employment

Risk factors include:

- Community disorganisation and neglect
- The availability of drugs and alcohol
- Lack of neighbourhood coherence
- Growing up in a deprived area within low income families, high rates of unemployment and a high turnover of population
- Areas where there are high levels of vandalism.

Personal and individual factors

Risk factors include:

- Alienation and lack of social commitment
- Early involvement in problem behaviour
- Attitudes that condone problem behaviour

- For young people, a high proportion of unsupervised time spent with peers and friends involved in problem behaviour

- Mental illness

- Early involvement in the use of drugs.

The Home Office list gives a number of factors that increase risk of involvement in ASB. However, it would be wrong to believe that the presence of one or more of these factors will inevitably lead to the person's involvement in such behaviour. Large numbers of the current population are born into dysfunctional families, grow up in deprived areas and never get involved in either anti-social or criminal activity.

The police must recognise that the intervention required to reduce the risk factor of a person becoming involved in anti-social behaviour may lie with another agency. Read the information provided in exercise 12B below and try to answer the questions following it.

Exercise 12B

Community intelligence has indicated that a number of young children are involved in vandalism and graffiti at a local youth centre. The local neighbourhood police officer has attended at the home and spoken to the mother of the children. The officer indicates that the mother is a lone parent who has learning difficulties and is on prescribed medication for depression. There are three children of eight, ten and 14 years. The two youngest children have a poor attendance record at school, the oldest child has been excluded from his school. The PSCO for the area reports that the older child is now becoming involved with a local gang of auto criminals.

In these circumstances, disregarding police enforcement, what do you think can be done to support the family and reduce the risk of offending?

What other agencies can you think of that need to be involved?

The information provided in exercise 12B could have made you think of:

- Support for the parent by joining a good parenting class

- Referring the matter to the social services department

- Speaking to the local education authority regarding the truancy and exclusion problem

- Attempts to engage the children in official youth activities.

Apart from some ideas such as those above, there are other official ways that anti-social behaviour can be tackled.

12.8 What can be done to deal with anti-social behaviour?

The CDRP/CSP will have in place a strategy to deal with the reduction of ASB; this strategy will have identified several areas of activity which will each contribute to the reduction:

- Prevention

- Intervention

- Victim and witness support.

Each of these areas will be discussed as separate sections below.

12.9 Prevention

The first and best way to deal with anti-social behaviour is, of course, to prevent it in the first place – something that is easier said than done. Only when this is either not possible due to the nature of the problem, or not sustainable due to the resources required to combat the issue, should the police and partners move on to intervention and enforcement.

Many problems of ASB are linked by communities to young people who are often seen as the main instigators of all social ills. The police practitioner will have to be careful to differentiate between youth presence and youth annoyance linked to anti-social or criminal activity.

Young people will choose to congregate in public areas and socialise. In doing so they often choose to avoid organised activities in search of a sense of freedom outside adult control. In itself this should not present a problem. However, the presence of large numbers of teenagers can be intimidating and can be seen as threatening by other parts of the community. The presence becomes a problem when the activity becomes associated with the consumption of drink or drugs, and where the boisterous behaviour becomes threatening, with individuals indulging in low-level criminality and rowdy behaviour. Again it must be remembered that young people themselves can become the victims of such behaviour. It is often the case that as a result of such problems they lose the ability to access parks and communal public spaces.

The first preventative method for the police practitioner must be to engage with the youths through highly visible patrolling. Public spaces must remain public and not the territory of any one particular group. The youths need to be part of the solution, their confidence needs to be gained. Is it a matter of choice, or a lack of suitable activities that leads to youths congregating in a particular area?

In the course of any information-gathering exercise and PACT process, young people need to be included and their views sought. If a lack of youth facilities of the required type is an issue, then agencies and the community need to address the matter as a priority. This may be one step in a fully integrated partnership approach to crime and disorder reduction in a particular area. If it is to be successful, it will need the active support of the young people themselves. The provision of such facilities is a key issue across both England and Wales. When developing the PACT process the local authority and police must make sure that the panel reflects not only an ethnic mix, but also all ages within that area.

Individuals themselves may need to be supported to reduce the risk of engaging in ASB. Increasingly, young people are living outside the old nuclear family with little or no parental support. Their accommodation requirements will need to be addressed by the local authority and social housing agencies. In providing such accommodation, support may be needed to assist the young person at this stage of their life.

Educational support is another area where agencies working together can reduce the risk by improving the educational attainment of young people. Encouraging the improvement of life skills and improving the employability of people all work towards reducing the risk of offending. Schools also have a significant role to play, whether it is working with the younger siblings of older offenders, or addressing the negative attitudes of some children towards educational attainment.

12.10 Intervention

When prevention is ineffective then agencies will naturally move towards the second way to deal with ASB: intervention; this taking place at a number of levels. The aim of such intervention is to stop the detrimental effects of anti-social behaviour at the earliest opportunity. The aim of such early intervention must be to:

- Protect victims, witnesses and the community. This must be the primary aim of all activity

- Enable the perpetrator to recognise the consequences of their behaviour

- Work to ensure that the perpetrator changes his or her behaviour.

In practice, interventions can take a number of forms, such as mediation between the perpetrator and victim, family group conferencing and community conferencing. These processes seek to draw in those affected by the behaviour and, through an appreciation of the negative effect of such activity, reduce it by collective action. To work, the offender must not only recognise the negative effect of their actions, but also actively change their behaviour for the better. In using such methods, care must be taken to put the needs of the victim first. No pressure should be put on victims to face those who carry out these acts – if difficulties arise then consider the use of a mediator.

Multi-agency conferencing often takes place, chaired by the ASB coordinator for the local CDRP/CSP. These conferences are attended by the police, local authority and its agencies and the social housing landlords, all of whom can and do share information under a data sharing protocol. In this arena individuals and families can be discussed and action plans coordinated to deal with any ongoing issues.

It will often be the case that a person who is a persistent young offender may be linked to problems associated with schooling, and the family itself may become a problem family for the relevant housing agency. On their own, each agency would have a limited view of the overall problem. Its ability to respond would be restricted to its own particular area of responsibility, and the effectiveness of any intervention might not address any underlying issues. Together, the agencies can pool resources and in so doing record their actions. This in itself would be good evidence to present to a court if applying for Anti-Social Behaviour Orders or possession or closure of a particular property.

Mentoring is an increasingly popular process that seeks to place an individual with a person at risk. The mentor will hopefully be seen as a positive role model and inspire a person at risk to turn away from offending.

12.11 Acceptable Behaviour Contracts

We have discussed the importance of high visibility patrolling in preventing ASB. It also has a role in intervention. It is one means of identifying who is actually present in an area and who is engaged in the anti-social behaviour. Using both uniform and plain clothes police officers and staff, the identities of those causing anti-social behaviour is established. This information is collated and warning letters are sent out to those individuals and, if appropriate, their parents.

This will target those who are on the periphery of such activity and, with parental support, the majority of individuals come to no further notice. A second warning may be appropriate. If this fails then an Acceptable Behaviour Contract (ABC) can be pursued. It should be remembered that the ABC which was initially designed to deal with children and young persons, can now equally apply to adults. The individual or individuals responsible for ASB are targeted for action and a file of evidence collected relating to their activity. The information gathered will outline the nature and extent of the ASB. Good practice dictates that in the event of an exclusion area being sought, a simple map delineating this area is included in the file. The ABC is then prepared and clearly outlines to the individual what they have done, where and when. It will require them not to carry on with certain behaviour, not to visit certain areas or even not to meet and be with other named individuals.

The next stage is to arrange an appointment between the individual, if appropriate a suitable parent or guardian, and a police officer or Youth Offending Team member. At the meeting, these activities will be discussed with the offender and the effect of their actions on individuals or the community will be explained. At this stage the reasons for the restrictions to be applied will be outlined. The ABC is a voluntary agreement and needs to be signed by the individual. In so doing they agree to the conditions laid out in the ABC and agree to follow those restrictions for the period that the ABC will be in being. If there is an area or areas where the individual is not allowed to be then those should be detailed in the ABC and shown on a map.

Finally the ABC should include a section that clearly states that behaviour outlined is unacceptable and that if the individual breaks the terms of the ABC it may lead to agencies applying for a full ASBO. The ASBO will then further curtail the liberty and freedoms of the individual, but in this case it is backed by a power of arrest and imprisonment or detention.

The ABC is a powerful tool in dealing with ASB, and can be a successful intervention tool. It also empowers the community to report breaches of the ABC. At this stage, and with parental support, many persons comply and the ASB is reduced.

12.12 Youth Offending Teams

We have discussed the importance of families working together to address ASB. In ABC the effectiveness will often depend on the involvement of the parents in enforcing the change in behaviour. At this stage it may be necessary to support the parents in building up their skill levels to cope with the challenge. It is here that the role of the Youth Offending Team becomes central.

The Youth Offending Team (YOT) is made up of both police officers and probation staff who work specifically with young offenders. They engage with the offender and they also work with parents. There are three ways in which parents can work with the YOT. These are:

- **Voluntarily** Here the parent wants to work to deal with their child's offending behaviour. They can do this without signing a parenting contract or being subject to a parenting order.

- **Voluntarily with a parenting contract** On this occasion the parent may be unwilling to cooperate with the YOT, so a contract will need to be made. A refusal to enter into such a contract can mean that agencies apply for a formal parental order.

- **Parenting order** On these occasions a parent has refused to cooperate and an element of compulsion is needed to gain that cooperation.

12.13 Parenting contract

The parenting contract is a written document which has been negotiated with and then signed by a YOT member and the parents of a child involved in, or likely to be involved in, crime or ASB. This is a voluntary document which parents cannot be forced to sign. It consists of two parts:

- An agreement by the parent of the child or young person that they will comply with the specific requirements of a programme designed to prevent their child committing specified criminal or anti-social behaviour. The contract lasts for a specified time.

- A statement by the YOT stating that they will support the parent or guardian for the period of time to ensure that the contract is complied with.

For the police practitioner this means a child or young person will have been identified as either being involved in crime or ASB, or is at risk of becoming so involved. The child or young person is then referred to the YOT. The YOT will work with the family to either end or prevent the child's behaviour. Because the agreement is voluntary the parent's cooperation is more likely to be successful. But, the parents will be aware that a failure to cooperate could be used as evidence for applying for a Parenting Order.

12.14 Referring a child for a parenting contract

The following children can be referred to a YOT for consideration of their parents being offered a parenting contract:

- A child convicted of an offence

- A child referred to a YOT following a reprimand or final warning. Some multi agencies wait until the final warning stage is reached before triggering such action

- A child under ten years old (the age of criminal intent), who a YOT member has reason to believe has committed an act which, had the child been older, would have constituted an offence

- A child identified as being at risk by a Youth Inclusion Support Panel.

The parenting contract can include a number of specific requirements for the parents to monitor and control their child, the requirements being intended to prevent the child from committing criminal or anti-social behaviour. For example this could include:

- The parent ensuring the child attends school

- A commitment not go to a certain location unless accompanied by the parent, e.g. local shops

- A commitment stay away from persons they may have been harassing

- An agreement not to continue to see or be with certain named individuals.

The YOT will provide parental support during this period, thus helping the parent or guardian to manage the child's behaviour in a positive manner. The contract needs to be realistic and something which both the child and parent can comply with. A contract stating that the child is not allowed to see any other friends or step outside the family home may be too restrictive with little hope of success. Indeed, the contract can be amended to take into account any reasonable adjustments. It should be remembered that the contract is designed to stop particular types of behaviour and not force either parent or child into a particular type of behaviour.

12.15 Failure to comply

The process is voluntary and so if the parent fails to comply there is no punitive action taken. However, such breaches of the contract (and there could be several) need to be recorded by the YOT and police. The reason for this is that such a failure to comply can be used as part of the evidence needed when applying to the court for a Parenting Order.

12.16 Different types of Parenting Order

Parenting Orders, if granted, are not voluntary agreements and their statutory basis is found under sections eight to ten of the Crime and Disorder Act 1998 and sections 25 to 29 of the Anti-Social Behaviour Act 2003. The Orders can be granted by a criminal court, family court or a magistrate's court acting under a civil jurisdiction. There are two types of Parenting Order: free standing and those linked to conviction or other orders.

Free standing Parenting Order

If the child or parent has either failed to agree to, or failed to comply with, a parental contract, then the YOT can consider applying to the court for a free standing Parenting Order. The objective is, of course, to get the child or young

12.19 Anti-Social Behaviour Orders

Anti-Social Behaviour Orders (ASBOs) were a much-heralded product of the Crime and Disorder Act of 1998. Initially the police were slow to implement the process, but by August 2006 over 7,300 ASBOs had been issued by the courts. The powers to deal with anti-social behaviour were extended under the Police Reform Act 2002 when the courts were given the power to make such orders on conviction in both criminal and county court proceedings. The courts were also given the power to make interim orders where it was felt the community needed to be protected. The ASBO can now apply across the whole of England and Wales, a measure of particular assistance to the British Transport Police.

The use of an ASBO is not intended to stop the investigation of criminal offences. If a person commits theft, criminal damage or assaults someone, then the police must investigate that offence. If the evidence is sufficient to meet the charging test for crown prosecutors, then that offence must be charged. We will see that ASBOs can be added to an offence on conviction, or be used to deal with offenders where the police and others are not in a position to charge a substantive offence.

ASBOs are civil orders and contain conditions that prohibit an offender from carrying out certain anti-social acts or from entering certain areas. The order is effective for a minimum of two years.

It should be noted that the definition is quite wide and there is no definitive list of what amounts to ASB. The act has been used by the police service to deal with increasing numbers and types of situations: common sense must apply to any law enforcement in this area. What the act has done is give some sense of empowerment back to victims. A breach of an ASBO can be, and often is, reported in the first case by members of the offender's own community.

12.20 Who can apply for an ASBO?

An ASBO can be applied for by a 'relevant authority', the term includes the following:

- Local authorities, which in England means the council of a county district or London Borough, the Isle of Wight or the Isles of Scilly, and in Wales a County or County Borough

- A police force which includes the British Transport Police

- Registered social landlords under section 1 Housing Act 1996;

- Housing action trusts.

The order can be applied for as a standalone order at a magistrate's court or as a bolt-on ASBO after conviction. It is also possible to apply for an ASBO at the county court. It remains a civil order irrespective of which court grants the order. This is an important point to remember as it affects the way evidence can be gathered, allowing both hearsay evidence and professional witnesses to give evidence.

The agency applying for the ASBO must show that:

- The defendant behaved in an anti-social manner, and

- An ASBO is necessary for the protection of people from further anti-social behaviour by the defendant.

The criminal standard of proof remains for the prosecution agency, but that agency does not have to prove the intent of the individual defendant to cause harassment, alarm or distress. The policing agency will need to gather information and record material to prove that either persons were caused harassment, alarm or distress, or the actions of the defendant were likely to cause such an effect. The practitioner setting out to gain ASBO can only do so against an individual and not an organisation.

12.21 Against whom can an ASBO be made?

An ASBO can be made against anyone aged ten years or over who either has acted in an anti-social manner, or is likely to act in such a manner. The ASBO is needed to protect people or the wider community from further anti-social acts. The agency will need to record their actions in trying to resolve these problems. As we have seen, the failure to comply with an ABC is good evidence on applying for an ASBO. The case study below provides an example of what can be done.

Case study

A group of youths were causing problems at a youth club on a local authority housing estate. Their actions consisted of abusive language, criminal damage and intimidating adults into purchasing alcohol. This resulted in rowdy behaviour until the early hours of the morning. Police patrols had dispersed and identified the youths, but the problem continued. Local residents came forward and, together with professional witnesses from the local authority and CCTV, identified three persons as the ringleaders. Intervention failed and the police applied for ASBOs against each of the three named individuals. The evidence was presented and the court agreed to the ASBO with a condition that the youths could no longer associate with one another or go within a named area surrounding the youth club. Having removed the ringleaders, the problems ceased and the numbers of persons attending the centre greatly increased.

12.22 Who can make an Anti-Social Behaviour Order?

An ASBO can be made by:

- Magistrates' courts when they act in their civil capacity
- County courts
- Magistrates' courts when a person has been convicted of an offence ('bolt on ASBO')
- Crown courts on conviction in criminal proceedings ('bolt on ASBO')
- Youth courts on conviction in criminal proceedings ('bolt on ASBO')
- Eleven county courts (in August 2006) where trials were being held for ASBOs against children and young people.

An ASBO lasts for a minimum of two years and can be for an indefinite period. They can be varied or discharged on the application to the court by either party. The ASBO cannot be discharged during the first two years without the consent of both parties. For children and young persons it is now seen as good practice to review the order every year to see if it is still applicable and still needed to deal with the offending behaviour of the individual.

12.23 What does an ASBO do?

The courts can impose prohibitions on individuals either on the recommendation of an agency such as the police, or it can decide upon its own restrictions. In effect, the court can prohibit someone from doing something, but it cannot impose positive restrictions on an individual.

There are a number of prohibitions that a court can impose which should:

- Cover the range of anti-social acts committed by the defendant
- Be necessary for protecting person(s) within a defined area from the anti-social acts of the defendant
- Be reasonable and proportionate
- Be realistic and practical
- Be clear, concise and easy to understand
- Be specific, stating clearly where a person is not allowed to go, the times when a prohibition will apply

- Protect all people in the area from the specified anti-social behaviour

- Be clear enough to make it easy to prosecute breaches of the ASBO.

Prohibitions can also prevent the person encouraging others to commit such acts and can prohibit a person approaching or harassing any named witnesses. ASBOs can also prohibit activity that is a precursor to a criminal act, such as a person entering licensed premises if this is, for that individual, a precursor to them assaulting persons when under the influence of alcohol.

An ASBO will have a major impact on the freedoms of an individual and should prevent the individual from carrying out acts which have caused harassment, alarm or distress. When the ASBO is publicised, the community can play an active part in reporting any breaches: the community becomes empowered, with pressure being placed on the partner agencies to both 'police' the ASBO, and prosecute such breaches.

A note of caution – the prohibitions placed on the individual can be quite extensive, but they need to be realistic and proportionate. An ASBO could be requested that prevented an individual from carrying out an act at any time, in any place, but how would it be enforced?

12.24 Breach of ASBO

If the individual fails to comply with the prohibitions outlined by the court they are in breach of the ASBO. This is a criminal offence and the standard of proof is that required by the criminal court. Guilt must be established beyond reasonable doubt. The penalty for an adult offender is five years in prison. For a young person a full range of punishments is available. The young person can be given a community order (for 10–11 year-olds) through to the most serious breaches where a Detention and Training Order for up to two years can be imposed (for 12–17 year-olds).

The ASBO, once granted, can apply anywhere in England and Wales. The difficulty in enforcement is identifying and policing those individuals subject to such orders.

12.25 Types of ASBO

There is a standalone ASBO where agencies apply for a prohibition on an individual to prevent them from acting in a manner likely to cause harassment, alarm or distress. In these cases the agency applying for the order must show that the defendant not only behaved in an anti-social manner, but that an order is needed to protect other persons from such anti-social behaviour caused by the defendant.

The courts can also impose an ASBO after a person has been convicted of an offence in court; this could be termed a 'bolt on' ASBO. The application for such an order is considered after the conviction and is a civil hearing. It is not considered as part of the sentence for the specified offence, but an instrument designed to prevent further such behaviour by the defendant, so protecting the community from such acts. The court can impose the ASBO on the basis of the evidence heard in the criminal case, or with additional information supplied by the police or partner agency. The ASBO can come into effect either from the date of conviction or, if the defendant is remanded in custody, when they are released.

Interim orders for ASBOs can also be made by both the magistrates and county courts. It applies to the first hearing of the application prior to any full hearing being arranged. The courts can therefore order an immediate end to anti-social behaviour. The defendant need not be aware of the interim hearing but, for the order to come into effect, a copy of the order must be served on the defendant. The police have seven days to serve the order, otherwise the interim order will lapse. A positive effect of taking out such an order is that witnesses can be protected and thus feel safer in providing the evidence for the full application. If an interim order is granted, a priority must be to serve the notice. If an interim order were to lapse due to a failure to act, public confidence in law enforcement would be severely affected.

12.26 Dispersal Orders

Section 30 of the Anti-Social Behaviour Act 2003 gives the police service powers to deal with groups of people who are behaving in an anti-social manner. The section states that where a relevant police officer has reasonable grounds for believing that any members of the public have been intimidated, alarmed or distressed as a result of the presence or behaviour of two or more persons in a public place or locality, the officer can authorise a police officer in uniform to require the persons to disperse, to require non residents to leave the locality and to prevent them from returning to the locality within 24 hours. The authorisation can last for up to six months.

In addition, a constable can patrol the relevant locality between the hours of 9pm and 6am and, if the officer has reasonable grounds for believing a person is under 16 years of age and not under the effective control of a parent or responsible person aged 18 or over, take the child back to their home, away from the relevant area. The case study below provides an example of this power.

> **Case study**
>
> In the run-up to Halloween, groups of youths are roaming an area of town causing damage, annoyance and intimidating people as a result of both their numbers and behaviour. CCTV and police patrols put the numbers in excess of 80 young persons, many of whom live in other areas but go to a local community school. Local councillors and residents have expressed alarm and refer to previous years when this behaviour resulted in assaults and an arson attack on a local shop. Local community officers are patrolling the area, youths are moving between streets and officers have had missiles thrown at them.
>
> The local police commander, in consultation with community leaders, authorises a dispersal order that is publicised in the local press and radio and at the school assembly. Uniformed officers deploy into the area assisted by mounted staff and colleagues from other sectors. Uniform officers instruct the youths to move away from the locality; many do; several of those who remain are then arrested.
>
> Local community officers identify several younger children who are taken home and warned in front of their parents. The operation is sustained for a four-week period until the incidence of anti-social behaviour is drastically reduced and a state of normality is achieved.

12.27 Other measures that can be used against anti-social behaviour

In addition to the above powers there are several other tactics available to partners to deal with anti-social behaviour. These include:

- Actions by landlords to deal with problem tenants such as injunctions or possession arrangements

- The use of Fixed Penalty Notices for Disorder to deal with offences on the street there and then

- The seizure of music equipment from persons who are acting in an anti-social manner.

12.28 Victim and witness support

The third aspect of dealing with ASB concerns how the police and partner agencies deal with the victims of and witnesses to anti-social behaviour. If witnesses are intimidated, victims ignored and both receive either little or no support, they are unlikely to support cases, give evidence or have faith in the fairness of the criminal justice system.

ASBOs are civil instruments – they allow the police and partners to make use of hearsay evidence and professional witnesses, and can now access special measures for the witnesses and victims of such behaviour.

12.29 Hearsay evidence

In essence, this is evidence of some activity that is not first-hand knowledge to the witness giving the information to the court. An example could be of a police officer giving evidence of the effect on local residents of the activities of individuals in an area. Hearsay evidence must, of course, be relevant to the case and concern the anti-social behaviour at issue. It should contain dates, times and the specific conduct alleged to have been committed by the defendant(s). It is down to the judge or magistrate to decide on how much weight to give the hearsay evidence in the trial.

12.30 Professional witnesses

The Home Office guide to ASBOs states:

> 'professional witnesses can be called to give their opinions as to matters within their expertise and can give evidence about their assessments of the respondent or his/her behaviour.'

The idea is that persons such as police officers, housing officers or teachers could give evidence of what they have seen or gathered. This could be the physical state of the victim, the attitude of the defendant, or the general effect of the anti-social behaviour on the community.

Whilst the police practitioner can use these measures, the best evidence is that provided by the witnesses and victims themselves. In the past, this group has been neglected and, indeed, ignored by the criminal justice agencies. Now their needs are recognised and we have witness care units in all police areas. These measures, a development of the 'No Witness No Justice' programme, are designed to give victims and witnesses a single point of contact and assist them in giving evidence. Amongst other measures, they will arrange child care or travel, keep witnesses updated regarding court dates and developments, arrange court visits and finally ensure they are thanked for their efforts.

12.31 Special Measures

The Serious and Organised Crime and Police Act 2005, allowed the Special Measures available to victims and witnesses in criminal trials to apply to those who are involved in cases of anti-social behaviour. The 'Special Measures' are just that, measures that can be requested from the court that will assist intimidated or vulnerable witnesses to give evidence. These measures include:

- Giving evidence behind a screen so their identity is protected

- Giving evidence by video link to the court

- Giving evidence in private, the court being cleared of people other than those required to be in attendance, e.g. defence and prosecution lawyers, court ushers, jury, etc.

- Removal of wigs and gowns to make the court less intimidating

- The provision of intermediaries – people approved to help the witness communicate with the police, prosecution or court.

Naturally such measures are the exception and can only apply in a restricted number of cases.

Vulnerable witness

The definition includes all witnesses aged under 17 years or those witnesses whose quality of evidence is likely to be diminished because they have a mental disorder or who have a physical disability or physical disorder.

Intimidated witness

These are the witnesses whose quality of evidence is likely to be diminished because they are in fear or distress about giving the evidence in court. Whilst the police may argue that a witness has been intimidated, it is for the court to decide if that is the case and whether special measures can apply.

When dealing with victims and witnesses the police must look after their interests and treat them with respect. But the police must not promise that special measures will be used as the court may take a different view. The crown court has all special measures available to it, except video recorded evidence, which is not available to vulnerable witnesses. In the magistrates' court the picture is more complicated and the police need to ensure their staff know what is, and what is not, available to the victims and witnesses to crime and disorder. Whatever happens, victims and witnesses need support, before, during and after any anti-social case. They are particularly vulnerable to threats from the defendant or their friends as in most cases their identities are known.

To maintain confidence in any police action relating to breaches of ASBOs, positive support and action need to be both given and maintained. Victims and witnesses are often known to offenders and are targeted. If the community sees that the police and their partners are not addressing the issue; if they see victims suffering or if they believe they will not be supported if they give evidence, then public confidence will be eroded and the cycle of anti-social behaviour, with all its negative effects, will continue. A failure to act is not an option.

12.32 Conclusion

Anti-social behaviour can occur anywhere at any time to anybody. The police and their partners have the power to tackle these issues particularly with the support of the community. The more joined-up the strategy, the more inclusive the partnership between agencies and the community, the more likely it is that a positive outcome will be achieved.

There are now a number of offences created by different Acts of Parliament such as the Crime and Disorder Act 1998 that enable the police and their partners to tackle persistent offenders. If used wisely by partnerships, this should ensure that recurring calls to the same problem should disappear and free up valuable police resources for other matters.

Suggested further reading

Rogers, C., *Crime Reduction Partnerships* (Oxford: Oxford University Press, 2006)
Home Office, *A Guide to Anti-Social Behaviour Orders* (London: Home Office, 2006)

Useful websites

www.homeoffice.gov.uk
Home Office website

www.together.gov.uk
A resource for practitioners working to tackle anti-social behaviour across England and Wales

www.respect.gov.uk
A website aimed at tackling anti-social behaviour and its causes

www.crimereduction.gov.uk
Providing information and resources for people working to reduce crime in their local areas

Chapter 13

Operational Response

This chapter supports the following National Occupational Standards which describe the performance and competence required of a probationer officer.

Unit No.	Unit title
1A1	Use police actions in a fair and justified way.
1A4	Foster people's equality, diversity and rights.
1B9	Provide initial support to individuals affected by offending or anti-social behaviour and assess their needs for further support.
2A1	Gather and submit information that has the potential to support policing objectives.
2C2	Prepare for, and participate in, planned policing operations.
2C3	Arrest, detain or report individuals.
2G2	Conduct investigations.
2G4	Finalise investigations.
2J1	Prepare and submit case files.
2J2	Present evidence in court and at other hearings.
4C1	Develop your own knowledge and practice.
4G2	Ensure your own actions reduce risks to health and safety.

13.1 Introduction

This chapter will introduce you to the idea of police operations. It will explain why the police conduct such operations and also introduce you to several useful mnemonics to assist you in learning and remembering how the police respond to different incidents. Firstly we need to consider what we mean by a police operation. Think about this for a few moments and see if you can answer the question in exercise 13A.

> **Exercise 13A**
>
> What do you think is meant by the term 'police operation'?

You may have thought of a few events such as major sporting occasions or a royal visit. In many senses you would be right. An operation within the police service, however, can mean almost anything. It can range from unforeseen disasters involving loss of life such as a plane crash or terrorist bomb, to dealing with local issues such as a parade or large village fete.

13.2 Safety and liability

Before we start to look at the police response to planned and unplanned operations, it is worth remembering that issues of safety and liability should be considered at all times when dealing with incidents. On many occasions, organisers of events will turn to the police for assistance because of their experience in organising events. However, it may be that on most occasions, the responsibility for public safety at events rests with the organisers themselves, or the owners of land upon which the event takes place and possibly the local authority. In fact many local authorities run safety advisory groups which comprise senior officers from the fire and rescue service, ambulance service, highways authorities and police.

Generally, in terms of deployment of police staff, they are normally confined to their core responsibilities. The core responsibilities include those identified in table 13.1.

Core responsibilities

■ Prevention and detection of crime.

■ Prevention or stopping a breach of the peace.

■ Traffic regulation.

■ Activation of a contingency plan to combat immediate threat to life and coordinate emergency service activities.

Table 13.1	Core responsibilities of the police

Liabilities

When police operations are being planned, the police have to consider carefully their liabilities and responsibilities. The following are important.

■ **Civil liabilities** There exists a duty of care for police officers when preparing for foreseeable events under civil law. This duty of care exists towards themselves, their colleagues and the public for injuries arising from foreseeable events. Civil cases are sometimes heard years after the event, so there is an obvious need for meticulous recording and storage of evidence.

■ **Criminal liabilities** Where police officers are responsible for the death or injury of others, they may be prosecuted in the criminal courts.

■ **Police personnel procedures** Police officers who fail to perform to expected levels of competency may also be liable to be dealt with under the unsatisfactory performance procedures – see Chapter 5 on ethical policing.

Safety and risk assessment

Many police operations are dependent upon the reliability of information and the establishment of the level of risk that may be involved. One way of assessing this is by using a matrix or table that identifies risks and then considers their likelihood and the seriousness of their impact. By using this approach, the person in charge of the police operation can concentrate on those risks that appear to be more serious and likely and, therefore, provide for a response to either negate or greatly reduce their impact. Table 13.2 below illustrates this approach by considering some of the risks associated with an incident where a person has been assaulted outside a nightclub late at night.

Risk	Likelihood	Impact
Injury to officers, the crowd and the suspect	High	High – possibly fatal
The crowd may become aggressive towards the police	High	High – there is the potential for further assaults, injuries and disorder
Reliable witnesses may have absented themselves from the scene	High/Medium	High – this could impact upon attempts to apprehend the offender

Table 13.2   An assessment matrix

However, it is not good enough simply to identify what the risks are. The police need to manage the risks.

Risk management

There are a number of approaches that are used to allow the police to manage risk effectively. Firstly the risk, having been identified, is accepted. Secondly, try to reduce its impact. Thirdly, try to reduce its likelihood. The final attempt to manage the risk is to displace it to those better trained to handle it. We can employ this approach to the risk we have already identified in table 13.2 – that of injury to officers at the scene of the disturbance. Table 13.3 illustrates this point.

Accept the risk	But brief the team to exercise caution and arrange for back-up of other officers.
Reduce its impact	Ensure officers are aware of risk and are wearing body armour and carrying protective equipment.
Reduce its likelihood	Use plain clothes officers at scene to minimise impact of uniform presence.
Displace the risk to some other party.	Try to get a trained public order unit to the scene to ensure proper control of crowd.

Table 13.3   Risk management matrix

It may be that under the circumstances, all or some of the above approaches can be employed at the same time. In exercise 13B below, and using the above information, identify the risks that may be associated with the information provided. Having done so, use the matrix above to try and manage the risk.

Exercise 13B

Information has been received that a male person has stolen property at his home address. The person has a vicious dog which he uses to protect the property.

The main point that needs to be remembered is that *all* police operations contain elements of risk. However, there are methods available to reduce or negate these risks and contribute to the success of the operation as a whole.

In general, police operations fall into two main categories. Those that follow *unexpected* or *unplanned* incidents such as a serious assault or major disturbance, and those for which there is a *planned event*, such as a drugs raid or attending a carnival/fete. Both these will now be considered.

13.3   Responding to unplanned events

Sometimes the police have to deal with unplanned and serious incidents. They have to be quick to respond and organise that response effectively and efficiently. One way of doing so is by using the mnemonic **SCENE** and **CHALET**. This way the police respond through a framework that enables them to cover the most important aspects of what they need to do *initially* at the scene of a major incident. For example, look at the following exercise and write down what you think you should do.

Exercise 13C

You are the duty sergeant at midnight on a Friday night when you receive a report of a disturbance at a nightclub. A male customer at the nightclub has been seriously assaulted, with what appears to be a bottle or glass. The offender has left the scene.

At first, perhaps, you may think of such things as getting an ambulance, going to the scene and finding out what has really happened. These are all natural reactions and none of them is wrong. However, to help ensure that the correct response is applied to the incident, the police turn to a mnemonic called CHALET. It is quite an easy mnemonic to remember as can be seen in figure 13.1 below.

CASUALTIES	Approximate no. of casualties: dead, injured, not injured.
HAZARDS	Present and potential: debris, terrain, chemicals, fire, danger
ACCESS	Best routes for emergency services, suitable RV point
LOCATION	Ensure precise location of incident known to all concerned.
EMERGENCY SERVICES	What other resources do you require – how you can get them?
TYPE	Accurately establish type of incident, its extent, number of people, vehicles, buildings, etc.

Figure 13.1 CHALET

Using the information in exercise 13C, try to apply this to our example of the incident in the nightclub in the following exercise. The first two boxes have been completed for you.

Exercise 13D

CASUALTIES	One male person, apparently seriously injured by bottle.
HAZARDS	In nightclub, people intoxicated and perhaps not, availability of weapons, i.e. glasses and bottles, witnesses and culprit left scene
ACCESS	
LOCATION	
EMERGENCY SERVICES	
TYPE	

As you can see, this framework will help you consider how to respond to an incident, what you need to do, who to contact and also provides a well thought-out response that covers the important issues at the beginning of an unplanned serious incident.

Having done so, the police need to consider the wider response to unplanned incidents as they may have to use other emergency services such as the fire and rescue department or the ambulance service. Again, there is a useful mnemonic to assist in this process. This is called SCENE. This is an easy mnemonic to remember as it relates to the scene of the incident itself as shown in figure 13.2 below.

SEAL AREA	Seal off area, establish cordons, provide access routes, control persons entering, rescue is a priority.
CONTROL	Establish a control point, and possibly a joint emergency control point, issue identification tabards, ensure a log is maintained.
EMERGENCY SERVICES	Coordinate their arrival, provide escorts if needed.
NOTIFY	Control room of actions, be accurate, clear and concise. Be prepared to brief others and to be briefed by specialists.
EVACUATE	The injured. If serious risk, evacuate the scene, leave the dead.

Figure 13.2   SCENE

If we consider our original information about the disturbance and serious assault in the nightclub we could apply SCENE to this set of circumstances. This is illustrated below in table 13.4.

SEAL AREA	The nightclub has now become a crime scene. Therefore the scene will need to be preserved. Cordons may have to be put in place and officers placed at entrances and exits to restrict access.
CONTROL	Contact the operations room so that the control room supervisor is aware. Establish one person at the scene to receive radio calls and mobile phone calls in the initial phases. One police officer or police community support officer may be designated to record decisions in a log of events.
EMERGENCY SERVICES	Ensure the ambulance knows where to attend. If injury is life threatening enquire with ambulance service if they need escort.
NOTIFY	Keep control updated with information. There may be the need to inform specialist squads or teams to take over the enquiry. Briefing of other personnel is an important job that you may have to consider.
EVACUATE	Ensure all injured are evacuated from the scene. In our scenario, you may have considered a police officer attending the hospital with the casualty to obtain as much information as possible.

Table 13.4   Application of SCENE

The mnemonics SCENE and CHALET are quite useful in responding to any type of unplanned incident in the early stages.

13.4 Planned events and targeted operations

The National Intelligence Model

The NIM is vital in feeding intelligence into the preparation for a planned event. There is a lot more information about NIM in Chapter 10 and elsewhere in this book.

The role of intelligence in setting pre-planned objectives

One of the most vital ingredients in a pre-planned operation is the setting of clear objectives. In order to ensure that the objectives are the right ones, intelligence gathered from the National Intelligence Model process and other information helps to formulate them. For planned events, gathering information is easier because there is more time. If intelligence is to be gathered using covert methods, it is important to remember that this is covered by the Regulation of Investigatory Powers Act 2000 (RIPA).

To help set good objectives you would need to consider what sources of information you can draw on before the operation begins. Figure 13.3 illustrates what you need to consider when setting objectives.

Points to remember that will help set objectives

State in simple terms what you want to achieve (objectives).

Make sure your objectives are balanced.

Make sure your objectives are lawful and lie in the area of core police business.

Make sure that the risks involved have been examined.

| **Figure 13.3** | Points to remember when setting objectives |

Much of the information provided from the NIM and elsewhere will form the basis for planned operations against criminals and other people involved in illegal activities. These operations are all more or less planned using a pre-defined layout. This layout is used for many planned operations, not just crime, and is used for operations such as major sporting events. Before you continue, however, try to complete the exercise below, using the information provided.

Exercise 13E

The police are told that a man is dealing drugs from his home address, which is situated opposite a school. Intelligence suggests that he has a rottweiler dog which he keeps in order to protect his drugs, which are stored in a box beneath the floorboards in the front room of his home. Write down how you think you would carry out this pre-planned operation. What do consider are important things you need to consider and how would you plan for them?

You may have considered several important points such as, for example, the fact that the suspect has a potentially dangerous dog. How do you think that may be dealt with? We will discuss a way of effectively communicating your ideas now.

13.5 Communicating pre-planned operational information

The way that police staff are briefed for any operational activity is very important. The briefing and how it is communicated can dictate how successful the operation may turn out to be. Some people find it very difficult to brief one or two individuals, let alone large numbers of people. A common problem with briefings is that they are sometimes too long or contain too much information. People are on the whole only able to absorb about seven items of information at one time, so we need to remember this when preparing our briefing. Practice is obviously important, but remember, 'the 5 Ps': **proper preparation prevents poor performance!**

For pre-planned operations a good format that can be used is one which uses the mnemonic IIRMACC.

This mnemonic provides for a very useful framework when it comes to planning an organised event. IIRMACC stands for the following:

Information – What we know about the event, venue, who is coming, what are the allegations, etc. Any intelligence brief will be updated on a separate sheet.

Intention – How we intend to police the information. For example, working in line with the chief constable's policy or guidelines minimises disruption to the public, etc.

Risk assessment – For example, it's important to assess the security threat level of the event or incident, or the likelihood of public disorder or injury, etc. We have seen earlier how we can identify and manage risks for the safety of everyone involved in the operation.

Method – How the event will be policed. Who will do what, when and how? Policies regarding the 'what if factor' – for example, a pitch invasion at a major sporting event – need to be considered here. Perhaps cordons will need to be established. The deployment of specialists would come under this heading.

Administration – Here we need to consider such items as tours of duty for individuals concerned. Also what is the mode of dress? Perhaps full uniform is needed for royal visits, for example, or riot clothing for major disturbances. Overtime claims forms and their submission need to be considered. Also officers need to be designated as being responsible for exhibits and their recording.

Communication – Important information – such as what radio channel is to be used – is indicated in this section. Further, we need to consider where the control room is located and who will operate it. Consideration is needed about such matters as where radios are to be booked out and returned to, the issue of mobile phones and their numbers and so on.

Community impact assessment – This is a very important section which may be completed as a separate document and attached to the briefing document. It considers how the operation will affect the community. For example, prolonged closure of roads, the impact of stop and search on ethnic minorities within the target area, and the impact upon a community's fear of crime, may be some issues for consideration. Consultation with local community leaders should be considered here as well as the impact on partnership members, e.g. drug rehabilitation workers after a drugs raid.

Let's look at a specific scenario in the light of the IIRMACC framework. Using the information provided in exercise 13E you may consider some of the following:

INFORMATION	Intelligence on the suspect and associates. Information about the numbers of people on the premises. Layout of the building. Previous information about the premises. Entrance and exit routes.
INTENTION	To gain safe entry, to contain the suspect and other people in it. To gather evidence on entry, and to locate and arrest drugs offenders.
RISK ASSESSMENT	Make aware of risks/hazards such as drugged people, violent offenders, the rottweiler dog and potential weapons, e.g. glasses, whereabouts of school pupils and staff.
METHOD	The instructions given to staff including how entry is to be made, the deployment of staff to particular jobs, gathering of evidence, dealing with any prisoners, equipment required and its location, covering of exits, etc.

▶

ADMINISTRATION	Briefing times. Dress to be worn by staff, e.g. full riot gear by entry teams may be a necessity. The numbers of staff required, dedicated control team, amount of force to be used, injuries on duty, welfare and refreshments.
COMMUNICATION	It may be that different radio channels need to be used for the duration of the operation, and certain mobile phone numbers need to be made available. It could also include different code names assigned to different individuals/teams.
COMMUNITY IMPACT	Preparation of a media release, meeting with community leaders to calm the community, liaison with school staff.

All police pre-planned orders must comply with human rights legislation and must be proportional in its response to the problem, and respect individual's rights under The Human Rights Act 1998 which has been written about in Chapter 5 on ethical policing.

Having seen how this approach can be used to formulate a briefing for a pre-planned operation, try to apply this information to the following exercise.

Exercise 13F

Information has been received that a small demonstration is to take place outside a meat packaging factory by a group who think it is inhumane to eat meat. They are not expected to cause any disturbances, but they will number around 30 people. The factory is situated on a busy B class road which has lorries travelling along it quite frequently.

You may have come up with some ideas such as those shown in the box below.

INFORMATION	Intelligence on any suspects and associates. Information about the numbers of people taking part in the demonstration. Layout of the area, including a map. Previous information about the group demonstrating. Intended routes and exits for procession.
INTENTION	To ensure the demonstration passes off peacefully. To prevent any disorder or disruption to the normal course of citizens' activities. To deal with any person committing any offences.

RISK ASSESSMENT	Make aware of risks/hazards such as traffic hazards along the intended route, potential violent offenders, and potential weapons. To ensure officers are suitably clothed and in possession of all necessary equipment.
METHOD	Ensure that all staff are informed of the intention of the demonstration, the numbers involved and the route to be taken. Ensure sufficient officers are located at the points allocated along the route. The deployment of staff to particular jobs, gathering of evidence, dealing with any prisoners, etc. should the need arise.
ADMINISTRATION	Briefing times; dress to be worn by staff e.g. high visibility reflective tabards may be a possibility. The numbers of staff required; dedicated control team; amount of force to be used; injuries on duty; welfare and refreshments.
COMMUNICATION	Ensure that radio channels to be used for the duration of the operation are known by all officers, and certain mobile phone numbers need to be disseminated. Code names may need to be assigned to different individuals/teams.
COMMUNITY IMPACT	Preparation of a media release; meeting with the leaders of the demonstration in order to ensure cooperation of demonstrators; liaison with staff from within the factory.

13.6 Debriefing police operations

At the conclusion of any operation, whether pre-planned or not, it is always useful to conduct a debrief of the event. The reasons why a debrief is carried out are as follows:

- It summarises information following an incident

- It identifies good work practice

- It also identifies poor work practice

- It ensures all information is disseminated to all those involved

- It identifies points for learning/development for future operations

- It motivates staff and can be used to praise them

- It identifies any support required for staff as well as any training needs.

It is important that all staff involved in the operation are brought together for the debrief session. There are several important areas that a debrief needs to cover. These include such things as who attended at the incident, where it happened, what happened, why it happened, what was learned and how it will affect future actions.

This can be shown as a typical debrief model in figure 13.4 below.

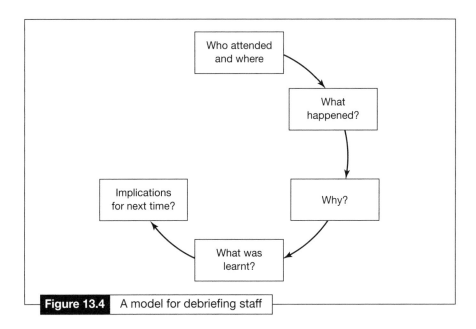

Figure 13.4 A model for debriefing staff

This approach is very similar to that known as the experiential learning cycle, as discussed in Chapter 2, with the purpose of identifying good practice and also ineffective practice. The idea is to see whether we can learn for the future. This does not just have to be any negative aspects of the incident, but also the positive aspects that can be highlighted as good practice. This is a simple model to remember and can be adapted in its use for any type of debrief.

13.7 Conclusion

The police have to respond to many unplanned incidents in an efficient and effective manner. Many times they are the first at the scene of serious incidents and have to make judgements relating to such things as casualties, level of response required and the setting up of local rendezvous points. In these instances, application of the mnemonics SCENE and CHALET assist in this vital first response.

Pre-planned incidents are those operations that the police and other agencies may have been working on for some time. They have predefined objectives and take into account the risks and hazards involved as well as the impact on the community and are very often based upon information and intelligence gleaned from a number of sources. One of the main sources used in these operations is the National Intelligence Model that ensures good quality intelligence for implementation of operations.

Whatever the type of operation the police are involved in, whether pre-planned or unexpected, there should always be a debriefing session in order to learn the positive and negative points from the operation. This should then be used to help formulate future operations.

Suggested further reading

Edmunds, M., Hough, M. and Urquia, N., *Tackling Local Drug Markets*, Crime Detection and Prevention series paper 80 (London: HMSO, 1996)

Maguire, M. and John, T., *Intelligence, Surveillance and Informants: Integrated Approaches*, Crime Detection and Prevention series paper 64 (London: HMSO, 1995)

Mawby, R. I., *Burglary* (Cullompton: Willan, 2001)

Stockdale, J. E. and Gresham, P. J., *Tackling Street Robbery: A comparative evaluation of operation Eagle Eye*, Crime Detection and Prevention series paper 87 (London: HMSO, 1998)

Tilley, N., Community Policing, Problem Oriented Policing and Intelligence Led Policing, in *Handbook of Policing*, ed. Newburn, T, (Cullompton: Willan, 2003), pp. 311–339

Emergency Preparedness (London: H.M.Government, 2005) available from The Emergency Planning College, Easingwold, York

Useful websites

http://www.acpo.police.uk/
The Association of Chief Police Officers. This site includes numerous policies on police response to emergencies, etc.

http://www.popcenter.org/
The Problem Orientated Policing centre. Here you will find examples of the problem orientated approaches to issues such as drug abuse, etc.

http://www.soca.gov.uk/
The Serious Organised Crime Agency

http://www.jdi.ucl.ac.uk/index.php
The Jill Dando Centre. This site contains useful information and guidelines regarding problem solving and intelligence-led policing

http://www.crime-scene-investigator.net/
How to recover evidence at scenes of crime

http://www.hse.gov.uk/index.htm
The government's health and safety website. This is a useful site to read and contains the latest information regarding hazards

http://www.ukresilience.info/index.shtm
The government's response to emergencies website, it includes some useful information regarding initial responses to emergencies

Chapter 14

Arrests

This chapter supports the following National Occupational Standards which describe the performance and competence required of a probationer officer.

Unit No.	Unit title
1A1	Use police actions in a fair and justified way.
1A4	Foster people's equality, diversity and rights.
1B9	Provide initial support to individuals affected by offending or anti-social behaviour and assess their needs for further support.
2A1	Gather and submit information that has the potential to support policing objectives.
2C2	Prepare for, and participate in, planned policing operations.
2C3	Arrest, detain or report individuals.
2C4	Minimise and deal with aggressive and abusive behaviour.
2G2	Conduct investigations.
2G4	Finalise investigations.
SH1	Interview victims and witnesses.
2H2	Interview suspects.
2I1	Search individuals.
2I2	Search vehicles, premises and land.
2J1	Prepare and submit case files.
2J2	Present evidence in court and at other hearings.

▶

Unit No.	Unit title
2K1	Escort detained persons.
2K2	Present detained persons to custody.
4C1	Develop your own knowledge and practice.
4G2	Ensure your own actions reduce risks to health and safety.

14.1 What is an arrest?

From a police perspective, making an arrest is virtually an everyday occurrence. However, from the perspective of a member of the public, it can be a distressing experience. It has been said (in the case of *Lewis* v *Chief Constable of South Wales Constabulary* [1991] 1 All ER 206), that an arrest involves depriving a person of his or her liberty to go where he or she pleases.

An arrest begins at the time the arresting officer informs the person of it, or when his/her words or actions suggest that the person is under arrest (*Murray* v *Ministry of Defence* [1988] 1 WLR 692).

There are many reasons for making an arrest and it does not always follow that when a police officer makes an arrest, the person will later appear in court. For example, a police officer may arrest a person:

- for their own safety (under the Mental Health Act 1983), or

- to prevent a breach of the peace (when the person may later be released when the breach of the peace has been averted).

However, in the majority of cases, an arrest will be made with a view to taking a person to the formal environment of a police station, for the purposes of investigating an offence the person is suspected of committing.

14.2 Reasonable grounds to suspect

Generally, when making an arrest for an offence, a police officer must be able to demonstrate that he or she held a reasonable suspicion that the person had committed the offence. Reasonable suspicion is known as an 'objective standard' and the courts have accepted that this will be determined according to what the constable knew at that time. The courts have also determined that the circumstances of the arrest should be such 'that a reasonable man, acting without passion or prejudice, would fairly have suspected the person of committing the offence' (see *Allen* v *Wright* (1838) 8 C & P 522 per Tindal CJ).

There is no need for the arresting officer to show that he or she knew beyond reasonable doubt at the time of arrest that the person was guilty of the offence. This is the test that will be applied in a court when it decides whether or not the person should be convicted of the offence. Now try to complete exercise 14A below.

Exercise 14A

Try to think of some situations that would give a police officer 'reasonable suspicion' to make an arrest.

You may have considered some of the following:

- Information received from a colleague
- Information received from a member of the public (whether anonymously or not)
- Information an officer receives on his/her radio
- Information an officer receives by telephone
- Information an officer receives from the Police National Computer
- Information an officer sees in a document
- Information an officer receives from an informant
- Circumstances which are observed by the officer himself/herself.

The list is not exhaustive and the main thing the police officer will have to show is that the arrest was made for a proper purpose.

14.3 Powers of arrest

The Police and Criminal Evidence Act 1984 (PACE) divides powers into two general areas :

- Arrests that may only be made by constables (s.24 of PACE)
- Arrests that may be made by any person (s.24A of PACE).

Unsurprisingly, the first category under s.24 provides constables with far greater powers of arrest than members of the public. The second category, s.24A, allows for members of the public to make a so-called 'citizen's arrest'. We will now examine the difference between the two powers.

Constable's power of arrest

The power of arrest given to a constable is divided into three general scenarios:

1 Where an offence is about to be committed

2 Where an offence is being committed

3 Where an offence has been committed.

The first two points above are covered by s.24(1) of PACE, which states:
A constable may arrest without a warrant:

(a) anyone who is about to commit an offence;

(b) anyone who is in the act of committing an offence;

(c) anyone whom he/she has reasonable grounds for suspecting to be about to commit an offence;

(d) anyone whom he/she has reasonable grounds for suspecting to be committing an offence.

Section 24(1) above is best explained by examining some scenarios shown in table 14.1 opposite.

You must remember that in relation to all of the above scenarios, the constable does not have to prove beyond reasonable doubt that the person is guilty of an offence. The arrest of the person in each case is only a means of preventing them from either committing an offence or continuing to commit an offence. It would be wrong if the constable had actually to wait for an offence to be committed before arresting the person.

In relation to the third point above, s.24(2) and 24(3) of PACE state:

2 If a constable has reasonable grounds for suspecting that an offence has been committed, he/she may arrest without a warrant anyone whom he/she has reasonable grounds to suspect of being guilty of it.

3 If an offence has been committed, a constable may arrest without a warrant:

(a) Anyone who is guilty of the offence;

(b) Anyone whom he has reasonable grounds for suspecting to be guilty of it.

Scenario	PACE Section
A constable is on patrol and as he approaches a person, he overhears the person say to a friend that he is going to throw a brick through a window. The constable sees the person picking up the brick and holding his arm back in a throwing motion. The constable is close enough to grab hold of the person's arm and prevent him from throwing the brick. The constable arrests the person for attempting to cause criminal damage.	Section 24(1)(a) (the person is *about* to commit an offence)
A constable on patrol stops a person and searches them. The constable finds a cellophane bag containing white powder in the person's pocket and the person admits that the bag contains heroin. The constable arrests the person for being in possession of controlled drugs.	Section 24(1)(b) (the person *is in the act* of committing an offence)
A constable has a call from a member of the public who has seen a person acting suspiciously near a car. The constable searches the person and finds a screwdriver, which the constable believes the person is about to use to break into the car. The constable arrests the person to prevent him from breaking into the car.	Section 24(1)(c) (the constable has reasonable grounds to suspect the person *is about* to commit an offence)
A constable is on patrol and stops a car. The constable notices that there is damage to the door lock and further damage to the ignition. The constable conducts a radio check, but the vehicle is not listed as being stolen. However, the constable arrests the person on suspicion of taking the vehicle without the owner's consent.	Section 24(1)(d) (the constable has reasonable grounds to suspect the person *is in the* act of committing an offence)

Table 14.1   Illustrating powers under section 24 of PACE

Again, let us examine some further scenarios in table 14.2:

Scenario	PACE Section
A constable is called to an alarm at a factory. As the constable arrives at the scene, she hears the alarm sounding and sees a person running away from the rear of the building. The constable chases the person and arrests them on suspicion of burglary.	Section 24(2) (the constable has *reasonable grounds for suspecting* an offence has been committed and has *reasonable grounds to suspect* that the person is guilty of it)
A constable on patrol has been called to a shop by a store detective who has seen two people acting suspiciously. The store detective has seen one of the people stealing an item of clothing and suspects that the other person has also stolen some clothes. The store detective cannot be certain about the second person as she has not had a chance to view the CCTV evidence. The constable arrests both people for theft.	Section 24(3) (an offence has been committed and the constable has arrested one person *who is guilty of the offence* and another whom he has *reasonable grounds to suspect* is guilty of the offence)

Table 14.2 Further powers under section 24 of PACE

Once again, the constables in the scenarios have arrested people using reasonable suspicion that they have committed offences. These actions are perfectly correct within the law.

Arrests made by other people

Arrests can be made by people other than constables in far narrower circumstances. Section 24A of PACE states:

1 A person other than a constable may arrest without a warrant:

   (a) Anyone who is in the act of committing an indictable offence;

   (b) Anyone whom he has reasonable grounds for suspecting to be committing an indictable offence.

2 Where an indictable offence has been committed, a person other than a constable may arrest without a warrant:

   (a) Anyone who is guilty of the offence;

   (b) Anyone whom he has reasonable grounds for suspecting to be guilty of it.

The first thing to note is that members of the public are not given 'preventative' powers of arrest. They may only make an arrest where an indictable offence is being committed or where such an offence has been committed. The member of the public does not have the power to arrest a person who is about to commit an offence.

The second point to note is that a member of the public may only arrest a person for an indictable offence. They have no power to arrest a person who has committed a summary offence. These offences may be described as follows:

- **Summary offences** Offences which may only be tried in the magistrates' court (minor offences such as driving offences).

- **Indictable offences** Offences that may be tried only in the crown court (serious offences such as murder, robbery, rape) and these include

- **Triable either-way offences** Offences that may be tried either in the crown court or the magistrates' court (less serious offences such as theft and criminal damage).

Quite simply, only police officers may arrest for summary (minor) offences.

14.4 Human Rights Act 1998

In the 1950s, the European Convention on Human Rights was signed by most European countries. Since then, citizens have been provided with the opportunity to take cases to the European Court of Human Rights if they feel their human rights have been infringed by the State. The Human Rights Act 1998 incorporated most of the Convention rights into UK legislation and provided an opportunity for people from this country to seek justice in our domestic courts for alleged breaches of human rights by a public authority (including the police). You can read more about this in general in Chapter 5, ethical policing.

How does the Human Rights Act 1998 affect people who have been arrested in this country? This particular Act provides that a public authority may act in a manner which is contrary to a person's human rights only if their actions are:

- Proportionate

- Legally based

- Necessary.

This means that the Human Rights Act 1998 does not actually prevent a person from being arrested; however, Article 5 of the European Convention on Human Rights states that every person has the right to liberty and security of person. In order for someone acting on behalf of a public authority to comply with Article 5, any arrest made must be both lawful and necessary.

14.5 Necessity test

Until recently, in order to comply with PACE, a constable only needed to show that an arrest was lawful and, whilst most arrests were probably justifiable, there was no specific requirement to show that they were also necessary. However, the Serious Organised Crime and Police Act 2005 amended s.24 of PACE so that now, when a constable makes an arrest, he or she must be able to show that it was necessary to do so, bringing s.24 in line with Article 5 above.

'Necessary' means 'essential, required, needed or obligatory'; in other words there was no other way of achieving the objective by less obtrusive means. More often than not, it will be necessary to arrest a person at the scene and this is recognised in s.24(5) of PACE, which lists a number of occasions when the necessity test is passed. This is illustrated in figure 14.1 below.

You will see from the figure that there will be many reasons where the arrest of the person is necessary at the time of the offence. The two most commonly used powers are where it is necessary to allow the prompt investigation of the offence – for example, evidence may be lost if the person is not arrested at the time – and when the disappearance of the person might hinder the investigation.

For police officers, there are other alternatives to actually arresting a person and taking them to a police station there and then. These alternatives should be considered, provided they do not interfere with any of the reasons listed in s.24(5) above.

Exercise 14B below describes some of the alternatives to making an arrest and has been partially filled in. Try to fill in the last column.

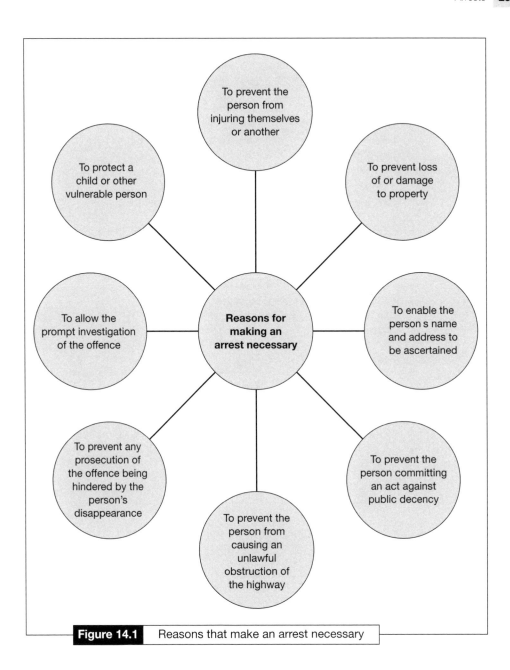

Figure 14.1 Reasons that make an arrest necessary

Exercise 14B

Power	Description	Benefits	Negatives
Street bail	The person may be bailed from the scene of the offence by a constable, to appear at a police station at some future date.	■ Allows the police time to investigate the offence while the person is on bail; ■ Allows the police to plan their workload more effectively; ■ Allows the police to spend more time on patrol.	
Fixed Penalty (or Disorder) Notice	The person may be given a fixed penalty notice at the scene, for minor criminal offences. They must pay the fine directly to the court.	■ Allows the police to spend more time on patrol; ■ Does not clog up the court calendar; ■ A quick remedy for more minor offences.	
Summons	The person may be summonsed to appear in court without ever being arrested.	■ Allows the police time to investigate the offence while the person is waiting to appear in court; ■ Allows the police to plan their workload more effectively; ■ Allows the police to spend more time on patrol.	

You may have considered some of the following issues:

Power	Description	Benefits	Negatives
Street bail	The person may be bailed from the scene of the offence by a constable, to appear at a police station at some future date.	■ Allows the police time to investigate the offence while the person is on bail; ■ Allows the police to plan their workload more effectively; ■ Allows the police to spend more time on patrol.	The person may: ■ fail to appear; ■ have given a false name; ■ interfere with witnesses or other evidence; ■ commit other offences before answering bail.

Fixed Penalty (or Disorder) Notice	The person may be given a fixed penalty notice at the scene, for minor criminal offences. They must pay the fine directly to the court.	■ Allows the police to spend more time on patrol; ■ Does not clog up the court calendar; ■ A quick remedy for more minor offences.	The person may: ■ fail to pay the fine; ■ have given a false name; ■ interfere with witnesses or other evidence; ■ commit other offences before paying the fine.
Summons	The person may be summonsed to appear in court without ever being arrested.	■ Allows the police time to investigate the offence while the person is waiting to appear in court; ■ Allows the police to plan their workload more effectively; ■ Allows the police to spend more time on patrol.	The process is lengthy and can take several months. Also, the person may: ■ fail to answer the summons; ■ have given a false name and address for the summons to be served; ■ interfere with witnesses or other evidence; ■ commit other offences before the court case.

The main barrier to the police using the above powers is often one of culture. For example, police officers may think:

'We've always arrested people for offences, so why should we change?'
'We'll get around it somehow.'
'We have a power of arrest, so why not use it?'

The government has driven through several changes in legislation to compel officers to seek alternatives to arresting people at the scene of offences and conveying them directly to the police station and, while the arresting officer can still make a choice at the scene, he or she will still have to demonstrate why the arrest was necessary at some future date.

Finally, under s.24A of PACE when members of the public make an arrest, they may only do so if:

1 they have reasonable grounds for believing that it is necessary to do so, to prevent the person in question from:

- causing physical injury to him/herself or any other person;

- suffering physical injury;

- causing loss of or damage to property; or

- making off before a constable can assume responsibility for him/her

and

2 it appears to the person making the arrest that it is not reasonably practicable for a constable to make the arrest instead.

The obvious practical difficulty in implementing these aspects of s.24A is that most members of the public will be completely unaware of their powers and responsibilities and they will assume they have the automatic power to conduct a 'citizen's arrest' without any other considerations.

14.6 What an arrested person must be told

Reasons for the arrest

Under s.28 of PACE, a person must be told of the fact that he or she has been arrested, and why he/she has been arrested as soon as practicable. This information must be given even if it is obvious, so that the person has a clear understanding that he or she is not free to leave. The information must be given in simple, non-technical language that the person would understand. The information can even be given in colloquial language: for example, in the case of *Christie* v *Leachinsky* [1947] AC 573, the court was satisfied when the officer told the defendant 'You're nicked'. The arrested person does not need not be told if he or she has escaped before the information can be given.

The Caution

When a constable has made an arrest, he or she must caution the person, unless it is impracticable to do so by reason of that person's condition or behaviour at the time, (in other words if they are violent, drunk or attempting to escape). The person must be cautioned using the following words:

'You do not have to say anything. But it may harm your defence if you do not mention when questioned something which you later rely on in Court. Anything you do say may be given in evidence.'

Unfortunately, unlike s.28 above, the arresting officer is not required to explain the caution in simple terms, in a language that the person would understand!

Try exercise 14C.

Exercise 14C

Try to explain what you think the caution means.

You may have considered something like this:

You do not have to say anything at this time. However, if at a future court case you attempt to rely on a fact or facts that you fail to mention now or during interview, the court will be entitled to ask itself, 'Why did they not mention these facts when given the opportunity to do so?' If the court comes to the conclusion that you could have mentioned the fact or facts when given the opportunity to do so, it may be entitled to believe that you have made those facts up since the interview. If you do say anything now or during an interview, what you say may be presented to the court as evidence.

There is no definitive answer to this question, but police officers are often asked to explain the caution in interviews, especially when the arrested person is considered to be vulnerable. In simple terms, the caution is intended to meet a balance of needs for the individual (and their right to remain silent) and the needs of the criminal justice system (and its right to hear all the evidence available).

14.7 Use of force when making an arrest

Under s.117 of PACE, a police constable may use reasonable force in order to arrest a person. There is no specific definition of what might be 'reasonable' force at the time of the arrest, but the courts may consider a range of situations faced by police officers from the trivial (where a police officer may simply place a hand on someone's arm), to the use of firearms and possible use of lethal force.

Exercise 14D

What might the courts consider in deciding whether force used was reasonable?

You may have considered some of the following:

- The nature or seriousness of the offence

- The person's behaviour at the time

- The risk to the officer, other colleagues or other members of the public

- Whether or not the person had a weapon with them (and the type of weapon)

- Whether the person was trying to escape

- Whether or not the person had a previous history of violence and the officer was aware of this fact

- Whether the arrested person was accompanied by other people who were likely to use force

- Whether the arresting officer was alone or accompanied

- The skills of the arrested person (i.e. trained in martial arts)

- The skills of the arresting officer

- The age, size or gender of the arrested person

- The age, size or gender of the arresting officer.

There is no definitive answer, but some of the above situations may cause the court to consider whether the force used was necessary. Members of the public have the same powers under s.117 to use force when making arrests. However, whereas police officers are issued with appropriate equipment and receive regular conflict management training, private citizens often do not. There are often incidents when members of the public over-extend their powers, which receive adverse publicity. These cases often prompt considerable debate as to what force is 'reasonable' in the circumstances.

14.8 Searching arrested people

In this final section, we will examine the powers given to police officers to search arrested people. The powers to search such people are contained in s.32 of PACE.

Where a police officer has arrested a person elsewhere than at a police station, he or she may search that person if there is reason to believe the person may:

- Present a danger either to himself/herself or other people (including the arresting officer)

- Be in possession of any object which that person may use to injure himself/herself or another

- Be in possession of anything which that person might use to escape from lawful custody

- Be evidence in relation to an offence.

The searching officer may seize and retain anything found in any of the above categories.

The power of search in such circumstances is vital to ensuring the safety of the arresting officers and other people, as well as retaining evidence. It is normal practice to conduct such searches as soon as possible after arrest, and in any case before the individual is placed in a police vehicle.

There are strict guidelines as to how such searches are conducted. For example, s.32(3) states that a search may only be conducted to the extent that is reasonably required for the purpose of discovering any such thing or evidence. This means once a police officer discovers the item he or she was looking for, there must be a good reason to continue to search a person for other items.

Finally, when a constable conducts a search in public, he or she may only require a person to remove their outer clothing, such as their coat, jacket or gloves, to ensure a person's privacy. A constable may conduct a more thorough search at the scene of the arrest if necessary, but this may only be done out of the view of the public.

Suggested further reading

Doak, J. and McGourlay, C., *Criminal Evidence in Context* (Exeter: Law Matters Publishing, 2005)

Johnston, D. and Hutton, G., *Blackstones Police Manual 2007, Vol 2 Evidence and Procedure* (Oxford: Oxford University Press, 2006)

Sampson, F., *Blackstones Police Manual 2007, Vol 1 Crime* (Oxford: Oxford University Press. 2006)

Useful websites

http://www.cps.gov.uk/index.html
The Crown Prosecution Service website which has much interesting information regarding criminal investigations, proof, etc.

Chapter 15

The Custody Suite

This chapter supports the following National Occupational Standards which describe the performance and competence required of a probationer officer.

Unit No.	Unit title
1A1	Use police actions in a fair and justified way.
1A4	Foster people's equality, diversity and rights.
2C2	Prepare for, and participate in, planned policing operations.
2C3	Arrest, detain or report individuals.
2G2	Conduct investigations.
2G4	Finalise investigations.
SH1	Interview victims and witnesses.
2H2	Interview suspects.
2I1	Search individuals.
2I2	Search vehicles, premises and land.
2J1	Prepare and submit case files.
2K1	Escort detained persons.
2K2	Present detained persons to custody.
4C1	Develop your own knowledge and practice.
4G2	Ensure your own actions reduce risks to health and safety.

15.1 Police detention

Reference was made in Chapter 1 to the passing of the Police and Criminal Evidence Act (PACE) 1984 and its effect on policing since the mid-1980s. This Act of Parliament created a whole new set of rules for the police service in respect of the treatment of people who come into contact with the police. Perhaps the most significant area of policing affected by PACE is the detention, treatment and welfare of people who have been arrested and taken to a police station. PACE is accompanied by the Codes of Practice, a set of rules which give guidance to the police as to how PACE should be implemented by police officers.

The Human Rights Act 1998 incorporated most of the European Convention on Human Rights into UK legislation and provided an opportunity for people from this country to seek justice in our domestic courts for alleged breaches of human rights by a public authority (including the police). The Human Rights Act is also discussed in Chapter 5 Ethical Policing Values and in other chapters throughout this book.

How does the Human Rights Act 1998 affect people held in police detention in this country? This particular Act provides that a public authority may act in a manner which is contrary to a person's human rights only if their actions are:

- Proportionate
- Legally based
- Necessary.

This means that the Human Rights Act 1998 does not actually prevent a person from being arrested and detained at a police station; however, before accepting a person into custody the police must be satisfied that the arrest was proportionate and necessary and that there was a legal reason for doing so (for example the person was arrested for theft).

The European Convention on Human Rights contains a number of Articles, which are reflected in the Human Rights Act 1998. Exercise 15A below contains the articles that mostly affect people detained in police custody. Try to think of an example for each Article as to how the actions of the police may infringe a person's human rights. Article 2 has been completed for you.

Exercise 15A

ARTICLE NUMBER	COMMENT	EXAMPLE
Article 2 The Right to Life	Everyone's right to life shall be protected by law.	A person in police detention was allowed to commit suicide due to the negligence of the people working in the custody office.
Article 3 Torture	No one shall be subjected to torture or to inhuman or degrading treatment or punishment.	
Article 5 The Right to Liberty and Security	Everyone has the right to liberty and security of person.	
Article 6 The Right to a Fair Trial	In the determination of his civil rights and obligations or of any criminal charge against him, everyone is entitled to a fair and public hearing within a reasonable time.	
Article 8 Right to Private Life	Everyone has the right to respect for his private and family life, his home and his correspondence.	

You may have considered the following:

ARTICLE NUMBER	COMMENT	EXAMPLE
Article 2 *The Right to Life*	Everyone's right to life shall be protected by law.	A person in police detention was allowed to commit suicide due to the negligence of the people working in the custody office.
Article 3 *Torture*	No one shall be subjected to torture or to inhuman or degrading treatment or punishment.	A person in police detention has had their clothing confiscated and has been forced to be interviewed in their underwear.
Article 5 *The Right to Liberty and Security*	Everyone has the right to liberty and security of person.	A person has been detained in a police station when the original arrest was unlawful.
Article 6 *The Right to a Fair Trial*	In the determination of his civil rights and obligations or of any criminal charge against him, everyone is entitled to a fair and public hearing within a reasonable time.	A person has been arrested and detained in police custody and has been released on bail for further enquiries. Because of the inefficiency of the investigating officer, the person's bail was extended several times causing a delay to the trial.
Article 8 *Right to Private Life*	Everyone has the right to respect for his private and family life, his home and his correspondence.	A person has been arrested and detained in police custody and the police conducted a search of their home. The searching officers confiscated items that were private to the individual and were not connected to the case.

As a general rule of thumb, if a person who has been detained in police custody is treated in accordance with PACE and the Codes of Practice, their human rights should be protected. If, however, the police fail to comply with PACE and the Codes of Practice, they may well find themselves being taken to court under the 1998 Act, not to mention the fact that the case against the individual may be lost.

Returning to PACE, this particular Act of Parliament and the Codes of Practice have been amended many times since 1984, often to allow the police to take advantage of progress made in science and technology. With this in mind, try to complete exercise 15B.

Exercise 15B

Think of two examples of advances in science or technology in the past 20 years that have assisted the police and which may have affected people being held in police detention.

You may have considered:

- Video conferencing

- DNA profiling

- Automated fingerprinting

- X-rays or ultrasound scans of people arrested for drug trafficking offences

- Intimate searches of people arrested for drug trafficking offences

- Taking fingerprints on mobile data devices away from police stations

- Taking footwear impressions for comparison with electronic databases

- Testing samples from detainees for the presence of Class A drugs.

15.2 Custody officers

In Chapter 14, Arrests, we saw that an arrested person must generally be taken to a police station. When that person arrives at a police station, he or she must be brought before a custody officer as soon as possible. The custody officer is a key individual in protecting an arrested person's right to liberty as he or she is responsible for deciding whether or not that person should be charged with an offence, released from police custody, or held at the police station for a period of time (we will be examining the reasons why a person may be held in custody without being charged later in this chapter). When a person is held in police custody, he or she is classed as being 'in police detention'.

As we saw above in the exercise on human rights, there is always potential for a police force to be sued for their treatment of individuals held in police detention. For this reason, there are firm rules as to who may act as a custody officer. There is a requirement under PACE for a custody officer to be 'appointed' by the chief of police for an area. This person must have the required experience and training to perform this role. Section 36(3) of PACE states that the person appointed as a custody officer must be 'at least the rank of sergeant'.

PACE goes on to say that the custody officer must remain impartial and independent from the investigation of a person in police detention. However, if the custody officer must be a sergeant, in other words a police officer, how does this affect their impartiality and independence? Consider this for a moment and try to answer the question in exercise 15C below.

Exercise 15C

Can police officers acting as custody officers be truly independent? Try to provide reasons to support your answer.

This question has caused significant debate and, perhaps, some of the answers lie in more recent legislation. In Chapter 1, we saw that the police service is made up of more than just police officers. The agenda of modernisation also applies in the custody office. The Police Reform Act 2002 allowed the 'civilianisation' of jailers and allowed police forces to appoint 'detention officers' who are non-police officers. Whilst this measure was mostly designed to allow the return of police constables (who used to act as jailers) to front-line policing, the appointment of police staff instead of police officers in the custody office creates some degree of impartiality.

However, detention officers are not given the same decision-making powers as custody officers – they are mainly employed to take care of the welfare needs of detainees. This brings us back to whether or not police officers can be independent and impartial when acting as custody officers. The Serious Organised Crime and Police Act 2005 caused a significant change to PACE. The alteration now allows the 'civilianisation' of custody officers. Police forces may now appoint 'staff custody officers' who are non-police officers and who will be given the same powers of detention as a police sergeant. Once again, this measure will free up police officer posts to front-line policing but, more importantly, decisions in the custody office in the future will be made by people who are independent of the police service.

15.3 Custody records

Under PACE, when a custody officer makes a decision to hold a person in police detention, he or she must make a written record of the reasons. This information will be recorded on a custody record. Most police forces now have electronic versions of custody records that are completed at the time decisions are being made. Before this technology was available, custody records were hand-written and could take a considerable amount of time to complete.

Custody records must be completed for each detainee even if several people have been arrested for the same offence at the same time. The custody record will act as a diary of events for the whole time the person is held in police detention and the custody officer (or detention officer) must update the record each time a decision is made about a detainee and sign the record for accuracy (this includes electronic custody records where an electronic signature may be used). Figure 15.1 shows a typical example of the front page of a custody record.

Custody record

Police Station: ....   **Reference Number:** ....

Arrest & Detention

Time and Date of Arrest:	Arresting Officer(s)
Place of arrest:	O.I.C.:
Time Arrived at Station:	Detention Authorised Yes / No
Grounds for arrest:	
Necessity criteria:	
Reason for Detention: Prisoner's comment:	

Custody Officer:	Time and Date:

Name: Maiden Name:	

DOB: Place of Birth:	Occupation:

Address:

Male /Female	Ethnic appearance:		Height:	Build:
Colour of Eyes:	Colour of Hair	Visible Injuries:	Illnesses:	Nationality:
If School Pupil School attending:			Parent or Guardian:	

Figure 15.1 A typical custody record

Prisoners Property

Prisoners Property	Property Subject to Charge
The above list is an accurate record of my property. **Signature:**	The above list is an accurate record of property that has been taken from me. **Signature**
The above property numbered ......to....... has been retained for the following reason: Rank and Number:	Searched by: Rank and number:
Property Returned: I confirm that I have received the above listed property number ..... to ..... **Signature:** Time and Date:	

Figure 15.1   Continued

Prisoners Rights

You have the right to free and independent legal advice. Do you wish to consult with a solicitor in person or by telephone? **Yes / No**	**Signature:**
If Yes which solicitor? or Duty solicitor?	**Signature:**
Time and Date informed / spoken to by telephone:	
If no, what is your reason for declining legal advice?	
Do you wish to have anyone informed of your arrest? **Yes / No**	**Signature:**
If Yes Who do you want informed? [For vulnerable persons details of person to be informed] Name: Address: Telephone Number:	
Time and Date requested:	Time and Date informed:
Do you wish to consult with a copy of the codes of practice concerning your rights and your treatment during your detention? **Yes / No**	**Signature:**
For **foreign Nationals** did you wish your consulate to be informed? **Yes / No**	**Signature:**
I can confirm that I have been provided with a form explaining my legal rights	**Signature:**

Do you agree to have your fingerprints and photograph taken? **Yes / No**	**Signature:**
Do you agree to provide a sample for DNA profiling? **Yes / No**	**Signature:**

Disposal

Charged with offence(s) **Yes / No**	Officer Charging:
Time and Date:	Charge Accepted By:
Released on Bail: **Yes / No**	Bail Granted By:
Details of Magistrates Court: Date and Time:	
Time and Date left station:	Details of any complaint: **Signature:**

Figure 15.1   Continued

Detention Log

Date	Time	Record of detention	Name and rank

Figure 15.1 Continued

As you can see from figure 15.1 above, the first part of the custody record typically contains information about the person's arrest, such as the time, date and place and offence. Once this information has been given by the arresting officer, the custody officer must make a decision whether or not to detain the person or release them.

If the decision is made to detain the person, the custody officer must make a written record as to why it is necessary to do so and must also record the fact that the person has been given information about their rights (these are dealt with in more depth in section 15.5 Detainees' Entitlements below). Custody records must also contain information about any property confiscated from a detainee, property which was taken for safekeeping, any illness the detainee may have, and any medication that needs to be taken. Once the above formalities have been recorded on the custody record, the custody officer and detention officer will keep a running log of decisions made in respect of a detainee.

It will be obvious from the above that there is a considerable amount of administration attached to each person's detention.

Exercise 15D

Consider the advantages and disadvantages of keeping custody records.

You may have considered the following:

Advantages

■ There will be an accurate and up-to-date record of the person's detention.

■ If mistakes are made, they are highlighted in the custody record.

■ The detainee or their solicitor may wish to see a copy of the custody record in future.

■ The court may wish to see a copy of the custody record in future to ensure PACE and the Codes of Practice have been complied with.

■ If there is a complaint by the detainee about their detention, the custody record will show whether or not they have been treated fairly.

■ A new custody officer may come on duty midway through a person's detention. He or she will be able to view all decisions that have been made.

Disadvantages

■ Each record takes a considerable amount of time to complete.

■ In a large custody office, there could be 20 detainees – the custody officer has ultimate responsibility for the accuracy of all custody records.

- If the custody officer or detention officer is busy, entries on the custody record may be late and therefore inaccurate.

- If a computer crashes, entries may be lost and the custody officer will have to back up the information in written form.

On the whole, keeping accurate custody records will assist the custody officer. While the advantages above may seem like a list of things that may hang a custody officer out to dry, if the record is accurate, it will also provide protection from any future complaints made by a detainee about their treatment whilst in police detention. The Codes of Practice state that decisions on the custody record must be updated as soon as is reasonably practicable. This offers a solution to late entries on the records, where the custody officer or detention officer has been busy with other duties in the custody office.

It should be noted that a solicitor may examine their client's custody record at any time while that person is in police detention. Also, the detainee (or their solicitor) may ask for a copy of the custody record at any time after they have been released from police detention – this entitlement lasts for 12 months after their release.

15.4 Risk assessments and deaths in police custody

Ask most experienced custody officers what the most worrying aspect of their job is and they will invariably point to the risk of a person dying, or committing suicide while in their detention. Any death in police custody will be subject of a coroner's inquest. It will also be investigated by the Independent Police Complaints Commission (IPCC).

The impact for the police force involved is also likely to be significant. Inevitably, there will be poor publicity and possibly suspicion by family members, the community and the press that the police should have done more to prevent a tragedy, even if the custody officer is eventually exonerated at the conclusion of an inquiry.

The number of deaths in police custody in the UK rose steadily between 1981, when statistics were first counted and the recorded figure was 49, and the year from 1 April 2002 to 31 March 2003, when there were 104 deaths. However, it should be noted that the Home Office counting rules were changed during this period to include the death of any person who had been in contact with the police, not just those who are in police detention. The latest Home Office figures show that there was an overall decrease in people who died in such circumstances during the year from 1 April 2003 to 31 March 2004 when there were 100 deaths.

One area of concern for the Home Office has been the number of people from minority ethnic groups who die in police custody. This concern was heightened when the figures were produced in the years 2002–2003 when 22 such deaths occurred, compared with 7 in 2001–2002. However, a report published in July 2004 as a result of an independent investigation on behalf of the Home Office suggested that while there are grounds for concern relating to some aspects of the general treatment of all detainees, there is little evidence to suggest that this concern can be directly linked to racial stereotyping, perceptions or different treatment of those from ethnic minorities.

Table 15.1 below displays the figures for deaths in custody by minority ethnic groups:

Ethnic origin	Number of deaths in 2002/2003	Number of deaths in 2003/2004
White	82	90
Asian	4	2
Black	17	7
Other	1	1
Total	104	100

Table 15.1 Deaths in custody

The custody officer has a positive duty of care to persons being held in detention, to protect them from harm. Remember that the duty is reinforced by Article 2 of the European Convention on Human Rights (right to life).

So what assistance is given to custody officers to prevent deaths in police custody? The PACE Codes of Practice contains specific guidance and advice to custody officers relating to the care and treatment of detainees. Within this guidance are strict instructions that custody officers must risk-assess people in police detention who may be 'at risk'. In addition, Guidance on the Safer Detention and Handling of Persons in Police Custody is currently being produced by the National Centre for Policing Excellence (NCPE), on behalf of the Association of Chief Police Officers (ACPO) and the Home Office.

'At risk' detainees fall into three broad categories:

■ Those at risk from suicide and self-harm

■ Those at risk because of illnesses or injuries

■ Those at risk because they are under the influence of alcohol or drugs.

Custody officers are required to fill in medical questionnaires in respect of all detainees, which means that a person being detained who is ill may be seen by a doctor. This should reduce the risk of people dying in police custody through illness. However, the risk of death through suicide or as a result of alcohol or drug use is not so easy to control or assess. A number of inquiries and reports have been published on these subjects and table 15.2 provides a summary of them.

Contributing factor	Research results
1. Mental health problems	In the chapter focusing only on deaths in custody, the Commission described how 50% of all those people who died in or following police custody had a prior indication of mental health problems.
2. Alcohol/drunkenness	1,575 custody records were examined relating to three metropolitan police stations. During this research, it was discovered that alcohol was a factor in the arrest of almost a third of the detainees.
3. Alcohol/drunkenness	Between April 1999 and March 2000, 70 people died in 'police custody', though only 10% of these deaths took place in police stations. Alcohol was a contributing factor in the majority of the cases.
4. Alcohol/drunkenness	86% of deaths in police custody were linked to recent alcohol consumption or chronic alcohol abuse. In 81% of head injury deaths in police custody, the deceased was suspected of intoxication and in many of these cases the link may not have been apparent to officers at the time of arrest. Further, alcohol-related death was cited as the second most prominent cause of death in police custody following death by hanging, and 42% of those who died as a result of hanging were thought to be intoxicated with alcohol or drugs.
5. Suicide or self-harm	Statistics show that the first five hours of a person's detention time is a high risk period for suicide or self-harm.
6. Drug abuse	Research was conducted into 43 drug-related deaths in police care or custody between 1998 and 2002: ■ 90% of the sample were male and 86% were white with an average age of 32; ■ the most commonly used drug was cocaine which had been consumed by more than half; ■ 39 of the 43 deaths involved the use of more than one substance, (one person had consumed alcohol and six different drugs); ■ mental health problems were much more prevalent among drinkers and drug users; ■ On average individuals were perceived to have fallen ill about five hours after the initial contact with police.

Research findings:

1. Police Complaints Commission presentation of evidence to the Joint Committee on Human Rights inquiry into Deaths in Custody (2003).

2. Home Office Research Findings 171, 2003.

3. Dr David Best and Amakai Kefas—The Role of Alcohol in Police-Related Deaths between 2000 and 2001 (Home Office, 2000).

4. Giles and Sandrin (1992).

5. Lancashire Constabulary, 'Self-harm and Suicides by Detained Persons' (1992).

6. Association of Police Surgeons study (1998–2002).

Table 15.2   Summary of reports on deaths in custody

Apart from the factors of illness, suicidal tendencies and alcohol/drug abuse, custody officers must consider two other major factors known as positional asphyxia and excited delirium (also known as acute exhaustive mania). Table 15.3 provides an outline of these conditions.

Condition	Description	Symptoms
Positional asphyxia	Positional asphyxia can occur when the person has been involved in a violent confrontation, and they are suffering from exertion. The person may also be suffering from the effects of alcohol or drugs, or may be overweight.	The person may be in danger if left in one of the following positions which may affect their ability to breathe: ■ lying face down; ■ sitting against a wall, with their head forward restricting the windpipe; ■ slumped forward where the chest or abdomen is compressed.
Excited delirium/ acute exhaustive mania	People who suffer from this condition are often found to be under the influence of drugs (usually cocaine) and/or alcohol. They may also be suffering from a psychiatric illness.	A person suffering from this condition may show extraordinary strength and will struggle violently, with no apparent regard for pain or CS incapacitant sprays. The main danger from this condition is the person suffering from a heart attack or similar condition.

Table 15.3 Two major factors in death in custody

There has been recognition for many years that people who are incapable through drink or drugs, or suffering from mental illness, would usually be better and more safely cared for in dedicated, secure medical facilities rather than at a police station. However, since such facilities are not available, the custody officer has a central role in protecting 'at risk' detainees. Figure 15.2 shows the importance of the role of the custody officer in these circumstances.

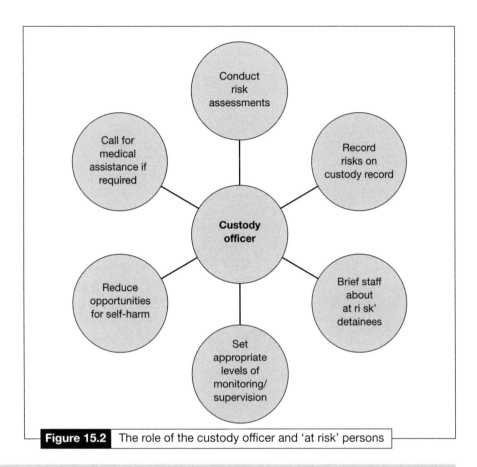

Figure 15.2   The role of the custody officer and 'at risk' persons

15.5 Detainees' entitlements

When a detainee is brought to a police station under arrest, the custody officer must make sure the person is told in a language that they understand about the following rights:

1 The right to have someone informed of their arrest

2 The right to consult privately with a solicitor for free independent advice

3 The right to consult the Codes of Practice.

The detainee will be given a notice similar to the one illustrated in figure 15.3 below.

The following rights and entitlements are guaranteed to you under the law in England and Wales and comply with the European Convention on human rights

Remember your rights
1 Tell the police if you want a solicitor to help you while you are at the police station. It is free.
2 Tell the police if you want somone to be told that you are at the police station. It is free.
3 Tell the police if you want to look at their rule-book called the Codes of Practice.

You will find more details about these rights inside

Figure 15.3 Notice of entitlement

The notice forms part of a booklet produced to help people understand their rights. It has been made available in 43 different languages by the Home Office to cater for people who do not understand English. In addition, the custody officer will have access to Language Line, a telephone service that provides an interpreter who may speak to the detainee in their own language to explain their rights. An interpreter will also be brought to the police station if the person is to be interviewed.

It should be noted that the above are **continuing** rights that may be exercised at any stage during the period in custody and, if the detainee is moved to another police station, he or she must be informed of these rights again.

In addition to the above rights, a detainee may also be allowed to make one telephone call and have access to writing materials. The custody officer also has the discretion to allow the detainee a visit at the cells.

Right to have someone informed of the arrest

The detainee may decline to have someone informed of his or her arrest, but if the person wishes to have someone told, it must be done as soon as is practicable.

Exercise 15E

Write down a list of individuals you think a detainee might ask to be informed of their arrest.

The Codes of Practice suggest that the following list of people may be notified:

- A friend

- A relative

- Another person who is known to the detainee or who is likely to take an interest in his/her welfare.

This means that if the person asks to have the Prime Minister or the Queen informed of their arrest, the custody officer may politely decline the request!

If a juvenile or vulnerable adult is detained, the police have a duty to inform an appropriate adult, who should be asked to attend the police station to act on the detainee's behalf.

Right to consult with a solicitor

This is a separate right to having someone informed of the arrest. Therefore, the detainee may exercise both of these rights. The difference between the two is that a friend or relative is simply informed of the person's presence at the police station and, unless the detainee is a juvenile or vulnerable adult, that person will not be attending the police station to assist the detainee. On the other hand, a solicitor will be expected to give advice to a detainee either by telephone or by attending the police station in person.

Delay in allowing a person their rights

Every person has a fundamental human right not to be held incommunicado at a police station (i.e. held without another person being aware that they are there), and to consult with a solicitor while at a police station. However, the police can lawfully delay these rights in certain, very restricted, circumstances. This is illustrated in figure 15.4 overleaf.

An indictable offence is one which is usually tried in the crown court. This means that such delays may only be authorised for more serious offences. Note that these rights may only be delayed (they may not be denied altogether) until the reason for the delay has ceased (i.e. there is no longer a risk of injury to a person, or property has been recovered).

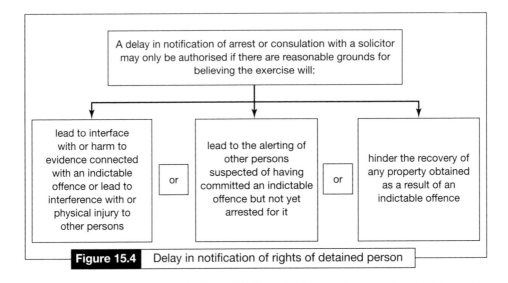

A delay in notification of arrest or consulation with a solicitor may only be authorised if there are reasonable grounds for believing the exercise will:

lead to interface with or harm to evidence connected with an indictable offence or lead to interference with or physical injury to other persons	*or*	lead to the alerting of other persons suspected of having committed an indictable offence but not yet arrested for it	*or*	hinder the recovery of any property obtained as a result of an indictable offence

Figure 15.4   Delay in notification of rights of detained person

15.6 Detention times

Unsurprisingly, a person may not be held in police detention indefinitely. PACE contains strict guidelines as to how long a person may be kept in police detention and, just as importantly, how their period of detention is monitored.

Extending detention

Generally, a person who has been arrested and brought into police detention must either be charged with an offence, or released from custody, within the first 24 hours. If a person is detained for longer than this period, their detention will be unlawful and the police could be sued. In most cases, 24 hours will be a sufficient period of time for the police to fully investigate an offence.

However, the police obviously deal with a variety of offences, some more serious than others. In the more serious or complex cases, the investigating officer may find that he or she needs more than 24 hours to deal with the detained person. In these cases, the officer may apply to a superintendent of police to authorise a person's detention time to be extended. The superintendent may authorise a further 12 hours' detention time.

The maximum period that a person may be held in police detention, where that detention has been authorised by the police, is 36 hours. If this period is insufficient, the investigating officer may apply to the magistrates' court for a further extension. If this request is granted, the person may be detained for a further 36 hours (total detention time of 72 hours to this point – or three days). The police may make one final request to the court for an extension to this time and if the application is successful, the detainee may be held for a further 24 hours. This means that the maximum time period that any one person may be held in police detention is 96 hours (or four days).

Much has been made recently of the police service's inability to deal with terrorism cases in the normal time period of four days. The provisions of the Terrorism Act 2000 allow the police, in terrorism cases, to hold a suspect in police detention for up to two weeks. This is broken down into an initial period of 48 hours (as opposed to 24 hours in ordinary cases), followed by an application to the court for an extended detention period of five days, followed by a further application to extend the detention to a maximum period of two weeks.

Proposals were made by the Home Office in December 2005 to extend the detention period in terrorism cases to three months. However, this move was rejected by the House of Lords. The issue is still under review and it is likely that sometime in the near future, the detention period of two weeks will be extended.

Table 15.4 provides a quick guide to the maximum detention times, and who may authorise them.

Type of offence	Maximum period of detention authorised	Authorised by whom?	Accumulated detention period
Indictable offence	Initial 24 hours	Custody officer	24 hours
Indictable offence	Additional 12 hours	Superintendent	36 hours
Indictable offence	Additional 36 hours	Magistrates' court	72 hours
Indictable offence	Additional 36 hours	Magistrates' court	96 hours
Terrorist offence	Initial 48 hours	Custody officer	48 hours
Terrorist offence	Additional 5 days	Senior district judge	7 days
Terrorist offence	Additional 7 days	Senior district judge	14 days

Table 15.4   Maximum detention times and authorising persons

Reviewing detention

When a person is held in police custody, PACE says that the person's detention should be reviewed periodically by an inspector. Section 40(3) of PACE states that the following timetable should be adopted:

1 The first review shall be not later than six hours after the detention was first authorised by a custody officer

2 The second review shall be not later than nine hours after the first

3 Subsequent reviews shall be at intervals of not more than nine hours.

The main function for the inspector conducting the review is to monitor the progress of the investigation. He or she has a duty to speak to the investigating officer and the custody officer to make sure that there is still a good reason for keeping a person in police detention. If the inspector believes that the detention is not necessary, he or she must make sure that the detainee is either charged with an offence, or released from custody immediately.

When conducting a review, the reviewing officer must adopt the following procedures highlighted in figure 15.5 below.

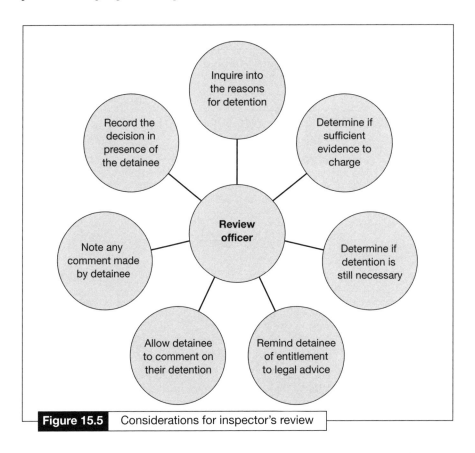

| **Figure 15.5** | Considerations for inspector's review |

Reviews are an important part of the detention process and provide additional protection of a detainee's human rights.

15.7 Methods of prosecution

From a police perspective, the main purpose of arresting a suspect and detaining them at a police station is to investigate whether or not they have been involved in a criminal offence. When it has been determined by the police that a person has been involved in a criminal offence, a decision must be made as to what legal action should be taken.

Not every person who is guilty of a criminal offence will be taken to court. If they were, the whole legal system in the UK would grind to a halt and police officers would probably find themselves appearing in court to give evidence more often than they are on patrol. Therefore, the legal system relies heavily on alternative methods of prosecution.

Figure 15.6 offers a quick guide as to how a person may be dealt with when it has been determined that he or she has committed a criminal offence.

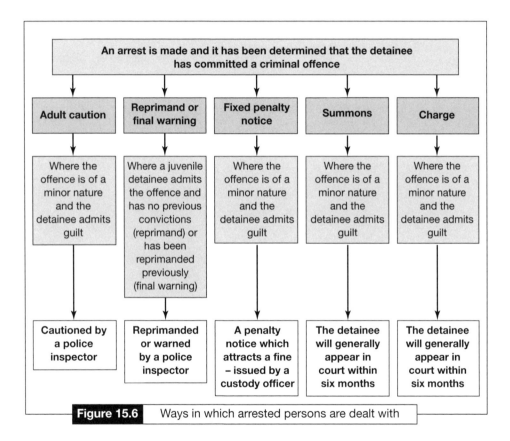

Figure 15.6 Ways in which arrested persons are dealt with

While any of the above methods may be used by the police to deal with an offender, the most common method of disposal is to charge a person with an offence, for which they will later appear in court.

15.8 Bail

When a person has been charged with an offence, the custody officer will normally release the detainee on bail. When a person is released on bail, it means that they have an obligation to appear in court at a time and date set by the custody officer. This period will usually be not more than two weeks and the custody officer can set conditions to the bail to prevent the accused from failing to appear in court, interfering with witnesses or committing further offences. Below are the types of conditions that may be imposed on a person charged with an offence by a custody officer in these circumstances:

- To report to his/her local police station (daily, weekly or at other intervals)
- To surrender his/her passport
- Not to enter a certain area or building, or to go within a specified distance of a specified address
- Not to contact (whether directly or indirectly) the victim of the alleged offence and/or any other probable prosecution witness
- A curfew between set times (i.e. when it is thought the accused might commit offences or come into contact with witnesses).

15.9 Detention after charge

Sometimes the custody officer may decide that the risk of the person re-offending, interfering with witnesses or failing to appear in court is too great to release them on bail. In these cases, he or she may decide to keep the person in police detention until the next available court. The police will then ask the court to remand the detainee in prison for the duration of the case.

The custody officer and the court will have to be mindful of the fact that such a decision will have an impact on a detainee's human rights; therefore, this decision may only be made in certain circumstances.

> **Exercise 15F**
>
> Write down what circumstances you think a custody officer would have to consider regarding granting bail to an arrested person.

The power for custody officers to detain people after they have been charged comes from section 38 of PACE, which states that:

'Where a person is arrested for an offence, the custody officer shall order his/her release from police detention, either on bail or without bail, unless any of the following reasons apply:

- His/her name or address cannot be ascertained or the custody officer has reasonable grounds for doubting whether the name or address given is correct

- The custody officer has reasonable grounds for believing that the person arrested will fail to appear in court to answer to bail

- The custody officer has reasonable grounds for believing that the detention of the person arrested is necessary to prevent him/her from committing an offence

- The custody officer has reasonable grounds for believing that the detention of the person arrested is necessary to prevent him/her from causing physical injury to any other person or from causing loss of or damage to property

- The custody officer has reasonable grounds for believing that the detention of the person arrested is necessary to prevent him/her from interfering with the administration of justice or with the investigation of offences or of a particular offence

- The custody officer has reasonable grounds for believing that the detention of the person arrested is necessary for his/her own protection.'

The court will have to consider the same grounds as a custody officer when taking the decision to remand a person to a prison while they wait for their court case to be dealt with. This decision will normally be reserved for people who have committed more serious offences, or where the person has shown in the past that they have a tendency to behave in a way listed above.

Suggested further reading

Doak, J. and McGourlay, C., *Criminal Evidence in Context* (Exeter: Law Matters Publishing, 2005)

Johnston, D. and Hutton, G., *Blackstones Police Manual 2007, Vol 2 Evidence and Procedure* (Oxford: Oxford University Press, 2006)

Sampson, F., *Blackstones Police Manual 2007, Vol 1 Crime* (Oxford: Oxford University Press, 2006)

Useful websites

http://www.cps.gov.uk/index.html

The Crown Prosecution Service website which has much interesting information regarding criminal investigations, proof, etc.

Chapter 16

Roads Policing

This chapter supports the following National Occupational Standards which describe the performance and competence required of a probationer officer.

Unit No.	Unit title
1A1	Use police actions in a fair and justified way.
1A2	Communicate effectively with members of communities.
1A4	Foster people's equality, diversity and rights.
1B9	Provide initial support to individuals affected by offending or anti-social behaviour and assess their needs for further support.
2A1	Gather and submit information that has the potential to support policing objectives.
2C2	Prepare for, and participate in, planned policing operations.
2C3	Arrest, detain or report individuals.
2G2	Conduct investigations.
2G4	Finalise investigations.
SH1	Interview victims and witnesses.
2H2	Interview suspects.
2J1	Prepare and submit case files.
2J2	Present evidence in court and at other hearings.
2K1	Escort detained persons.
2K2	Present detained persons to custody.
4C1	Develop your own knowledge and practice.
4G2	Ensure your own actions reduce risks to health and safety.

16.1 Introduction

The quotation below is taken from the Association of Chief Police Officers (ACPO) Roads Policing Strategy, published in January 2005, and sets the scene for this chapter:

> 'Virtually everyone in the country uses roads every day, as drivers or as pedestrians. With 30 million vehicles in Great Britain, the roads are busy and hazardous. Their unlawful and anti-social use affects people's safety and sense of security. Bad road use also contributes to the 3,500 people killed and 35,000 people seriously injured each year on the roads.'

The police service has a key role in enforcing the lawful use of vehicles on the roads and promoting road safety.

In late 1993, the Traffic Committee of ACPO and the Home Office jointly commissioned the first in-depth study of the activities of traffic police officers, together with the identification of the objectives, performance indicators and costs associated with traffic policing. The subsequent report – *Traffic Policing: Activity and Organisation* produced by the Police Research Group in 1994 – found that:

> 'Some eight percent of police personnel are dedicated to traffic duties making this the second largest speciality, exceeded only by CID which absorbs15% of police manpower. In the current financial year, it is estimated that approximately £400 million will have been required to finance road traffic policing. This level of expenditure forms a significant part of the overall police budget and is itself primarily accounted for by manpower costs. (Traffic cars, equipment and capital costs also attract significant expenditure.)'

The study focused upon six police forces selected as broadly representative of the 43 police forces of England and Wales. These six forces provided a total sample of 1,242 traffic officers, which represents approximately 14 per cent of all traffic officers in England and Wales. The researches discovered that the main objectives of traffic officers at the time were to:

- Support divisional policing and divisional objectives, both criminal and traffic

- Reduce road traffic accidents (RTAs) by encouraging safer driving

- Secure compliance with traffic law

- Provide a rapid response to incidents of all kinds

- Maintain the free flow of traffic

- Provide specialist expertise, e.g. accident investigation, incident management

- Detect and investigate vehicle related crime

- Provide advice and assistance to the motoring public

- Prevent/detect excessive speed on roads, where possible by advice/education

- Foster effective traffic management

- Participate in and support specific divisional operations.

While the above research is now somewhat dated, the main objectives will be similar to those of present day traffic departments (now mostly known as roads policing departments) throughout the country. What is absent from the report is the recognition that road policing forms a large part of the work of most non-specialist front-line officers, as well as the more specialist roads policing departments.

Advances in technology, such as speed detection devices, have assisted the specialist officers to become more proactive in achieving the wider objectives – such as casualty reduction and targeting criminals who use roads – which are required by the joint Department for Transport and ACPO Roads Policing Strategy. This strategy is discussed in depth below.

16.2 Road safety and roads policing strategy

The government's road safety strategy *Tomorrow's roads – safer for everyone* published in March 2000 set out a framework for delivering further improvements in road safety over the next decade and established new long-term casualty reduction targets to be achieved by 2010.

The strategy contained more than 150 measures across ten key themes:

- Theme 1 – Safer for children

- Theme 2 – Safer drivers – training and testing

- Theme 3 – Safer drivers – drink, drugs and drowsiness

- Theme 4 – Safer infrastructure

- Theme 5 – Safer speeds

- Theme 6 – Safer vehicles

- Theme 7 – Safer motorcycling

- Theme 8 – Safety for pedestrians, cyclists and horse riders

- Theme 9 – Better enforcement

- Theme 10 – Promoting safer road use.

The themes listed above can be divided into two general areas:

1 Road safety

2 Enforcement.

In January 2005, an agreement was reached between ACPO, the Department for Transport and the Home Office to address the main issues contained in the *Tomorrow's roads – safer for everyone* report. As a result, the ACPO Roads Policing Strategy was produced. The strategy required the police to develop a proactive approach to roads policing in partnership with other agencies and authorities, and to focus on the following areas:

■ Denying criminals use of the roads by enforcing the law

■ Reducing road casualties

■ Tackling the threat of terrorism

■ Reducing anti-social use of the roads

■ Enhancing public confidence and reassurance by patrolling the roads.

Each of these will be examined separately below.

16.3 Denying criminals use of the roads by enforcing the law

Road policing should not be viewed in isolation from other core policing functions of reducing and preventing crime and disorder.

Exercise 16A

List five criminal activities that take place using vehicles.

You may have considered some of the following crimes illustrated in figure 16.1.

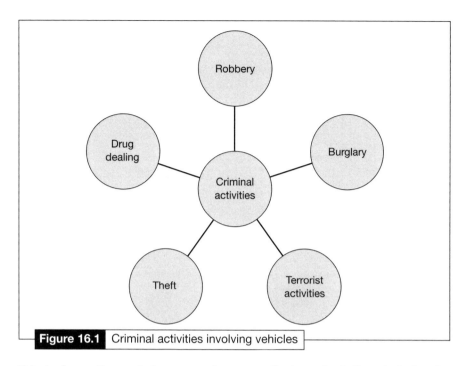

Figure 16.1 Criminal activities involving vehicles

Criminals use the roads to carry out a range of crimes, including theft, burglaries, robberies, drug dealing and terrorism. Research also shows that such people are likely to be:

- Driving illegally without driving licences

- Driving unroadworthy vehicles without an MOT – thereby causing a danger to other road users

- Driving without road tax – thereby adding to the cost of motoring for law-abiding road users

- Driving without insurance – again adding to the cost of motoring (estimated as adding £30 to the premium of each law-abiding motorist).

The police need to be proactive to target criminals and their vehicles, using some of the methods shown in table 16.1.

Enforcement strategy	Outcome
Target vehicles used by criminals to commit crime by proactive patrol.	Prevention and reduction in crime.
Target criminals who drive without licences.	Increased penalty points – leads to disqualification. Could also lead to confiscation of vehicles.
Target criminals who drive without MOTs.	Could lead to confiscation of vehicles.
Target criminals who drive without insurance.	Increased penalty points – leads to disqualification. Could also lead to confiscation of vehicles.
Target criminals who drive without road tax.	Financial punishment (up to five times the value of the tax), clamping and/or confiscation of the vehicle by the DVLA.

Table 16.1   Proactive roads policing

The police were given extended powers by the Serious Organised Crime and Police Act 2005 to confiscate vehicles being used without driving licences and insurance. This is in addition to the power to confiscate unroadworthy vehicles.

Police officers use intelligence to target known criminals and their vehicles, even when they are not suspected of committing crimes, in order to disrupt their activities. While this will not prevent crime altogether, such tactics should not be underestimated. The police can use legitimate methods to make sure criminals build up penalty points on their driving licences. This often leads to criminals being disqualified from driving and can lead to terms of imprisonment. The added bonus will be a financial cost if vehicles are confiscated.

16.4 Reducing road casualties

Performance measurement

In 2000, the Department for Transport and ACPO set challenging, joint casualty reduction targets to be achieved by 2010. The Road Safety Strategy includes three targets, to be compared with the average for 1994-98. A Road Safety Advisory Panel has been set up to help government in taking forward the road safety strategy and to review progress. Chaired by the road safety minister, the panel has members representing some of the main stakeholder bodies. Table 16.2 below shows the targets, and a review of achievements conducted in 2003.

Target	Achievement in 2003
40% reduction in the number of people killed or seriously injured in road accidents.	3,508 people were killed in road accidents and 33,707 were seriously injured. This is 22% below baseline – almost half way to the 40% target
50% reduction in the number of children killed or seriously injured.	171 children were killed in road accidents and 3,929 were seriously injured. This is 40% below baseline – over three quarters of the way to the 50% target
10% reduction in the slight casualty rate, expressed as the number of people slightly injured per 100 million vehicle kilometres.	For slight injuries the reported rate in 2003 was 17% below the baseline but it is possible that this is partly due to a drop in reporting of less serious accidents and casualties.

Table 16.2   Road safety targets and achievements

Research shows a higher incidence of road casualties amongst people from disadvantaged communities. To address this, the Department for Transport has placed pressure on Local Authorities, stating:

'For 'dealing with disadvantage', we want to see a faster rate of reduction in the total number of road casualties in the 88 local council areas that are eligible to receive Neighbourhood Renewal Funding (NRF) than for England as a whole. Total casualties in the 88 NRF areas in 2002 were 6.4% below the average for 1999–2001 compared with a 5.1% drop for England as a whole.'

Enforcement

One of the big tests facing the police service these days is how to meet the correct balance between enforcement and reduction. This is just as true for road policing as it is for crime. For example, should the service place a police officer or Police Community Support Officer (PCSO) on every street corner to reduce burglaries? Of course not – crime reduction figures are met with a mixture of:

- Targeting prolific offenders
- Sound investigation techniques
- Intelligence-led patrols
- Partnership work to educate young people
- Use of technology (e.g. DNA, fingerprinting)
- Target hardening and educating the public.

So how does the police service contribute to reducing casualties on the road? Try to think of some answers and attempt exercise 16B below.

Exercise 16B

How does the police service contribute to reducing casualties on the road?

Hopefully you didn't consider putting a police officer on every corner! Taking the burglary example a step further, how will more officers on patrol reduce road casualty figures? A current problem facing the service is tackling the use of mobile telephones by drivers. Almost everyone would agree that using a mobile phone whilst driving is dangerous – yet thousands of drivers do it. Of course if an officer sees someone using a phone while driving, they may issue a fixed penalty notice, but this relies heavily on the police being in the right place at the right time. The main tools available to officers are:

■ Enforcement wherever possible

■ Suitable punishments as a deterrent

■ Tactical and high visibility patrols when the roads are busy

■ Using CCTV to detect offenders

■ Members of the public reporting incidents

■ Education and publicity campaigns.

The list is not much different from the tactical options for reducing burglaries and will apply to most road traffic offences.

There are two main pieces of legislation available to assist the police in tackling offenders on the roads: The Road Traffic Act 1988, and The Road Vehicles (Construction and Use) Regulations 1986.

The Road Traffic Act 1988

The Road Traffic Act 1988 contains the main offences the police use to prosecute offenders. Table 16.3 offers a quick guide to these offences.

Section	Description	Punishment
1	Causing the death of another person whilst driving dangerously.	Maximum 14 years' imprisonment – *and* compulsory disqualification (minimum of 2 years).
2	Driving dangerously (without the element of causing the death of another).	Maximum 2 years' imprisonment – *and* compulsory disqualification.
3	Careless and inconsiderate driving.	Fine and discretionary disqualification.
3A	Causing the death of another person by careless and inconsiderate driving whilst under the influence of drink or drugs.	Maximum 14 years' imprisonment – *and* compulsory disqualification (minimum of 2 years).
170	Failing to stop after an accident, or failing to report an accident.	Fine and penalty points.
4	Being in charge of a motor vehicle whilst unfit through drink or drugs.	Three months' imprisonment – discretionary disqualification.
5	Driving or attempting to drive a motor vehicle while over the prescribed limit.	Six months' imprisonment *and* obligatory disqualification.
143	Driving without insurance.	Fine – discretionary disqualification.
81	Speeding.	Fine, penalty points or discretionary disqualification (for excessive speeds).
36	Failing to comply with a traffic sign (e.g. red light, give way, stop or direction sign).	Fine, penalty points, discretionary disqualification under certain circumstances.
87	Driving otherwise than in accordance with a driving licence (e.g. no licence, provisional licences, HGV licences).	Fine, penalty points, discretionary disqualification under certain circumstances.
103	Driving while disqualified.	Six months' imprisonment and/or fine – discretionary disqualification.
14 and 15	Contravention of seat belt legislation.	Fine, penalty points.
47	Using a motor vehicle without a test certificate.	Fine.

Table 16.3   Main offences under the Road Traffic Act 1988

Of course, there are many other offences under the Road Traffic Act 1988, but the above are the main enforceable sections, which can contribute to casualty reduction.

The Road Vehicles (Construction and Use) Regulations 1986

The Road Traffic Act 1988 deals mainly with the use of vehicles on roads, where offences may be committed. Although the Road Vehicles (Construction and Use) Regulations 1986 can cover the use of a vehicle on a road (as in the case of driving a motor vehicle while using a hand-held phone, causing an obstruction and unnecessary reversing), the Regulations also cover the state of motor vehicles and their roadworthiness. The Regulations contribute to road safety by creating offences when the following are not in good working order:

- Brakes
- Tyres
- Mirrors
- Steering.

The Road Vehicles Lighting Regulations 1989 deal with the maintenance and suitability of all lights on vehicles.

Using technology

Technology cannot completely replace the police – as discussed above, a visible police presence on the road is also vital. For example, cameras and other technology cannot always be used to detect certain offences, such as drink and drug driving, careless and dangerous driving, failure to use safety belts and using mobile phones.

However, regardless of the poor publicity received by the use of cameras to detect speeding and traffic light offences, the tactic has proved an important element in reinforcing the national Road Safety Strategy. There are approximately 5,000 fixed and mobile camera sites in Great Britain. An independent review of the first three years of the national safety camera programme found that there was a 32 per cent reduction in the number of vehicles exceeding the speed limit at camera sites; the number of personal injury collisions was cut by 33 per cent; and the number of people killed or seriously injured by 40 per cent over and above the UK's overall general downward trend in numbers killed or seriously injured.

In terms of reducing criminality, the pilot 'Operation Laser' project introduced Automatic Number Plate Recognition (ANPR) technology. The ACPO ANPR Steering Group published its paper *Denying Criminals the Use of the Road* in March 2005. It stated that the ANPR Strategy will help to meet primary police service aims to:

- Reduce crime

- Increase the sanction detection rate

- Increase the number of offences brought to justice

- Enhance intelligence in accordance with NIM principles.

The continuing improvements made by the Driver and Vehicle Licensing Agency (DVLA) to the vehicle and driver databases, and the data links between them and the Police National Computer (PNC), mean that operational officers can receive data direct from these computer systems to their patrol vehicles, enabling them to identify stolen vehicles and other vehicles of interest, whether for breaches of road traffic law or general criminal matters. This growing use of technology is proving invaluable in the pursuit of criminals using the roads.

16.5 Tackling the threat of terrorism

The threat of terrorist activity in the UK remains high, and is likely to be so for the foreseeable future. Terrorist networks need to use roads, and can be detected in doing so by proactive road policing. Terrorist networks are also involved in organised crime including smuggling, which also involves use of the roads, and is thereby vulnerable to police activity. The police will use the Road Policing Intelligence Forum to enhance the gathering and use of intelligence. The use of ANPR technology will enhance opportunities at border controls to identify potential terrorist vehicles entering the country. However, all of these methods will rely on the police receiving intelligence on terrorist activities both internationally and from within our own communities. You can read more on terrorism in Chapter 17.

16.6 Reducing anti-social use of the roads

One of the key priorities for the National Policing Plan 2005–2008 is:

'reducing people's concerns about anti-social behaviour'.

The ACPO road policing group believes that addressing road crime is part of that task. Their strategy is based on the intelligence-led analysis contained in ACPO's *National Strategic Assessment on Road Policing*.

The assessment was carried out in accordance with the National Intelligence Model (NIM), and the strategy will be implemented through a 'Control Strategy' – also in line with the principles of the NIM, which ACPO is developing. ACPO have also established a Road Policing Intelligence Forum to support the implementation of the strategy.

As discussed in section 16.3 above, the Serious Organised Crime and Police Act 2005 gave police the specific power to confiscate vehicles being used without driving licences and insurance. The Police Reform Act 2002 created further powers for police officers and PCSOs to confiscate vehicles, where their use is likely to cause harassment, alarm or distress to residents. This power enables the service to deal more effectively with the real issues that affect communities, such as motor cycles being used on common land and playing fields, as well as 'car cruisers' who choose to drive dangerously in large numbers, usually in car parks.

Another power given to the police and local authorities is to recover abandoned vehicles under the Refuse Disposal (Amenity) Act 1978. Abandoned vehicles have been identified in the ACPO Road Policing Strategy as:

'unsightly and hazardous and a particular problem in housing estates, disfiguring residents' surroundings, undermining confidence in the community, and challenging efforts to establish a crime free environment.'

In order to improve police powers, the End-of-Life Vehicles (Producer Responsibility) Regulations 2005 have also been introduced. These Regulations impose a series of requirements on vehicle manufacturers and importers to register their interest with the Secretary of State. The Regulations also require such people to declare a responsibility for vehicles they have produced or placed on the market. The overall purpose of the Regulations is to allow the Secretary of State with the assistance of the Environment Agency to effectively 'track' vehicles which are manufactured, imported or sold, so that if they become waste, companies are in a position to receive them back. The programme is in its infancy, but when fully implemented it should contribute to the overall aim of clearing the streets of abandoned vehicles.

Lastly, there is a specific offence under s.2 of the Refuse Disposal (Amenity) Act 1978 of abandoning on any land in the open air, or on any other land forming part of a highway, a motor vehicle or anything which formed part of a motor vehicle and was removed from it in the course of dismantling the vehicle on the land. This offence is enforceable by the police and local authorities.

16.7 Enhancing public confidence and reassurance by patrolling the roads

The ACPO Road Policing Strategy identifies that roads are part of our public space and that:

'unlawful and unruly behaviour on the roads and in vehicles needs to be challenged and lawful standards need to be asserted, as they are on the streets and in other public places. 'Road rage' is a serious and unacceptable problem.'

Under the Strategy, the visible presence of the police is important in protecting the public, maintaining safer communities and supporting law-abiding motorists. To this end, high visibility patrols are important not only for enforcement purposes, but also to provide reassurance to the public. This should ultimately lead to increased public confidence in the police.

16.8 Working in partnership

We should remind ourselves that research shows a higher incidence of road casualties amongst people from disadvantaged communities (see section 16.4 above). Elderly people, children, and people from economically and socially disadvantaged communities are five times more likely to be killed on roads than those from more fortunate communities. It has long been recognised that the police service cannot work in isolation from its partners to achieve results. This principle is the same in respect of road policing and achieving casualty-reduction targets, in particular in socially-disadvantaged communities, who should be given priority for funding at a local level.

Figure 16.2 identifies a hierarchical structure for the delivery of the Roads Policing Strategy.

National Partnerships

The National Highways Agency is the vehicle for the Secretary of State for Transport to deliver his or her strategy for road policing. The Highways Agency has primary responsibility to develop the strategic road networks throughout the country. This will include improving traffic management on Britain's motorways and delivering projects such as active traffic management schemes to reduce congestion. These will include actively managed hard shoulders on motorways (where hard shoulders are used during busy periods as an extra lane), as well as other lane control initiatives and the illumination of road markings.

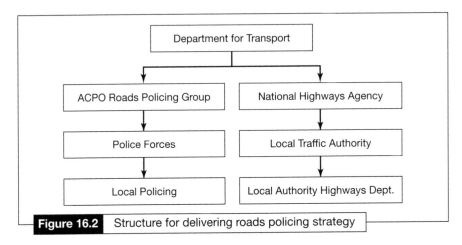

Figure 16.2 Structure for delivering roads policing strategy

The Traffic Management Act 2004 introduced the concept of civilian traffic officers who will wear uniform and work in partnership with the police to enforce legislation, deal with obstructions and other operations such as the movement of abnormal loads.

Local Partnerships

Under the 2004 Act, Local Traffic Authorities are required to appoint a traffic manager to manage the movement of traffic in its own area and neighbouring areas. For example, a Local Traffic Authority has the power to create 20mph zones in certain areas, such as outside schools, to reduce the risk of harm to children.

Under the Crime and Disorder Act 1988, local authorities have an obligation to liaise with other partners, such as the police, to reduce crime and disorder. This obligation extends to consulting with the police on road safety and enforcement issues. This is generally done through highways departments and will include consultation on such matters as positioning of road signs, speed reduction issues and preventing road traffic collisions.

The delivery of effective traffic management nationally and locally is crucial to maintaining safety on the roads and reducing casualties.

16.9 Human rights

Since one of the key aims of the Roads Policing Strategy is to reduce fatalities on the roads, the link with the Human Rights Act 1988 cannot be discounted. Take the following case study as an example:

The police are called to a fatal road traffic collision at a busy junction on a main road. A van has entered the main road by turning right illegally, against a 'No Right Turn' sign. The driver of the van failed to see a motorcyclist travelling along the road and the two vehicles collided, killing the motorcyclist instantly. The van driver was convicted of causing death by dangerous driving.

Six months later, a similar road traffic collision occurred when the driver of a car turned right illegally onto the main road, killing the driver of a car which was travelling on that road.

The local police consulted with the local authority to find ways to improve road safety at the site. It was agreed that the junction would be made safer either by building a roundabout or by introducing a traffic lights system. A report was submitted to this effect; however, the proposals were turned down due to the cost involved.

Would either of the public authorities involved be liable if a third fatal road traffic collision occurred at this junction?

To answer this question, we have to turn to Article 2 of the Human Rights Act 1988, which states:

'Everyone's right to life shall be protected by law.'

Public authorities (which include police and local authorities) have a positive obligation to *protect* people's human rights. In order to protect itself from falling foul of Article 2, a public authority would have to show that its actions were proportionate, legal and necessary.

Although the above scenario is fictitious, the local authority involved would find it hard to justify its actions were a third fatal collision to occur at the same junction after it had considered the risk and rejected proposals to improve the junction on the grounds of cost. As with all issues relating to human rights, we would have to wait for another tragedy to occur before such a matter is tested before the courts.

Suggested further reading

Sampson, F., *Road Policing, Blackstones Police Manual 2007* (Oxford: Oxford University Press, 2007)

Useful websites

http://police.homeoffice.gov.uk/operational-policing/road-traffic.html
The Home Office site dedicated to road policing

Chapter 17

Terrorism

This chapter supports the following National Occupational Standards which describe the performance and competence required of a probationer officer.

Unit No.	Unit title
1A1	Use police actions in a fair and justified way.
1A2	Communicate effectively with members of communities.
1A4	Foster people's equality, diversity and rights.
1B9	Provide initial support to individuals affected by offending or anti-social behaviour and assess their needs for further support.
2A1	Gather and submit information that has the potential to support policing objectives.
2C2	Prepare for, and participate in, planned policing operations.
2C3	Arrest, detain or report individuals.
2C4	Minimise and deal with aggressive and abusive behaviour.
2G2	Conduct investigations.
2G4	Finalise investigations.
SH1	Interview victims and witnesses.
2H2	Interview suspects.
2I1	Search individuals.
2I2	Search vehicles, premises and land.
2J1	Prepare and submit case files.

Unit No.	Unit title
2J2	Present evidence in court and at other hearings.
2K1	Escort detained persons.
2K2	Present detained persons to custody.
4C1	Develop your own knowledge and practice.
4G2	Ensure your own actions reduce risks to health and safety.

17.1 Introduction

The purpose of this chapter is to provide a background to terrorism and the actions that government and agencies – including the police – have taken in response.

Terrorism is not new. In 1867 a gunpowder charge placed at the outside wall of Clerkenwell Prison in London killed a child and an elderly resident in neighbourhood housing and damaged 400 houses. Suicide bombings and assassinations, now the tactics of choice by some terrorist organisations, have been used by the Tamil Tigers and Palestinian groups for decades. Recent terrorist activity includes the World Trade Centre and Pentagon attacks in 2001, the Bali Bombing in 2002 and the Madrid Train Bombings in 2004. On 7 July 2005, terrorists attacked London, killing 52 people and injuring hundreds more. Alarmingly, the recipe for the illegal manufacture of many explosives from everyday materials is freely available on the internet.

Most terrorist groups have common features. Terrorist groups claim to represent minorities. They usually prefer random violence because it causes greater fear (and so greater impact) than discriminate violence. Publicity is essential to the terrorists' cause: Mrs Margaret Thatcher, former Prime Minister, called publicity 'the oxygen of terrorism'. Contrary to some expectations, the leaders of terrorist organisations are often well educated.

The motivation of terrorists has been the subject of much research. In general, terrorists are motivated by political not religious grievances, although they may express their grievances using the ideology of religion and they may use religion to simplify their cause into one of 'good against evil'. The current terrorist threat to the UK is international in nature and the terrorist communities, including Al Qaeda, usually have excellent communications with their associates in other countries. This means that counter-terrorism, aided by rapid electronic communications, is a truly international activity.

Exercise 17A

How would you define terrorism? (This is actually much more difficult than at first appears.)

There is no one definition of terrorism to which all observers subscribe. Examples of simple definitions include:

- Politically motivated violence intended to influence the views of the public

- The use of violence or threats of violence to advance a political, religious or ideological cause

- The deliberate threat or use of force to bring about a change in the political structure of a country.

There are many more and they vary in sophistication and comprehensiveness.

In the UK, terrorism is legally defined in section 1 of the Terrorist Act 2000. The definition comes in two parts which may be simply classified as 'purpose or design' and 'action'. In this Act 'terrorism' means the use or threat of action where:

(a) the action falls within any of the definitions (d)–(h) below;

(b) the use or threat is designed to influence the government or to intimidate the public or a section of the public; **and**

(c) the use or threat is made for the purpose of advancing a political, religious or ideological cause.

Action falls within (a) if it:

(d) involves serious violence against a person;

(e) involves serious damage to property;

(f) endangers a person's life, other than that of the person committing the action;

(g) creates a serious risk to the health or safety of the public or a section of the public; **or**

(h) is designed seriously to interfere with or seriously to disrupt an electronic system.

According to this law, a terrorist offence is proven if (b) and (c) are present with any of the 'actions' (d)–(h). However, the use or threat of action involving firearms or explosives is considered to be terrorism whether or not subsection (b) is satisfied. Note the use of the word 'serious' and 'endanger' in (d)–(h): it prevents indictments which are based on less serious actions.

17.2 Government response to terrorism

The UK tackles terrorism using the criminal justice system with some military intervention as required, supported by intelligence and information gathering agencies. The governmental responses to terrorism may be grouped under the following headings:

- Organisational
- Legislative
- Operational.

Organisational

The organisational response has been to develop the role of the security services, Interpol and Europol to combat terrorism. The Metropolitan Police's Anti-Terrorist Branch co-ordinates the investigation of acts of terrorism throughout the UK. The special branches of police forces are now increasingly co-ordinated nationally and have strong links with the security service. Broadly speaking, the police have the lead role in responding to terrorism in the UK, whilst governmental and security agencies have the lead in responding to terrorism abroad.

Legislative

The legislative response has been to enact laws that define terrorist-related acts and make it easier to prosecute those attempting or carrying out acts of terrorism and to permit surveillance of suspects. The increasing emphasis of legislation is to allow investigators to protect the public before any planned terrorist activity is executed. Examples include:

- The Intelligence Services Act 1994 – which allows the issuing of warrants for surveillance and the interception of mail, etc.
- The Criminal Law Act 1977 – which covers bomb hoaxes
- The Terrorism Act of 2000 – which makes it illegal for certain terrorist groups to operate in the UK
- The Anti-terrorism Crime and Security Act 2001 – which covers the deportation and detention of suspects and includes offences related to weapons of mass destruction

- The Prevention of Terrorism Act 2005 – which enables the Secretary of State to make a control order against individuals who are suspected of being involved in terrorist activities. Control orders are designed to restrict, prevent or disrupt involvement in terrorist-related activities, e.g. by curfew and travel restrictions. The control orders are subject to judicial oversight

- The Terrorism Act 2006 – which includes offences relating to the encouragement of terrorism, the dissemination of terrorist publications, the training of terrorists and which broadens proscribed organisations to include those that encourage terrorism. The Act also increased the maximum period for which a suspected terrorist could be detained before being charged with an offence from 14 to 28 days.

Note that PACE and The Regulation of Investigatory Powers 2000 (RIPA) apply to all police investigations, including those that are terrorist-related.

Operational

At the national level, the operational response has been to engage in specific and coordinated investigations and surveillance so as to gather intelligence on terrorist networks. About one thousand suspects are believed to be under surveillance in the UK on a regular basis, requiring unprecedented levels of staffing and technical support. Anti-terrorist operations also use special forces in sieges and hostage-taking operations.

The UK government's 2006 strategy for countering international terrorism (http://www.ukresilience.info/publications/countering.pdf) deals specifically with Islamic Terrorism as a response to the 2005 London Bombings. The strategy includes the improving of intelligence-gathering, strengthening border security and also aims to reduce the radicalisation of individuals within the Islamic community. The last part of the strategy may be called a 'hearts and minds approach' and is a recognition that simple law enforcement strategies cannot succeed by themselves.

The Joint Terrorism Analysis Centre (JTAC) is based at the Security Service's (MI5) headquarters in London. JTAC reports threat levels based upon the latest intelligence information. There are five threat levels which inform decisions about the levels of security needed to protect UK infrastructure (e.g. power stations, and vital communication facilities):

- **Low** – an attack is unlikely

- **Moderate** – an attack is possible, but not likely

- **Substantial** – an attack is a strong possibility

- **Severe** – an attack is highly likely

- **Critical** – an attack is expected imminently.

17.3   The police officer's role in anti-terrorism

Police officers are involved in a wide range of anti-terrorism activities that includes:

- Developing community ties that will reduce disharmony and mistrust and improve the flow of information that will isolate terrorists and disrupt terrorist action. No police force can substitute for the 'eyes and ears' of thousands of vigilant members of the public. With the cooperation of the public, information about suspicious activities will be forthcoming; without such cooperation the flow of information will be drastically reduced.

- Advising the public to be vigilant and to provide advice on the ways in which property can be protected.

- Maintaining the flow of intelligence that is essential to fight terrorism before it results in deaths.

- Securing the scene of a terrorist attack or attempted attack so as to minimise loss of life and to maximise the retrieval of forensically-valuable information.

- For specialist police groups in liaison with security agencies, investigating terrorist groups, carrying out surveillance and interrupting their development or operations.

- Supplying specialist skills, e.g. firearms identification.

- Maintaining awareness of the basic materials that could be used to manufacture explosives at home. (In a series of attempted terrorist acts committed in 2006, very large quantities of hydrogen peroxide were bought from suppliers. Hopefully, such purchases would now attract considerable attention.)

The rise of Islamic terrorist groups and their support within a small minority of the UK population has focused attempts to build better relationships between Muslim communities and the police service. One suggestion is that the police service provides Muslim representatives with access to sensitive intelligence information in order for them to defuse anxieties in their communities by being able to confirm that police action (for example, mass searching of properties) was justified within the context of the intelligence received.

Exercise 17B

You are first at the scene of a suspect parcel bomb (i.e. a bomb sent in a parcel which explodes upon opening) in a small factory. What actions do you take?

The first priority is the safety of the public and even the preservation of forensically valuable evidence is of secondary importance until that has been achieved. With this in mind:

- Quickly determine the position and nature of the suspect device. Do not touch it

- Give clear instructions to senior members of staff to evacuate the factory. Staff should seek substantial protection several hundred metres away from the package

- Do not use personal radios or mobile phones within ten metres of the object. Move away and confirm the presence of the package to your police control room

- Retire to a safe distance, noting the best point of access for further investigators

- Reassure members of the public and staff whilst keeping them away from the scene until help arrives. Check in case a suspicious person was seen in the area; if so, pass on their description

- Remain calm: calmness is contagious.

17.4 Protecting businesses against terrorism

The MI5 document at http://www.mi5.gov.uk/files/pdf/protecting.pdf contains lots of advice on dealing with specific threats from terrorist attacks including bomb attacks. It also gives the following advice to businesses:

1 Carry out a risk assessment of the threats you might be facing and their likelihood

2 If possible, consider security at the planning stage

3 Make security awareness part of your organisation's culture.

4 Ensure good housekeeping throughout your premises

5 Keep access points to a minimum and issue all staff and visitors with passes

6 Install appropriate physical measures

7 Examine your mail-handling procedures

8 When recruiting staff or hiring contractors, check identities and follow up references

9 Take proper IT precautions and examine methods for disposing of confidential waste

10 Plan and test continuity plans.

Exercise 17C

Give one example of each of the points given in the MI5 advice for businesses.

---

1 Risk assessment: e.g. IT sabotage if an IT-based company or deliberate food contamination if a confectionery manufacturer.

2 Planning stage, e.g. when planning a new office.

3 Security awareness as part of your organisation's culture: the health and safety portfolio of a company is usually held by a senior executive – why not security too?

4 Good housekeeping throughout your premises, e.g. maintain clutter-free public areas and install good lighting.

5 Keep access points to a minimum, e.g. close some doors on a more or less permanent basis.

6 Install appropriate physical measures, e.g. alarms and CCTV surveillance.

7 Examine your mail-handling procedures, e.g. should your mail room be in an isolated building away from your main premises?

8 When recruiting staff or hiring contractors, check identities and follow up references, make it clear to applicants that this will always be done.

9 Take proper IT precautions and examine methods for disposing of confidential waste, e.g. shred important documents.

10 Plan and test continuity plans, e.g. backup IT systems which store valuable client information.

17.5 Example of a terrorist group: Al Qaeda

Al Qaeda is an international terrorist group with 'cells' in over 60 countries. Al Qaeda has attacked the USA, UK and their allies and it aims to expel non-Muslims from the Middle East. It does not have the vertical management structure of many terrorist groups. Instead, it operates loosely linked cells in different countries. The absence of a 'central control system' makes it more difficult to disrupt Al Qaeda.

Al Qaeda has used no-warning coordinated suicide attacks to kill people, destroy property and create a climate of fear. Its most high profile attack was on the World Trade Centre and the Pentagon on 11 September 2001, in which over 3,000 people were killed. It was also responsible for the bomb attacks on the transport system in London in July 2005.

Al Qaeda is well funded and its sources of money include drug smuggling, voluntary payments from businesses and individuals, profits from legitimate 'front' organisations and money laundering.

The international response to Al Qaeda has involved a US-led coalition against terrorism (with military intervention in Afghanistan), the suppression of terrorist finances and the cultivation and use of the media to illustrate the horrors of Al Qaeda's terrorist attacks. At the same time, governments have begun to try and alleviate the cause of much discontent in the Middle East that is used by Al Qaeda to justify some of their actions. This is one reason for the extra government emphasis upon political initiatives, particularly in Palestine.

17.6 Anti-terrorism: accountability and control

The use of police powers and the increasing volume of anti-terrorist legislation have raised concerns about the erosion of individual rights and freedoms and the accountability and control of police actions. We know that the terrorists make use of the freedoms of modern British life to conceal their plans and actions and that the freedom of the internet has made the development of the 'virtual community' of terrorists possible.

The government has an overriding responsibility to protect its citizens from the fear of disorder and violence. Put another way, the government has to protect its citizens from the horror of civil chaos. The question is always there as to what extent the rights of individuals to go about their daily lives without interference and surveillance should be balanced with the need of security and police organisations to obtain even more information on citizens, of which terrorists form a tiny but largely unidentified minority. William Blackstone once said that 'it is better that ten guilty escape than one innocent suffers'. But the costs of a failure to disrupt terrorist activities may now be so serious that even this 'principle' – if inconvenience and individual monitoring are classed as suffering – is under threat. The Report on the London Terrorist Attacks of July 2005 by the Intelligence and Security Committee continued this theme:

'The debate continues as to the appropriate balance between the protection of lives against terrorist atrocities and the protection of civil liberties against increased intrusion into those lives, aimed at preventing such attacks. If we seek greater assurance against the possibility of attacks, some increase in intrusive activity by the UK's intelligence and security agencies is the inevitable consequence. Even then it seems unlikely that it will stop all attacks.'

It may be thought that it is in the interests of the police and security services to minimise the information about terrorism that is provided to the media and the public, but there are strategic advantages in providing the public with as much information about police enquiries and the terrorist threat as possible. These advantages include:

- The provision of the public with sufficient information to enable them to supply valuable information, which may lead to the arrests of suspects

- A demonstration of the inhumanity of terrorist groups set against an otherwise fairly stable and tolerant society

- The reassurance of the public that the police and security services are using their rights of surveillance justifiably, sparingly and properly

- Convincing all parties, including groups who have been sympathetic to terrorist action in the past, that the principles of 'rule of law' and a 'fair trial' apply to terrorism as they do to other crimes.

Exercise 17D

What complicates the accountability of information-gathering law enforcement agencies involved in anti-terrorism?

Accountability is best achieved by transparent auditing. This is hardly possible where law enforcement agencies wish to keep some of their methods and 'information gains' secret so as not to aid future terrorist groups. Nevertheless, law enforcement agencies must still conform to the law. Complaints regarding police action are well established via the Independent Police Complaints Commission. The National Intelligence Machinery (including the Secret Intelligence Service (MI6), the Security Service (MI5) and the Government Communications Headquarters (GCHQ)) is overseen by commissioners appointed under the Regulation of Investigatory Powers Act 2000. Such commissioners review the issue of warrants for various forms of surveillance and the interception of mail and telecommunications.

The cost of counterterrorism is also of concern if in the long-term it drains police resources from their conventional 'daily roles'. The use of technology in police work comes at a high price. National databases are particularly expensive and capital and personnel costs are frequently measured in hundreds of millions of pounds, raising questions about alternative ways of spending sums which are equivalent to the annual turnover of a small police force. Yet, the balance in arguments about 'value for money' has shifted because of real fears of the damage that terrorist organisations might wreak upon society.

┌───┐

Case study

Operation Kratos

The mistaken shooting of Jean Charles de Menezes in July 2005 has focused attention on the tactics used by the police service in dealing with suspected suicide bombers.

The 27-year-old was shot on a train at Stockwell tube station, London, by police who wrongly suspected him of being one of four men wanted over attempted bombings on London's transport system the previous day.

The tactics so tragically used in this incident are believed to have been agreed in January 2003 and are coded 'Operation Kratos'.

In fact, Kratos is a generic operation that embodies a range of separate plans:

- Operation Andromeda: police response to the spontaneous sighting by a member of the public of a suspected suicide bomber

- Operation Beach: an intelligence-led covert operation to locate and arrest suspect terrorists

- Operation Clydesdale: police response to the receipt of intelligence about a pre-planned event involving a suicide bomber.

The precise tactics used by police in implementing these plans will depend upon the circumstances. The type of explosive used by many suicide bombers raises fears that if Tasers, baton rounds or bullets strike the material that there is a risk of initiating an explosion. Additionally, suicide bombers are unlikely to surrender even if faced with overwhelming odds. The inference is therefore that shots must be directed to the head with the aim of killing the terrorist outright so that s/he cannot activate the device they are carrying and so as to prevent accident detonation. This is consistent with section 3 of the Criminal Law Act 1967: 'A person may use such force as is reasonable in the circumstances in the prevention of crime, or in effecting or assisting in the lawful arrest of offenders or suspected offenders or of persons unlawfully at large'.

Two other aspects of Operation Kratos are also worth emphasising. The first is that while it is usual for firearms officers to give a warning before firing, this is not always possible and, in the case of a suicide terrorist, may not be desirable since they might detonate the explosive before being shot. Second, while it is normally the sole decision of the firearms officer whether or not to shoot, in circumstances suspected to involve suicide terrorism a shot may have to be fired on the command of a senior officer since only s/he may have knowledge of all the available information.

└───┘

What of the future? The possibility that a terrorist group could detonate a weapon of mass destruction may force governments to sweep aside more human rights. The national security of one country will only be protected by international action in many countries. Terrorism is altering our world and the world will not easily return to the way it was. One person commenting upon the security that now surrounds government and ministerial buildings in London noted that 'I can no longer take my daughters, as my father once took me, to the door of No 10 Downing Street. I can only watch at a distance. Whatever the security situation in the next ten years, it would be a brave person who would throw the security risk assessment away, turn back the clock and allow the public access to such governmental sites. That saddens me.'

Suggested further reading

Richardson, L., *What Terrorists Want* (London: John Murray, 2006) Richardson's thesis is that we must understand terrorists if we are to be successful in combating them.
Whitaker, D. (ed.), *The Terrorism Reader* (London: Routledge, 2002) Chapter 1 includes an exhaustive discussion of the definitions of terrorism used by authors.

Websites

http://www.psr.keele.ac.uk/sseal/terror.htm
A collection of websites on terrorism

http://www.opsi.gov.uk/acts/acts2000/20000011.htm
The Terrorism Act 2000. This describes the range of offences and police powers that can be brought to bear in cases of terrorist activity

http://www.archive.official-documents.co.uk/document/caboff/nim/0114301808.pdf
The National Intelligence Machinery, including MI5 and MI6. For information on JTAC see http://www.mi5.gov.uk/output/Page421.html

http://www.ukresilience.info/index.shtm
A UK government website dedicated to emergency responses and contingencies

http://www.ukresilience.info/publications/countering.pdf
The government's strategy to counter international terrorism (July 2006)

http://www.fas.org/irp/threat/nsct2006.pdf
The National US strategy for combating terrorism (September 2006)

http://www.cabinetoffice.gov.uk/publications/reports/intelligence/isc_7july_report.pdf
Intelligence and Security Committee Report on the 7 July 2005 London attacks, published May 2006

http://www.mpa.gov.uk/committees/mpa/2006/060223/08.htm
An update on Operation Kratos to the Metropolitan Police Authority

http://www.acpo.police.uk/asp/policies/Data/ACPO%20(TAM)%20(PUF)%20Review.doc
'The UK Police Service Response to the threat posed by suicide terrorism': review by Association of Chief Police Officers Use of Firearms Committee

http://www.demos.co.uk/publications/bringingithome
Think tank Demos' report on a community-based approach to counter terrorism

Chapter 18

Future directions

18.1 Introduction

In recent years policing has undergone an enormous amount of reorganisation in response to changes within society. There has been the expansion of private security and a growth in realising that trans-national policing is important when tackling major, organised crime and terrorism, for example. Further, the way the police are organised and managed has also been under scrutiny within the government's drive for reform in all the public services. Perhaps one of the biggest changes in the police service as a whole can be seen in the introduction and use of technology, coupled with an increase in the intelligence-led, or targeted, approach to the use of police resources.

18.2 Demands on the police

Within all these changes there is an increase in the demands on policing. We see a continued increase in the local governance of crime, with communities being encouraged to report incidents and work with the police and criminal justice system as part of the citizen-focused response to crime and disorder. The introduction of neighbourhood policing teams and the use of police community support officers, special constables and other volunteers in the extended policing family throw down new challenges at the local level for the police. Working within Crime and Disorder Reduction Partnerships (Community Safety Partnerships in Wales) the police are exhorted to communicate better and wider with the community they serve. Public expectations of the police are high, so maintaining standards is of vital importance if the police are to retain popular public support.

At a middle level, the police organisation is expected to deal with national problems such as increased serious criminality involving firearms and illegal drugs. Cross-border cooperation in the case of serious crimes has led to a call for regionalisation, which has now turned into the demand for collaboration between forces particularly in the use of resources for serious offences such as murder, and in particular when it comes to the sharing of intelligence and information.

At an international level, the police service, working with other government agencies both in this country and throughout the world, have to try and tackle the ongoing problem of terrorism, whilst engaging with diverse communities in the UK without alienating them.

All of these roles and others are to be carried out in an accountable, transparent and responsible manner, with ethical policing at the forefront of all police activities, be it a stop search on a street or a major anti-terrorist operation. How can society rely on the individual police officer to perform such a wide range of diverse and, on occasions, complicated roles to the best of their abilities? One answer may lie in the education and training of the officer.

18.3 Police training

In line with the ideology of change, the government white paper, *Building Communities, Beating, Crime*, has addressed the concept of police training. The report firmly places police training into the sphere of higher and further education and many universities and colleges are preparing courses to accommodate the new clientele. Furthermore, many police forces are carrying out their probationer training programmes within these educational establishments. Behind these educational and training changes lies the idea of professionalism. The police service has always at best been regarded as a quasi professional organisation, or one that is not quite what is considered to be a professional organisation in the truest sense of the word. Most professions work to the highest possible ethical standards within a recognised body of professional knowledge. That is why doctors, lawyers and others regarded as professionals spend a considerable amount of time in higher education getting thoroughly acquainted with this body of knowledge and understanding how to dispense it in an ethical manner. Currently, policing is neither a graduate profession nor is there a life-long culture of learning and reaccreditation. Whilst there is no current code of ethics written for the police role, there are several important documents such as the ACPO statement of common purpose to guide the police. The police service must continue to invest in better training, understanding what works, and ensuring that good practice is spread throughout the different police forces.

Consequently there is a need for a book that goes some way to satisfy this demand, as many police officers, student police officers, PCSOs, and others interested in the police service as a career will have limited or no knowledge of the new approach to a professional police service. Above all, police officers will need to become far more knowledgeable, professional, and flexible in their roles which will constantly be changing to meet the demands of politicians and public alike.

One major aspect of distinguishing the police officer from other members of the extended policing family will be the professional status endowed upon that role by the accomplishment of higher educational qualifications, supported by an ethical approach to their work. The current volume, an *Introduction To Police Work*, supports the beginning of the journey towards a professional police service

Index

Letters from the Trenches